The School
of
Sun Tzu

The School
of
Sun Tzu

Winning Empires without War

David G. Jones

iUniverse, Inc.
Bloomington

The School of Sun Tzu
Winning **Empires without War**

iUniverse books may be ordered through booksellers or by contacting:

iUniverse
1663 Liberty Drive
Bloomington, IN 47403
www.iuniverse.com
1-800-Authors (1-800-288-4677)

ISBN: 978-1-4697-6911-0 (sc)
ISBN: 978-1-4697-6913-4 (e)
ISBN: 978-1-4697-6912-7 (dj)

Library of Congress Control Number: 2012902323

Printed in the United States of America

iUniverse rev. date: 3/28/2012

provided with no evidence why this book was written and what it was ultimately used for.

My Rosetta Stone for *Ping-fa*[1] was the *Tao Te Ching*. It is believed to be the second most frequently translated book in the world, with as many as a thousand Chinese commentaries and possibly a hundred translations. It is a key to *Ping-fa's* front door. Though some of the commentary suggests a possible *Tao Te Ching/Ping-fa* relationship, to date nobody has defined that relationship. In fact, like *Ping-fa,* no one has definitively resolved the *Tao Te Ching's* authorship, age, and application. There are, therefore, two mysteries. Both mysteries will be exposed in *The School of Sun Tzu.*

The notion that the *Tao Te Ching* was written by a wanderer named Lao Tzu in one evening as he rested at a border post is as silly as the notion that Sun Tzu, a retired general, took pen in hand and set down a treatise that has been read, analyzed, and studied for over two thousand years. The very idea that two very famous works were scratched out in a few days by individuals with no specialized learning or previous literary achievement is patently absurd.

The School of Sun Tzu carefully examines and defines the *Tao Te Ching/Ping-fa* relationship, the period and context within which they were created, and what use they were intended to serve. The inherent harmony of the two is obvious. The form and flow of the two are the same, and the principles and values identical. There is really only one difference: one is practice, and the other is philosophy. With the benefit of a *Tao Te Ching* perspective, *Ping-fa* is transparent and metaphorical. With *Ping-fa* decoded, freed of its military metaphor and retold in plain language, it emerges as a concise, comprehensive manual for strategic management. Now, one can revisit the *Tao Te Ching* and see quite clearly

---

1   *The Art of War* is also called *Thirteen Chapters* in some publications.

that it is a statement of values and principles intended to guide human activity.

The context for these works begins in the period known as the Warring States[2] and carries through the peace that followed and the emergence of the first empire of China. In this journey, we encounter the short-lived Qin dynasty, its "Legalist" administration,[3] and the Han dynasty that followed it.

The key player in this remarkable story is China's first emperor, Qin Shih Huangdi. A brilliant and immeasurably successful champion for Chinese nationhood, he has been discredited for two millennia by his successors and history dilettantes. Because of these sins of omission and commission, we know as much today about the first emperor as we do about "Lao Tzu" and "Sun Tzu"—that is, almost nothing at all. Most of what is written today about the first emperor is fabrication.

The emergence of China is a story of elegant and gentle nation building. The small kingdom of Qin, exploiting the talents of the greatest body of strategic knowledge that the world has ever assembled, crafted an empire for the millennia.

Today's political leaders, journalists, and intellectuals seem convinced that life without conflict and periodic combat is a naive dream. They imagine they have seen it all, and though they might think wistfully of a world without distrust, polarization, and war, they are convinced they will not live to see it happen.

It is time to challenge these assumptions and deeply held beliefs. The state of Qin, which gave us the great nation of China, did just that over two thousand years ago. The evidence is there for all to see. All one needs do is look.

---

2   From 770 to 476 BCE is the Spring and Autumn period; From 475 to 221 BCE is the Warring States period.
3   The theory of government practiced in Qin was called "Legalism." It was secular, rules based and focused on management and change.

To Possess the Sky ... Practice Humility.
Stop the water and seize the river.

Take hold of the air and possess the sky.
Such foolish struggle.

To seize the river ... become river.
To possess sky ... become sky.

Practice humility and do not try to get
ahead of each other.

A winner requires a loser.
Retribution provokes reprisal.

What a foolish circle to be trapped within.

—Ray Grigg, *The Tao of Relationships*

The Militaristic Sun Tzu

- Bullets figure prominently in business language. This is no surprise, as practitioners like to think of themselves as military generals, plotting strategy and leaving occasional corpses in the battlefield. A favorite manual, for instance, is Sun Tzu's Art of War. (*Business World,* Philippines, February 1999)

- I believe *The Art of War* shows quite clearly *how to take the initiative* and combat the enemy—any enemy. Sun Tzu's truths can equally show the way to victory in all kinds of ordinary business conflicts, boardroom battles, and in the day-to-day fight for survival we all endure—even in the battle of the sexes! They are all forms of war, all fought under the same rules—*his rules.* (Clavell 1983)

- Speaking of Machiavelli—he recommends that when a new leader comes into rule, that he should start instilling fear. Sun Tzu, in "The Art of War" also recommends the same strategy—that a new leader should even kill off some of his followers. Sun Tzu's followers were not as lucky as you and your fellow employees, because when Sun Tzu said kill, he literally meant kill.[4] (Karen Salmansohn)

---

4   Online chat on ABC News, October 1, 1998, at 1:22pm ET.

- [The need for military readiness] will be as true in the future as it was during Desert Storm, and it has been true throughout the history of warfare. As Sun Tzu said, "It is a doctrine of war not to assume the enemy will not come, but rather to rely on one's readiness to meet him. It is a doctrine of war not to presume that he will not attack, but rather to make oneself invincible." I make those statements in the context of what is happening in the world today. When you glance around the globe you find that there is a potential trouble spot in literally every continent of the world with the exception of the two poles and perhaps Australia.[5] (General Bramlett 1998)

- Booz Allen & Hamilton Inc. built a war game based on the premise "war is hell." They released for public use a tool they had been using for military simulations at the Pentagon. Customers include General Electric, General Dynamics, Caterpillar, and Chevron. "It gets rough out there," says *Businessweek,* "at Chevron some 'enemies' took on their roles so thoroughly, they almost had trouble getting back into Chevron." George Thibault of Booz Allen was asked, "Is business war?" "More or less," said the thirty year navy veteran who worked in the CIA and headed the National War College's military strategy department."[6]

- By introducing [a Sun Tzu–based] system of 'high rewards and severe punishment', the joint venture of Fujian-Hitachi TV Ltd. of China

---

5   Memo entered into Congressional Record, September 10, 1998, on the subject of "Status Of Operational Readiness Of U.S. Military Forces."
6   *Businessweek* (February 1, 1995).

raised productivity. Top management was not exempted. Chronic late arrival and early departure was rooted out (Min Chen, professor of International Studies in Arizona).

- Four centuries before Christ, Sun-tzu wrote that waging war need not require killing people. More than two millennia later, military technologists are taking him at his word by developing sophisticated weapons to subdue enemy soldiers without killing or even permanently injuring them.[7] (*New Scientist*, reported in *Vancouver Sun*, February 1994)

- What is our long-range plan for space—military, civil, commercial, international? And once identified, how do we convince our fellow citizens to contribute their treasure, their time and their energy toward making the plan a reality? Joint Vision 2010[8] cannot be implemented without the capabilities space forces bring to the table. Investment is vital in the continued pursuit of our ability to conduct surveillance of both the Earth and space from space. In the ancient words of Sun Tzu, 'To know yourself, and to know your enemy is the ultimate indicator of success in battle.' Never before in the history of mankind has any nation come closer to actually implementing this philosophy. We migrated most of five major areas to space—missile warning, communications, weather, intelligence and navigation. The next major area could be surveillance—surveillance of

7   See discussion later on "non-lethality" in "Infowar."
8   Often linked to something called RMA (Revolution in Military Affairs), but not to be confused with "Space Cast 2025" or "New Vistas."

space, surveillance of things on or just above the surface of the Earth.[9] (General Howell M. Estes III 1997)

---

9 *Defense Issues*: Volume 12, Number 20. General Howell M. Estes III, commander, US Space Command, to the US Space Foundation's 1997 National Space Symposium, Colorado Springs, April 1997.

A Few Conventions

There are many references in this book to the so-called *Art of War*, referred to here as *Ping-fa*. And while convention has it that *Art of War* was written by a general named "Sun Tzu," *The School of Sun Tzu* holds that Sun Tzu was an institution of learning, not a person. Similarly, evidence suggests that the *Tao Te Ching* was written, not by a person named Lao Tzu, but by a school of that name. *Ping-fa* references will be shown as chapter and amonition. For example, the third admonition in chapter XI would be referenced as (XI.3). *Tao Te Ching* quotations will always appear like this: (*Tao Te Ching* 22) or simply (22). Here, we use "Sun Tzu" as the name of the alleged general; however, the reader will also see "Sun-tzu" and "Sunzi." "Lao Tzu" may also appear as "Lao-tzu."

Contents

Part I: A Journey Through Two Thousand Years

Chronology of Events

BCE

ca. 720–ca. 476	Spring and Autumn period
ca. 600–ca. 500	The time of Lao Tzu (conventional)
ca. 500	The time of Confucius (conventional)
ca. 500	A "soldier-statesman" writes *Thirteen Chapters* (conventional)
ca. 475–ca. 221	Warring States period
ca. 400	The Hundred Schools of Thought
370–290	Time of Mencius
361	Shang Yang arrives in Qin. Qin joins the conference of Warring States. Shang concentrates power of the king.
ca. 330	Jixia Academy established in Ch'i
318–312	Qin on campaign of conquest
284	Qin occupies Ch'i
264	Hsün-tzu comes to Qin
261	Lü Pu-wei meets Tzu-ch'u in Chao. Two years later, the wife of Tzu-ch'u presents him with a baby named Cheng.
256	Qin winds down Zhou dynasty
251	The king of Qin summons Tzu-ch'u and Lü Pu-wei to Xianyang
250	Tzu-ch'u becomes King Chuang-hsiang of Qin; Lü Pu-wei is made chancellor.
247	Chuang-hsiang dies. Cheng assumes the throne. He is thirteen. Li Ssu arrives in Qin.

246	Lü Pu-wei is named Regent. Li Ssu is made senior scribe. Chengkuo Canal completed, radically increasing Qin prosperity.
ca. 245	Flowering of the Qin Academies
240	Lü Pu-wei publishes his anthology (which may include the original *Ping-fa* and *Tao Te Ching*)
237	Lü Pu-wei is exiled. Li Si escapes deportation.
236	Li Ssu becomes justice minister
234	Han Fei-tzu arrives in Qin
233	Death of Han Fei-tzu—allegedly engineered by Li Ssu
230–221	Qin annexes Han, Chao, Wei, Ch'u, Yen, and Ch'i
221	End of the Warring States period. King Cheng becomes Qin Shih Huangdi
213	The (alleged) Burning of the Books
212	The (alleged) Burying of the Scholars
210	Death of Qin Shih Huangdi. Li Ssu and Zhao Gao engineer the ascension of Hu Hai to the throne as second emperor.
208	Li Ssu is killed.
207	Hu Hai dies. Zi Ying ascends as third emperor.
206	Collapse of Qin. Zi Ying submits to Liu Pang, destined to become emperor of the Han dynasty
85	*Shih Chi*, Records of the Historian, completed by Sima Qian

CE

1949	Proclamation of Zhonghua Renmin Gonghe Guo—the People's Republic
1972	Discovery of the Linyi *Ping-fa*
1974	Tomb of the terracotta soldiers discovered near Xi'an

Beginnings

This book is a diary. Or perhaps "ship's log" would be more accurate, for it records my intellectual travels from the moment when a colleague, hearing me speak at a conference, said, "You sound a lot like Sun Tzu!"

The conference subject was knowledge management. I had spoken with some passion about the need to gather intelligence, process it carefully, and then make decisions on what was known, not on what was imagined. My colleague said that was exactly what an ancient Chinese philosopher had said over two thousand years ago. I was intrigued enough to read Thomas Cleary's 1988 translation. I saw that elements of my "contemporary thinking" were in fact quite ancient.

But the text also spoke of the importance of clarity of purpose, role definition, communications, and the need for control. All of this was captured in cryptic instructions, ostensibly about military matters. I say "ostensibly," because most of the alleged military content seemed odd. I had served as an army officer in several organizations, including the infantry and artillery, and had done considerable reading on the subject. So despite the military language and the fact that the book was titled *The Art of War,* I could find nothing actually warlike about it. I read it again, and again, and while war remained elusive, I made new discoveries each time in subjects as diverse as teamwork, negotiation, and leadership.

I saw many odd admonitions. It says "Commanders should be wise, sincere, and benevolent." They are instructed to give careful thought, exercise cautious decision-making, and above all ensure they achieve their objectives without destruction. Instructions for being kinder and gentler, however, seemed overwhelmed by a lot of talk about besieging and being besieged, and assault by fire. Nevertheless, one comes away with a nagging suspicion that it isn't all what it seems. For instance, in contrast to what usually appears in the military genre, *The Art of War* does not address violence.[10]

Consider Machiavelli's admonition "Men ought either to be well treated or crushed, because they can avenge themselves of lighter injuries, of more serious ones they cannot; therefore the injury that is to be done to a man ought to be of such a kind that one does not stand fear of revenge" (Jay 1987, 18). This is combat talk of the sort that never appears in the *Ping-fa* that is required reading in military schools, and referenced in hundreds of textbooks and other media. The commentary used in these venues varies minimally.

Allowing for the distinct possibility that my understanding of the military genre was inadequate, I plunged into so-called "related works." I read Niccolo Machiavelli, Liddell Hart, Wutzu[11], George Silver[12], Carl von Clausewitz, and Antoine-Henri, Baron de Jomini. I read Sun Pin and Miyamoto Mushashi's *Book of Five Rings*.

Thomas Cleary, the author of thirty books on Eastern culture, was convinced the subject was war but frequently shared his doubt that was all there was to it.

---

10   *Ping-fa* has only one, clear advocation of violence—and that is in regard to the treatment of spies. That advocation is questionable, if for no other reason than that it proposes a punishment that exceeds the nature of the offense. As you will see later, *Ping-fa* has very likely suffered additions and "corrections" during its lifetime. This would be a likely candidate.

11   Calthrop's *Book of War*

12   *Paradoxes of Defense.* See: http://www.pbm. com/~lindahl/brief.html

Unfortunately, he didn't pursue what must have been nagging suspicions.

He did understand that *Ping-fa* had distinct roots in the *Tao Te Ching*. He said that readers could not get to the substance of *Ping-fa* unless they saw it as a work written in a Taoist land, from a Taoist perspective.[13] He said, "The importance of understanding the Taoist element of *The Art of War* can hardly be exaggerated." He called *Ping-fa* a "classic of Taoist thought" and a "Taoist practical philosophy."[14]

The very talented *Ping-fa* translator Lionel Giles said, "The great body of Chinese sentiment, from Lao Tzu downwards, and especially as reflected in the standard literature of Confucianism, has been consistently pacific and intensely opposed to militarism in any form." This "intense opposition to militarism" was most passionate when it came to combat, which might be deemed appropriate only when all other options have failed. Even then, it was not considered desirable or worthy of praise and reward. Combat represented failure.

Taoism has been an important element in Chinese philosophy from times of antiquity. And one of its key tenets is the concept of *wu-wei*, a belief that one should shun activity that disrupts the natural flow of the world—a condition known as "the Way." In its earliest Confucian iteration, *wu-wei* meant noninvolvement. The world will unfold as it wishes.

When Qin embarked on its path to empire, it reinvented Taoism with the publication of the *Tao Te Ching*. The horrendous effects of the Warring States period needed a tool that would help transform the ancient philosophical and cultural tradition of situation avoidance to legitimized social intervention. A number of significant shifts were achieved. The new Taoism of the *Tao Te Ching* delivered a social, philosophical, and political peace manifesto. It states—emphatically and

---

13 Though he will stray from that insight again and again.
14 Cleary 1988a, 29, 30

with clarity—that people must control their world. It recognizes that a world uncontrolled is a world of chaos. The *Tao Te Ching* tells us that while there is a preference for intelligent noninvolvement, there is a great value in people of learning and good will intervening when essential, ensuring that society does not fall apart. A talented Taoist will know what to do and what not to do to forestall unpleasant or unhelpful events, being highly skilled at working proactively to ensure that harmony reigns.

The *Tao Te Ching* is the authority under which one can—with the blessings of the gods—seek to change the ways of humankind. It declares that methods and events vary in their degree of goodness and that there is rightness to intervention when conditions are less than ideal. Less ideal conditions are those of disharmony and conflict. The dedication of people to achieving peace over war is both admirable and essential. This forms the moral ground. The methods by which these lofty goals could be achieved were the practices of *Ping-fa*.

Ping-fa is the operational manual for the application of the *Tao Te Ching*. It draws from the new authorities that made *wu-wei* a strategic vehicle. Intervention was appropriate and, in fact, essential under certain circumstances. But still, the preferred option was to do nothing whatsoever. Matters, it was believed, worked themselves out most of the time, and intervention might be helpful, or not.

The philosophy and practice of *wu-wei* sets out when and how leaders should act. *Wu-wei*—which is either "sensitive intervention"[15] *or not doing anything at all*—is

---

15   The science-fictional series *Dune* has the Bene Gesserit practicing sensitive intervention: "Throughout the Imperium the Bene Gesserit kept a low profile, but they were always to be found in vital areas, tilting the political equilibrium at crux points, watching, nudging, achieving their own aims. It was best when others under-estimated them; the Sisters encountered fewer obstacles that way."

what *Ping-fa* is all about. It is the vehicle for achieving great things, before the need for great things is even generally known. *Wu-wei* has a moral base and is driven by practical need. When one acts in accordance with *wu-wei*, one acts unobtrusively—without evident assertion or disruption.

> The skilled master of life never tries to change things by asserting himself against them; he yields to their full force and either pushes them slightly out of direct line or else transfers their energy so that it can be used against them. He accepts life positively, and when events must be changed, he negotiates rather than inflicting his will on others. (Norris 1996, 32)

Ping-fa models and methods are dependent upon, and validated by, the difficult concept of "benevolence."[16] This is the "benevolence" that was widely known, understood and accepted long before the state of Qin set out on creating the first empire of China.[17] As Confucius said,

> Only the man of humanity knows how to love people and hate people. A resolute scholar and a man of humanity will never seek to live at the expense of injuring humanity. He would rather sacrifice his life in order to realize humanity. (Bishop 1985, 17, 22)

Benevolence is an essential piece of the *Ping-fa* methodology. If states were to practice the new *wu-wei* and do it without offending the gods, then intervention could occur only when it was in the best interests of

---

16   As J. I. Crump (1964, 4) notes, *li* (literally "profit") really means "what is beneficial" in a Taoist context.

17   The Dalai Lama says all the teachings of Buddhism can be distilled into: "If you can, help others; if you cannot do that, at least do not harm them" (Norris 1996, 161).

all concerned. But the clearer the *Ping-fa* methodology became, the applications of it became more and more mysterious.

That there could be possibly significant inter-organizational implications and applications appealed to my interest in strategic planning. But this analysis was also shaping up as a quite divergent perspective on the legendary Sun Tzu and Lao Tzu. Sooner or later I knew I would be confronting the near unanimous commentary which was intractable. It seemed to agree even on the material that could not be found in any *Ping-fa* translation.[18] At this stage I had limited corroboration of my suspicions.

Then I discovered J. H. Huang. He worked with a newly discovered, earlier *Ping-fa*, known as the "Linyi" version. It was found to have much less of a war and much more of a peace flavor than what had been available until that moment. Huang also brought a new set of skills to the exercise. A talented academic and linguist, he had no allegiance to the military view of *Ping-fa*, and importantly, he translated according to the vocabulary and culture of the pre-Chinese period. So his skills and approach brought an entirely new perspective.

Huang's findings were illuminating and startling. When *The Art of War* was written, he says, it was known only as *Ping-fa*. Though that expression might be translated today as "art of war," at the time of its writing it meant "art of engagement," in the context of interstate diplomacy.[19] Here was an analyst brave enough

---

18 Commentators often say, "Sun Tzu must have meant ..."

19 Huang was not the first or only commentator to observe that the meaning of *ping* had changed in two thousand years. But he is the only one who has attached any significance to it. Tang Zi-Chang offered up seventeen military meanings for *ping*, none of which approximates "engagement" (1969, 14).

to suggest that *The Art of War* might not be about war exclusively, or at all.

At this point I needed additional perspective and insight. I sought out Eastern experts Ray Grigg and Alan Watts. Their advice was sound. Watts said to move slowly and carefully. One must learn, he said, to let Eastern philosophical works speak, rather than trying to force meaning out of them.

> I am much more interested in how these ancient writings reverberate on the harp of my own brain, which has, of course, been tuned to the scales of Western culture. Although I will by no means despise precise and descriptive information—the Letter, I am obviously more interested in the Spirit—the actual experiencing and feeling of that attitude to life which is the following of the Tao. (Watts 1975, xvi)

I came to see the great importance of metaphor and analogy in ancient Chinese writing. Stories were used to convey complexities and subtle values.[20] Images showed learners the meaning of concepts that were both new and difficult. I came to appreciate Ames's instruction:

> In our encounter with a text from a tradition as different from ours as is Classical China's, we must exercise our minds and our imaginations to locate it within its own ways of thinking and living. (Ames 1993, 6)

Just as Japanese drums utilize a beat quite distinct from Western traditions, so too do Eastern philosophical

---

20   As Stanley Herman observed about the *Tao Te Ching*, "the nature of Chinese character writing [which] can represent a large number of things and ideas, makes it literally impossible to translate verses without interpreting them" (1994, 2).

and cultural ideas spring from a realm far from Western experiences. Wisdom, success, and failure have variable meanings, I found. By now I was able to read *Ping-fa* as message and metaphor, not bound by what the commentary said "must be there."

Ping-fa sets out methods for delivering shared solutions where there are competing interests. It is about organizational management in an environment of actual and potential competition where skilled leaders, following a concise methodology, work to ensure that conflict does not occur. If it does, their efforts are directed at ensuring it is at the absolute minimum level. Contact is strategically considered and allowed to occur only when it is clear that the consequences will be mutually beneficial.

Ping-fa is simplicity and elegance. There is concept, detail, and comprehensiveness. There are crystal clear messages about leadership, organization, and communications, about the importance of strategies and adaptive behavior. There are instructions on issues as diverse as ethics, winning, and human nature. Control is evidently the central theme: "Engagements are critical. Manage them. Be benevolent. Don't screw up. Here's how you do that."

Those most skilled in engagement management achieve their objectives quietly, efficiently, and with minimum outlay. They realize gains without losses, victory without defeat. *Ping-fa* states that confrontation suggests incompetence and conflict indicates failure. Here finally is the explanation for one of the most misunderstood admonitions in *Ping-fa*: those who are competent achieve victory before war is begun. In other words, victory (for all) is achieved without evident intervention (the "war" of "art of war").

Collectively, the admonitions comprise a comprehensive, integrated framework for management. *Ping-fa* is a great deal more than mere battlefield tactics (though I was not prepared to deny that as one possible use). There are forty strident admonitions about managing interorganizational engagements. Good managers maintain control. Incompetent managers lose control and find themselves in situations of conflict. About these incompetents *Ping-fa* instructs, "Dismiss them." [21]

The "War" in *"Art of War"* is as J. H. Huang has pointed out, the practice of "diplomacy." There are no military instructions in *Ping-fa*, no wounded, and no loss of life. Armed combat is condemned again and again as the worst possible option for achieving objectives. If *Ping-fa* is not about battles and war but rather about diplomatic relations, just what could have been its possible use at the time of incessant war in the decades before the founding of China?

The *Intrigues of the Warring States (Chan-kuo Ts'e)*[22] exposed me to the "persuasions" that were developed by the same academies of learning in Qin that gave us the *Tao Te Ching* and *Ping-fa*.[23] These little stories are given little attention today, considered imaginative fables similar to the nursery rhymes of Old England. But their meaning and intent are far more profound than generally understood.

Persuasions were intended to convey complex training messages and were also used as propaganda. While the Qin academies were writing entirely new analyses about the beliefs and activities of individuals and groups, communications professionals were creating the training tools and messages that would enable Qin to reach out to the Middle Kingdom (what would eventually become China) with its messages of empire. Today, Qin's persuasions can be as helpful in enabling understanding

---

21   Lau and Ames (1996, 41) can't find that message in their *Ping-fa* analysis.
22   Referred to hereinafter as *Intrigues*
23   Academies that included what I refer to here as the School of Lao Tzu and the School of Sun Tzu

the concepts developed by Qin's academies as they were over two thousand years ago.

Consider the story of the Imperial Concubines, alleged to be "the biography of Sun Tzu" (See Annex 2). It is a charming story that illustrates the key concepts of leadership, delegation, control, and communication. "The Physician Best Known in the Land" has messages about benevolence, while providing incomparable insight into the practice of sensitive intervention.[24]

These concepts, values, and principles were highly significant in the context of the times—that is, the remarkable ending of the Warring States and the establishment of the first empire of China. Could such devices have come from individuals named Sun Tzu and Lao Tzu? This is the least likely scenario. *Ping-fa* and the *Tao Te Ching* are evidently beyond the time and talent of single individuals. They had to be the work of people of great wisdom, fired with the importance of their work, and mesmerized by the prospects of their orders. Their power and insight tell us they were the product of experts in organization, management, and process. As *Ping-fa* has complete resonance to the *Tao Te Ching* a strong argument could be made that the same people produced the two simultaneously.[25] My studies, however, suggest they came from different institutions, the *Tao Te Ching* from the Lao Tzu School, and *Ping-fa* from the Sun Tzu School.

How then did this notion of Lao Tzu, the philosopher, and Sun Tzu, the army general, emerge and gain credence? One possible explanation is that it may have been a literary device, a case of character invention, where near-mythical figures are endowed with great

---

24 Examination of the Lao Tzu–Chuang Tzu philosophical coincidence and the *Ping-fa–Intrigues* practical coincidence would be a valuable area of study.

25 Australian National University says *Ping-fa* and the Tao Te Ching are among the first works to use the dialectical process (http://marxists.anu.edu.au/).

wisdom to help people relate to new concepts, ideas, and messages. Such would have been consistent with the (created) legendary superhero Su Qin. According to the *Intrigues* and the *Shih Chi* of Sima Qian, Su Qin is an historical character who had great knowledge that had been gained from a secret book.

Su Qin was a marketing tool. It was part of Qin's vast socio-political-military propaganda construct that included fictitious details about at least four major alliances. The reluctant states of the Middle Kingdom had to be convinced they were in a minority that was doomed to failure, thereafter marginalized from the empire. Qin needed a folk hero to personify the emerging empire who would be the new China's "everyman." A caricature of the Qin dream and method, Su Qin was a persuader with *Ping-fa* in hand.

The *Tao Te Ching* and *Ping-fa* were tools—of many— that brought about a new social foundation, framework, and process. They were the products of an exciting time. A grand challenge had been defined in the context of an incredible dream. This was an epoch of greatness—the greatness of leadership and intellectual achievement.

Qin's *Tao Te Ching* and *Ping-fa* established (as yet unrecognized) benchmarks in leadership, teamwork, relationship management, and empowerment. A model for harmonious relations at the interpersonal and international levels, these works instruct us in role definition, communications, planning, and adaptability.

Ping-fa is important literature. It is also important political science, sociology, psychology, and organizational dynamics. Relegated to the military strategy shelves for centuries, its proper place is alongside the works of today's best theorists and management analysts.

But if *Ping-fa* and the *Tao Te Ching* were great works produced by a great nation on the path of creating the first empire of China, how can it be that historians and analysts have been utterly blind to that possibility? The answer is quite shocking. These works were debased, or disguised, because they were an embarrassment to the Han (Confucian) regime that succeeded the first empire.

The Qin regime had followed the tenets of "Legalism," from which evolved a political structure and process not much different from what is seen in almost every country today. Legalism was despised by the ruling Confucians. When they returned to power, they sacked the Qin capital, tore down the great creations of the first emperor, and discredited or burned its written works. The story of the first empire then is a story of both greatness and tragedy. The tragedy is that the greatness of Qin and its emperor, Qin Shih Huangdi, are now buried in layers of revisionist history.

Scholars will have confirmation of the origins, use, and consequences of the *Tao Te Ching* and *Ping-fa* when they examine the roots and foundation of the Chinese empire, but only if they approach the vast trove of archaeological and documented evidence with a fresh perspective.

When Chinese authorities uncover the tomb of Qin Shih Huangdi, first emperor, we will see what a unique event the founding of the Chinese empire was. And it will be clear that there was no "Sun Tzu" or "Lao Tzu," but rather there were schools of learning in the highly advanced Qin Kingdom that bore those names.

How *The School of Sun Tzu* Moves Us Away from the Art of War Canon

The Qin, Han, Sun Tzu, and Lao Tzu commentators have a calcified view of the epoch that featured the end of the Warring States and gave us Qin Shih Huangdi and the Chinese empire. Accordingly, they will find it difficult to appreciate that, with only a few exceptions, all that is reported and analyzed here is based on solid, published research. To date, the commentary has not examined that research in a cohesive manner, evaluating the evidence and recognizing the revisionist work of the second empire. The exceptions referred to are those few instances where I offer conjecture on events and the meaning of those events, because proof is not available.

The School of Sun Tzu exposes, for the first time, just how the empire of China came into being. It profiles a quite different emperor, Qin Shih Huangdi, from what is portrayed again and again: that he was a murderous illegitimate tyrant who was besieged by both devils and drugs. That "truth" has grown from a brilliant revisionist plan executed by the bitter Confucians when they regained control of China.

This thesis explores the organization, structure, content, and meaning of *Ping-fa*. It will be shown that it and the *Tao Te Ching*, products of the Sun Tzu and Lao Tzu Schools in Qin, were and are epoch-spanning works of literature and philosophy. When their origins become known and understood, what they achieved concerning the founding of China will be evident.

Ping-fa has languished in dusty corners because of a wonderful paradox. It uses the language of war to condemn the evils of war. As for military content, there are no wars, no casualties and no advocacy of destruction. War is simply a pedagogical device.

Tactile messages are used to pictorially communicate concepts. You can't define and describe the concept of "team" in a few sentences. But you can call it an army, and your audience will have an idea of what you are talking about. With the image of an "army" in mind, you can then discuss other very difficult notions, such as roles, leadership, authority, and delegation. Troop movements and battles help us visualize organization and process.

The Han's "Great Historian," Sima Qian, may be responsible for the notion that *Ping-fa* started out as a general's *Thirteen Chapters* and that its import was militaristic.[26] He apparently saw it, or was instructed to see it, as unimportant, relegating it to a list of lesser works. Perhaps he didn't understand it, or he may have understood it and made sure it was discredited as yet another evil work of the hated Qin Legalists. If he understood what it was about and what it had helped achieve, he may have felt driven to suppress it, as it could have posed a serious threat to the new dynasty.

> Because of its realistic approach [employing spies and deception] *The Art of War* was vehemently condemned by Confucian literati throughout late Chinese history. Sun Wu's existence and role as well as the book itself accordingly were viewed as late fabrications, unworthy of consideration except by the morally reprehensible.[27] (Sawyer 1993, 150 note 11)

Though Sima Qian and his *Shih Chi*, or *Records of the Historian,* are the most quoted "authentic" sources for the Qin and Warring States period, the lot should be taken with a grain of salt. The Great Historian ensured that everything noted about the Han was good and that most Qin references were bad.[28] The *Records* were the product of a regime not disposed to favor anything Qin. The Historian was a state appointee, working for a

---

26 Sima Qian was born about 145 BCE and in 107 BCE succeeded his father as Grand Historian of the Han court.
27 Sawyer's 1993 work says Sun Wu's name did not appear in the *Tso chuan* that reports Wu's history in great detail, because "many persons and events pivotal to the history of various minor states went unrecorded" (1993, 150 note 6).
28 One of the few to question the Historian's integrity is E. Chavannes, whose *Les Mémoires de Se-ma Ts'ien* asks just how sure we can be that Sima Qian's sources were truly from antiquity.

Confucian dynasty whose official policy was to document and promulgate the alleged "horrors" of the Qin.

Tang Zi-Chang was able to see the intrigue implicit in *Ping-fa*, though not its peaceful nature. "[During the Qin empire] and at the beginning of the Han dynasty, *Sun Zi* was treated as the secret rule for the conduct of war and revolution." He understood *Thirteen Chapters* to be a "crystallization of thousands of years of military experiences and documentation," including a number of "ancient war books such as *Ping Fa (The Art of War)*, *Jun Zheng (The Administration of War)* and *Zhian Fa (The Principles of Tactics)*" (1969, 165).

The commentators revere the Great Historian despite the known ambiguities about his life and work. His *Records* "became the inspiration of the twenty-six dynastic histories written up to the 20th century" (Pirazzoli-t'Serstevens 1982, 102, 206). J. I. Crump (1964, ix) notes that Sima Qian's rendering of Qin history has "never been seriously impugned."

Sima Qian's sparse, unsubstantiated reports on *Ping-fa* are deemed inerrant in all the commentary. He classed the work as a war manual, and there it has remained. He imagined that the fascinating persuasion called the "Imperial Concubines" was Sun Tzu's biography.

The one thing he got right was the passion in *Ping-fa*. He said "Sun Tzu" was someone who "had his feet cut off and yet continued to discuss the art of war." This is likely metaphor, and it would have described very well the commitment of Qin and its agents. The commentators who are not comfortable with metaphor are certain Sima Qian must have been talking about Sun Tzu's (alleged, but imaginary) footless nephew, Sun Pin.

Ping-fa is replicated here without the military metaphor, where one finds sovereigns, generals, spies, and armies. *The School of Sun Tzu* replaces these roles with civilian chiefs, leaders, observers, and teams. Understanding what the military imagery was used for brings an appreciation of a critical conceptual *Ping-fa* building block. With that, one can then see the emergence of *Ping-fa's* really exciting premise: that organizations can exist and relate to each other in ways that do not lead to chaos and conflict.

With demilitarization, the *Ping-fa* engagement management brilliance emerges. We see instructions on roles, responsibilities, and processes. We learn that when an engagement is warranted (and they rarely are), they should be entered into and concluded quickly and discreetly. The longer you are engaged, the greater the chance you will achieve visibility. And the more visibly engaged you are, the harder it is to maintain control. *Ping-fa* repeats these instructions again and again, but they are yet to register in a military commentary that assumes peace is brought about by war.

> Actually Sun Tzu and Clausewitz do not differ as much as is often assumed regarding the need to resort to the ultimate means of battle and bloodshed. They agree that the most rational way of waging war is usually to fight for the shortest possible duration and win as decisively as possible. (Handel 1992, 32, 75–76)

For the most part it was not overly difficult to replace the military language with civilian. That ease did not extend to the term "enemy." There are at least two parties to an engagement, and it is natural to speak of "the enemy" in a military model. For "enemy" I've used "other party" or simply "other." The literature on conflict management has also had to confront this issue. Albrecht (1993) speaks of "other party," while Carolyn Dickson (1997) uses the much less satisfactory and ambiguous "conflict partner."

Achieving a clear unencumbered understanding of *Ping-fa* takes more than a vocabulary change. It also demands stepping away from our own philosophical traditions, which include the mental straitjacket called "determinism." While the ancients in pre-China's Middle Kingdom believed that they could not and should not interfere with the natural unfolding of the world, many in the West today believe that human destiny is foretold and unchangeable. The widespread acceptance of the notion that "war is inevitable" is one illustration of this collective mind-set.

There is one final personal adjustment needed, and that is to accept the notion that change can be managed in a way that is beneficial for all concerned, and that when it is done in that manner, there are lasting effects. *Ping-fa* insists that it must be done that way, or not done at all. And the way of that change includes an insistence that there be no loss to any party and preferably no evidence that a managed intervention has taken place. These are huge expectations, not easily achieved. We are instructed that those who act for reasons other than defined necessity, those who do more than is required, and those who seek recognition for what they have done should be dismissed.

There are other admonitions and instructions in *Ping-fa* that challenge sacred assumptions about human interaction. We are asked to consider the possibility that competition and conflict are not integral to personal and social success, and that real values depend upon serving the needs of more than the self. These admonitions are clearly drawn from the wisdom of Taoism, in the way that Heider does. He says that when one knows "how polarities work, wise [Taoist] leaders do not push to make things happen, but allow processes to unfold on their own" (Heider 1988, 3).

Appreciating *Ping-fa* as a work of peace makes significant demands on the reader who must, at first, get beyond the military metaphor. Then, it is necessary to read the text in plain language, preferably with the benefit of some grounding in the *Tao Te Ching*. Recognize that certain assumptions about people and interpersonal relations are seriously flawed. Then, make a reach.

Imagine the possibility that there is a way that people can work proactively, and intelligently, to achieve a better society for all.

Ping-fa challenges an intractable belief structure. It is a great humanitarian work, railing against the outrageous costs of weapons, soldiers, and war that we are told symbolize uncaring and incompetent leadership. They exhaust organizational resources while delivering no assurance of benefit.

Ping-fa is an inspired methodology for the management of the organization and its environment. It presents a comprehensive strategic planning process that defines roles, relationships, dynamics, values, and methods for effective engagement management. As it is both intellectual and procedural, blending profound admonitions and succinct instructions. it can only have come from a team of philosophers and practitioners, strategists and tacticians, administrators and governors. *Ping-fa* was an instrument that helped create the empire of China. It was also an immeasurable gift to the future.

The School of Sun Tzu is an appeal for reexamination of certain facts and assumptions surrounding *Ping-fa*, the *Tao Te Ching* and the founding of China. Because the "official" commentary tirelessly repeats an unverified mantra about these works and the first empire, alternative perspectives and analyses are not being heard. Accordingly, opportunities to draw on what was taught and learned in the academies of Qin are being missed. There is a subtle promise in the *Tao Te Ching* and *Ping-fa*: there are messages and methods here that may have worked wonders once and may yet come to work those wonders again.

There is a market for peace and peaceful processes. *International Dispute Settlement* says, "The peaceful settlement of international disputes is the most critical issue of our time [given that] the use of force in certain disputes could result in the destruction of civilization"

(Merrills 1998, 292, 310). This was the exact realization that dawned on the intellectual elites of the Middle Kingdom as the period of the Warring States unfolded.

As today's academics and analysts seek new solutions to critical relationship issues, hallowed assumptions are being challenged. Vladimir Vassin's *The Eleventh Commandment* says, "It is almost universally assumed that the only way human society can make progress is through competition [but] competition is a barbarian's activity" (1995, p. 13,14). That was an early discovery in the academies of Qin that were established to solve the riddles of war and peace.

Part II: The Architects of Empire

Chinese legend says a king asked Mencius (370–290 BCE) how a country could be united. He replied that if a leader could be found who did not delight in killing, the people would flock to him in a rush. He declared that "those who delight in their skill in strategy are, in fact, great criminals" (Creel 1953, 81–89).

Mencius said that a people properly administered by a benevolent government should be able to overcome armed soldiers with sticks, because "morale was more important than armament." Such a country would have the "mandate of heaven" and would serve at the pleasure of Shang-ti, God-on-high.

The man who came to fulfill the Mencius prophecy was Qin Shih Huangdi, China's first emperor.[29]

The first emperor's story begins the day a very rich merchant from Chao named Lü Pu-wei arranged to meet a Qin prince named Tzu-ch'u, who was living in exile. Though in the line of succession, Tzu-ch'u was facing limited prospects. He was out of favor and impoverished. Lü Pu-wei became his sponsor and mentor. A clever man, he was able to engineer not only his return to Qin in 251 BCE, but also advancement to the top of the line of succession.

Within a year the king is dead. Tzu-ch'u becomes King Chuang-hsiang. Lü Pu-wei is now chancellor, then considered a noble achievement for a merchant. Only three years later, Chuang-hsiang is also gone, then to be replaced by his thirteen-year-old son Cheng who was born in 259 BCE. Cheng is guided by regents and tutors, the foremost of whom was Lü Pu-wei, until he achieves majority. In twenty-six years he will declare himself first emperor of China.

Sima Qian, China's "Great Historian," insists that Cheng was really Lü Pu-wei's child, born of a relationship

---

29 Zhou dynasty philosophers (1027–221 BCE) enunciated the doctrine of "mandate of heaven" (*tianming*), the notion that the ruler (son of heaven) is governed by divine right. Dethronement would prove he had lost the mandate.

with a concubine. The message in blunt terms is that a bastard child of a lowborn merchant became first emperor of China, and that everything the emperor knew came from that lowly merchant. This is all, of course, egregious insult to his memory. In the highly unlikely event that these stories are true, they are yet more evidence of just how remarkable the achievements of the amazing—and possibly ruthless—Lü Pu-wei were.

We have only second-empire (Han) historians to credit with this story. These Confucians were more propagandists than historians, committed to discrediting the name of the man who had achieved empire without them. They succeeded beyond their wildest dreams. The official Han empire position that the first emperor was a tyrannical despot who would stop at nothing to achieve his evil ends became well entrenched. One current commentator, for example, speaks of his

> demonical spirit [for military supremacy] that constituted a vast plan for espionage and corruption. Where bribery produced no results, Huangdi resorted to assassination. Once treachery was certain and the most loyal defenders had vanished, the Qin armies began their offensive. (Gernet 1968, 131)

Despite the Han rhetoric there is no doubt the first emperor had a vast plan and that he achieved great wonders in his short lifetime. The Han were able to color his achievements, but they could not erase them. Qin Shih Huangdi carved an empire out of an embattled collection of principalities. The commentary asserts he used "vast armies" and caused the deaths of hundreds of thousands in numerous campaigns. None of this has been confirmed. The "Great Unifier," first and August emperor of the Qin dynasty, brought generations of internecine conflict to an end and unified China. Whatever the means Qin used to achieve these ends, were they not significant achievements?

The first emperor owed much to a single act of pure genius. That act was the decision to search the known world for the brightest and best intellects. They were brought to the kingdom, and a noble purpose was placed before them: to set out the ways in which wars could be brought to an end, the states unified, and an empire created. This was the foundation of Qin's "university" of academies, designed to study policy, governance, and diplomacy.

Here is a great mystery. How did these elements come together in one of the Middle Kingdom's minor states in a way that would eventually lead to an empire of two thousand years? To answer that question, we need to go back two hundred years before that time.

In the "Spring and Autumn" period of the Middle Kingdom (ca.720–ca.476 BCE), there had been a tradition of gentlemanly jousting held during the summer months. These were recreational diversions conducted according to strict rules and causing no serious degree of social disorder or loss. They were ceremonial, "ritualistic" events, held when the growing season allowed time off and the weather was not too hot or too cold. It doesn't appear that there were any serious inconveniences or consequences.

For some reason all this changed. The period of Spring and Autumn became the period of the Warring States. Social activity evolved into all-out war. In time, the scope and scale of military activity became incredible, and the costs—human and otherwise—staggering. It is reported that there was war somewhere in China in 105 out of the 141 years from 363 to 222 BCE. States were either at war, preparing for war, or recovering from war during all of that time.[30]

The kingdoms established standing armies of frightening numbers. War and warriors became powerful,

---

30   *The Cambridge History of China*, Vol. 1, p. 20–25.

and conditions were in continuous disequilibrium. Military engagements now involved professional soldiers, with consequent huge costs and massive losses of life. "By the fifth century BCE, the only alternative to winning was to perish," says Roger Ames (1993, 3).

Conditions were

characterized by expansionism and imperialism, starting unjust military operations against innocent countries, killing innocent people, cutting off the heritage of ancient sages. Blood flows for a thousand miles, and skeletons litter the fields—all to satisfy the desires of greedy rulers and governments. (Cleary 1992a, 27, 61)

Sima Qian reported that one single campaign in 260 BCE cost 450,000 lives. While these numbers are likely exaggerated, the situation suggested to some that social dissolution was a real possibility.

The sages ... could not ignore the rising tide of violence, and avoid wondering where it might end. Their fingers of blame pointed in various directions, but all were united in decrying the brutality and destructiveness of the wars that surrounded them. (O'Connell 1995, 170)

The Middle Kingdom was in desperate straits. People were suffering. Living conditions had become dreadful as food, materials, and the strength of the people were absorbed into military activity. Young men, recruited from meager farm operations, were continually drafted for campaigns, only to return bruised and broken years later. Those left to eke out an existence were burdened with horrendous taxes, special war levies, and a constant threat of conquest and subjugation.

Though people of insight and intelligence may have seen that the delicate, natural balance of civilization was threatened and the common people were living shattered lives, there was little that could be done. The common will was driven by a belief in "the Way"—that events were unfolding as they should—and one should avoid entanglement in social engineering. So even if the issues were clear and the need for action evident, there was no widespread will to do anything about it. In short, the common folk considered the situation ordained and inevitable.

Some held the view that peace and justice had become dire needs. But there was no one they could turn to for salvation. The philosophers were mired in tradition, refusing to embrace the sacrilege of intervention. They were not about to offend the will of heaven. The military and their princes who felt driven to continue things as they were had no idea how to break the spiral of war even had they wanted to.

There was one island of sanity in the midst of this chaos. The small state of Qin was politically unimportant, situated on the fringe of the Middle Kingdom. For some time its resources had been focused on defending its borders and repelling barbarians. But Qin had ambition and a hardworking population gifted with imagination and confidence. They had long dreamed of peace and an end to war.

Qin's dreams started to take on a material aspect with the arrival from Wei, in 361, of Shang Yang. Qin may have already been exceptional and called Shang Yang, or Shang Yang made Qin exceptional, a cauldron for greatness. Whatever the sequence, this was not coincidence.

With Shang Yang at the helm, the kingdom joined the council of feudal rulers and the Warring States conference. A visionary, he saw that Qin could play a significant role in the Middle Kingdom, and he had the management and diplomatic skills necessary to set that course. He brought order and efficiency to the state government and economy. He lured statesmen, sages, and traveling teachers who brought the accumulated wisdom of the ages to Qin. His lessons and instructions were summarized in *The Book of Lord Shang* (*Shangjun shu*). Before he died in 338, he forged a new kingdom that was the first state in the Middle Kingdom to challenge feudalism. Lord Shang's administration authored a new government model and code that became known as "Legalism."

> The Chinese imperial political tradition is described by most Chinese historians as 'outside Confucian, inside Legalist' (*wairu neifa*). Although the Chinese imperial dynastic era ended in 1911, the influence of the Legalist tradition on Chinese political development can still be felt today. (Zhengyuan Fu 1996, 8)

Importantly, Lord Shang started the process of Confucian disenfranchisement. Persuasions legitimizing Legalism - some of which are reported as *The Master of the Hidden Storehouse* – started circulating in the Middle Kingdom.[31] With that, there was no turning back. Qin's resourceful people who would not be hobbled by tradition were convinced they had the "mandate of heaven" to rule the world. They set out to use their remarkable talents in the realization of a most extraordinary vision.

When Legalism became the official philosophy at court, the powerful Confucian reactionaries were discredited and denied access to the administration. Legalist methods were progressive even by today's standards: they involved study and analysis, professional management, and sound business practices. To date, China has seen no reason it should vary from that course. Legalism played a

---

31   *Thunder in the Sky* (Cleary 1993)

crucial role in laying the intellectual and ideological foundation of the traditional Chinese empire, which lasted more than two thousand years and was the prototype of the modern totalitarian state." (Zhengyuan Fu 1996, 7)

In Qin it became clear that a jihad—a true "holy war"—would be necessary if they were to move the world away from what was wrong and closer to what they knew to be right. All Qin needed was a strategy by which this could all be achieved. A major breakthrough occurred when Qin invaded and occupied Ch'l in 284 BCE. There, it took possession of the great Jixia Academy, which was pre-China's great intellectual capital.

Jixia Academy had focused on the theory of statecraft and other subjects, but Qin saw that theory had to be married to philosophy and practice. The academy was transformed to serve Qin. New analyses were authorized to determine whether, and how proactive intervention in social affairs might be appropriate. (Lin 1977, ix)

The roles and responsibilities of kings and officials were examined, as were forms of governance. Experts studied the nature and function of laws and alternate ways of settling disputes. New policy and procedural works were commissioned, and older works were revised to meet the new requirements. There were important new discoveries, earthshaking in their vision and power.

Because it dared to imagine a different world, Qin became a crucible for innovation, change, and enterprise. When those principles became known, the gifted, the adventurous, and the entrepreneurial came by the thousands. Learning became such a fashionable activity in Qin that the rich endowed their own academies to study subjects of interest to their benefactors.

Qin at this time was Camelot, a kingdom that valued intelligence and excellence, wisdom and leadership. The state's interests were not solely on ending war and building an empire. The needs of the state itself were also a prime focus. With an insistence on managerial and administrative competence, the state's wealth grew.

Qin undertook an ambitious program of public works. Canals and irrigation systems brought fertility to arid lands. Qin's strength, or *qi*, became worrisome to neighboring states, though it would be some time before they realized just how powerful Qin had become.

The king of neighboring Han thought he would deflect Qin's energies by conning the state into a wasteful and useless canal project. He loaned Qin an engineer to work on what was to be a futile exercise, but the plan backfired. Qin made the canal a major driver of the economy. Soon Qin wealth represented "six-tenths that of the empire" (Cottrell 1962, 111). By 256, Qin had evolved from an innocuous existence on the fringe, to the most powerful state in the kingdom.

Qin's leaders were brash. Fuelled by a sound economy, good planning, and developing expertise, they believed they had or could develop answers to the challenges of Qin and the Middle Kingdom. Their analysts took nothing for granted—not the wisdom of the ancients nor the pronouncements of the age's leading politicians, philosophers and militarists. They challenged everything that was known and believed. In short order, Qin achieved a series of miracles.

Qin understood that there would be no movement forward until the calamity of the Warring States period was addressed. Also, Qin saw that the end of war would necessitate methods involving low costs and with minimum losses. Sheer economics dictated those conditions. Drawing on the discoveries of the academies, Qin also understood that sustainability and longevity would not come about through death and destruction. These courageous heretics had no reservations in seeing old assumptions challenged. The Qin governors were ready to be shown, and test new ideas.

Observers—in Qin and beyond—saw the transformation of the Qin state as something quite mysterious, but the way Qin brought an end to war and the unification of China was pure magic. The methods developed by the Qin academies worked best when they were unseen, and when they were delivered by trained professionals.

> Everyone strives to be prepared to solve problems, but no one actually knows how to cause problems not to arise. It is easier to cause problems not to arise than it is to solve problems, yet no one actually knows how to work on this; so you cannot talk to anyone about such arts. (Cleary 1992a, 48)

Qin: Learning, Application, and Empire

Qin Shih Huangdi himself recruited more than 370 scholars and philosophers, including the brilliant Han Fei-tzu, a person many consider to have been an ancient Machiavelli. Dun J. Li says that Han Fei-tzu was a major influence on Qin Shih Huangdi, as was Li Ssu, one of his followers.[32] Li Ssu had radical ideas for the time. He

---

32 There are confusing analyses around the alleged role of Li Si in the death of Han Fei-tzu. I would argue there is more liklihood that if Li Si did play a part in his death, it was an act of loyalty to Qin rather than an act of self-interest, as most believe.

advocated the steps necessary to enhance the absolute power of the ruler, and the legal measures required for ensuring this goal. Simultaneously, he contemptuously rejected appealing to the sanctions of antiquity, favored by almost all the other schools of thought. (Rodzinski 1984, 37)

Qin left no avenue unexplored. Its academies searched for the means by which war between the states could be wound up—peacefully. They had learned enough to know that bringing peace to a unified Chinese nation would take leadership, courage, intelligence, and planning. Without doubt the military arts would have been studied. Of the many academies of learning, at least one would have been dedicated to this subject, studying what worked and what did not. Issues of importance would have included strategies and tactics, logistics and provisioning, offense and defense, weapons and war machinery. A great deal was learned from the (evidently) incompetent way that states had been managing their diplomatic and military affairs.

Qin academicians developed, tested, and perfected their theories and methods in schools of governance, philosophy, change management, law, medicine, agriculture, and diplomacy. Some of these academies were state operated, while others were private institutions. They were funded by benefactors from the administrative and business classes that considered it genteel to surround themselves with learned people creating inspiring new works to benefit the kingdom. These academies were not unlike a modern university comprised of colleges. But there were also stark differences. The academies were powerhouses with a defined focus. They were driven with a shared passion, the likes of which the world has never seen. Unlike the separation one normally sees today between government and academia, at this time they were intimately intertwined. The Qin government was corruption and warfare of his time and was extremely critical of superstition.[35]

Hsün-tzu provided an intellectual bridge between diverse philosophies. His first exposure to Qin was as a Confucian emissary (ca. 264 BCE). We are told he advised his home institution that there appeared to be a deficiency of Confucianism in the state and that it seemed an "uncivilized place" (Cottrell 1962, 112).

That first (and possibly revisionist) impression would have been quoted time and again by the home Confucians as evidence of Qin's disconnect from propriety. In the view of the Confucian establishment, Qin's focus on change and the future without the guidance of Confucian literati "might well lead Qin to ultimate disaster" (Twitchett and Loewe 1986, 48).[36] Counterrevolutionaries wanted no part of Qin's march toward empire, believing the whole movement heretical, if not completely insane. They could not have been pleased by Hsün-tzu's defection to Qin.

This was the time during which the Qin court was reducing the strength and social standing of Confucianism. Han Fei-tzu called those who didn't subscribe to the Qin vision or make an economic contribution "lice" or the "Five Vermin." They included "scholars, freelance politicians, independent knights, persons with connections to senior officials and merchants and craftsmen" (Zhengyuan Fu 1996, 92). Qin needed the support of everyone. It needed their resources, and it did not need voices of dissidence. At first, Qin declared the vermin to be security risks. Then, it made them outcasts.

---

35 Hsün-tzu's name sounds so much like Sun Tzu that the *Companion* was appalled at the prospect that someone might confuse the two (O'Neill 1987, 122, 300). But the similarities go far beyond the sounds of their names.
36 Here, and frequently, we have what could well be elements of the Han (second empire) campaign of discredidation of Qin, Qin Shih Huangdi, and the first empire.

advocated the steps necessary to enhance the absolute power of the ruler, and the legal measures required for ensuring this goal. Simultaneously, he contemptuously rejected appealing to the sanctions of antiquity, favored by almost all the other schools of thought. (Rodzinski 1984, 37)

Qin left no avenue unexplored. Its academies searched for the means by which war between the states could be wound up—peacefully. They had learned enough to know that bringing peace to a unified Chinese nation would take leadership, courage, intelligence, and planning. Without doubt the military arts would have been studied. Of the many academies of learning, at least one would have been dedicated to this subject, studying what worked and what did not. Issues of importance would have included strategies and tactics, logistics and provisioning, offense and defense, weapons and war machinery. A great deal was learned from the (evidently) incompetent way that states had been managing their diplomatic and military affairs.

Qin academicians developed, tested, and perfected their theories and methods in schools of governance, philosophy, change management, law, medicine, agriculture, and diplomacy. Some of these academies were state operated, while others were private institutions. They were funded by benefactors from the administrative and business classes that considered it genteel to surround themselves with learned people creating inspiring new works to benefit the kingdom. These academies were not unlike a modern university comprised of colleges. But there were also stark differences. The academies were powerhouses with a defined focus. They were driven with a shared passion, the likes of which the world has never seen. Unlike the separation one normally sees today between government and academia, at this time they were intimately intertwined. The Qin government was based on knowledge, and academies of learning were in service to government.

The academies examined all that was known and all that was being said about the nature of society and roles for government. The academicians, not bound by strictures or dogma, looked to history and reexamined and reshaped ancient hallowed truths. Where there were unknowns, they searched contemporary situations and literature and added those learnings to the rest.

They pored over huge volumes of information, knowledge, and commentary that had been gathered for centuries. Their sources were from antiquity, from the Zhou, Shang Yang, and other kingdoms and quite likely from lands beyond the borders of the kingdom. They commandeered the ancient *Book of Changes* and used it in their research, in their planning, and in their communications.

> The *Book of Changes* is the sage's way of probing what is profound to its limit, and of getting to the very gist of things. It is only through this profundity that the sage can come to understand the propensities of the world; it is only through its pivotal significance that he can be successful in the business of the world; it is only through its mystery that he can be quick without haste and can arrive without going. (Lau and Ames 1998, 41)

Mo Tzu (479–438 BCE) was a revered source. Not a fatalist like his Confucian brethren, he was known to favor an "open society in which individuals were constantly enlarging, not restricting consciousness of others" (Bishop 1985, 67). Mo Tzu had preached nonaggression, arguing that war could never bring real benefit, only hardship.[33] He passed on his wisdom through simple stories. He said that people insist on competence when they have a garment repaired or a sick horse looked after. But when it came to the affairs of state, "the ruler selects his relatives, the rich and noble without merit and those who are merely good looking. Does he care less for the state than for a sick horse or a suit of clothes?" Creel (1953, 50) notes

> [He taught that] rulers ought to care for their subjects ... and government ought to treat another state the same as its own state. By not threatening other states they would be left in peace, and by reducing military expenditures prosperity would result. The expenditures of warfare cripple the nation's livelihood and exhaust the resources of the people. Mo-tzu concludes, 'rulers and officials delight in carrying out such expeditions. In effect they are taking delight in the injury and extermination of the people of the world. Are they not perverse?'[34]

Hsün-tzu (298?–238?) was a noted scholar in Jixia Academy. According to the *Companion to Chinese History* he was

> the most prominent Confucian scholar at the end of the Warring States ... a synthesizer of Taoism, Legalism and Confucianism [who] deplored the

---

33 (Zhengyuan Fu 1996, 30)
34 http://www.west.net/~beck/WP1-Chinese.html

corruption and warfare of his time and was extremely critical of superstition.[35]

Hsün-tzu provided an intellectual bridge between diverse philosophies. His first exposure to Qin was as a Confucian emissary (ca. 264 BCE). We are told he advised his home institution that there appeared to be a deficiency of Confucianism in the state and that it seemed an "uncivilized place" (Cottrell 1962, 112).

That first (and possibly revisionist) impression would have been quoted time and again by the home Confucians as evidence of Qin's disconnect from propriety. In the view of the Confucian establishment, Qin's focus on change and the future without the guidance of Confucian literati "might well lead Qin to ultimate disaster" (Twitchett and Loewe 1986, 48).[36] Counterrevolutionaries wanted no part of Qin's march toward empire, believing the whole movement heretical, if not completely insane. They could not have been pleased by Hsün-tzu's defection to Qin.

This was the time during which the Qin court was reducing the strength and social standing of Confucianism. Han Fei-tzu called those who didn't subscribe to the Qin vision or make an economic contribution "lice" or the "Five Vermin." They included "scholars, freelance politicians, independent knights, persons with connections to senior officials and merchants and craftsmen" (Zhengyuan Fu 1996, 92). Qin needed the support of everyone. It needed their resources, and it did not need voices of dissidence. At first, Qin declared the vermin to be security risks. Then, it made them outcasts.

---

35   Hsün-tzu's name sounds so much like Sun Tzu that the *Companion* was appalled at the prospect that someone might confuse the two (O'Neill 1987, 122, 300). But the similarities go far beyond the sounds of their names.
36   Here, and frequently, we have what could well be elements of the Han (second empire) campaign of discredidation of Qin, Qin Shih Huangdi, and the first empire.

Free from fatalism and the mind set of millennia, Qin made extraordinary discoveries. Qin concluded that combat was both wasteful and useless as a tool for peacemaking. It would also not serve Qin's dreams of nation building. They discovered too that the people had to be behind this transformation of view. The people throughout the Middle Kingdom had to come to accept a key series of propositions. War was not a natural state. Beneficial change could be brought about by people with good intentions. A new social order could set the stage for generations of peace and prosperity.

It was not an easy sell. The peasants had known nothing but war and deprivation and believed it to be the way of the world. As the Master of the Hidden Storehouse observed,

war has existed ever since humankind has existed. All wars come from human force. Forcefulness in humans is received from heaven. Therefore war comes from above, and there is never a time when it is not in operation. (Cleary 1993, 158)

Against this dogmatic backdrop, Qin's academies exposed a radical new view of Taoism that was earthshaking in its ideas and suggestions. They had drawn on the philosophies and cultures of the ancient Middle Kingdom but they expressed that wisdom in a way that was intended to connect with people in a society bent on destruction. In time, these new views would be articulated in a document called the *Tao Te Ching*. It was the work of a Qin academy likely known as the "Lao Tzu School," just as *Ping-fa* came from the "Sun Tzu School."

The Lao Tzu School may have been the academy run by Lü Pu-wei who had engaged three thousand scholars. Around 240 BCE, it produced *Lü-shih ch'un-ch'iu* or Lü's *Spring and Autumn Annals* (Twitchett and Loewe 1986, 43); (Nienhauser 1994b, 314). Lü Pu-wei is said to have offered a fortune to anyone who could add or delete a word, it was so perfect.[37]

The resonance between the *Tao Te Ching* and *Ping-fa* in poetry and theoretical/practical synergy suggests a closely linked or combined institution. The *Tao Te Ching's* subject was foundation, philosophy, and mandate. The *Ping-fa* subject was delivery and achievement. Cleary called *Ping-fa* "practical Taoism" but then failed to explore either the implications or ramifications of that insight (1988a, vii). Key Sun (1995), in his study of Taoism and conflict, quotes Z. Li:

> *Tao Te Ching* can be viewed as a manuscript addressing human behavior at the metaphysical level, whereas *The Art of War* may be perceived as a practical guidebook dealing with human interaction.[38]

The development of a new Taoism that set out, and planned for social revolution sent the Confucians into a paroxysm of rage.[39] Neo-Taoism rejected Confucianism's blind subservience to the past and passivity. It legitimized

---

37 Mihaly Csikszentmihalyi (1997) at times sounds like the Lao Tzu School. He says that essentially one must engage or die. If you are going to engage, do it right. "Participate intimately in the complexity of the cosmos."

38 Li, Z. *Zhong Guo Gu Dai Si Xiang Shi Lun (On the Thought History of Ancient China)*. Beijing: Beijing Press, 1985.

39 Most commentators say the *Tao Te Ching* originated in antiquity, but Thomas Cleary quite rightly pegs it at the time of Qin's ascendancy. "The scripts used [in the oldest known *Tao Te Ching*] would also tend to identify them as relics of the third century BC Qin dynasty" (Cleary 1991b, 128).

social interventionism in the service of empire and set out both principles and best practices (*wu-wei*).[40]

While the philosophical battle lines were being drawn, the academicians were making discoveries. They rejected the notion of "human nature." Through another awesome intellectual reach, they exposed determinism as a human invention, not a natural condition. Now they knew that war was neither ordained by the gods or an inescapable fact of life. These "lessons learned" are evident in persuasions, such as the *Intrigues* story of T'ien Tan and Lu Chung-tzu (Crump 1964, 11).

Having cleared the decks of unhelpful "truths," the academies were ready to address their mandate. If war was not inevitable, and if social intervention was not only proper but essential, just how could war be brought to an end?

They started with a royal pronouncement. The king claimed that he was the rightful bearer of the "mantle of heaven" and gave notice that he intended to end war and usher in a period of eternal peace. This was the equivalent of a bombshell.

As those messages were going out, the academicians struggled with the profound political and philosophical issues raised by legitimized social intervention. They concluded that social intervention could happen only when it was absolutely benevolent. If intervention did not serve the needs and interests of all concerned, it should not be done as it would not be totally effective.

The only way to ensure absolute benevolence was to serve the Way and remain invisible. As Thomas Merton says, "Conscious striving [would have been] self-aggrandizement [that was] bound to come into conflict

---

40 Many confuse "traditional"—which is to say pre-Qin Taoism—with the Taoism of the *Tao Te Ching*. Taoism evolved during its millennia of existence before the founding of the first empire. One error perpetuated by this misunderstanding is the notion that "contemporary" *wu-wei* means "non doing."

orchestrated by able leadership into a productive harmony. (Lau and Ames 1988, 5)

Realization dawned that foreknowledge was essential for *wu-wei*, as it could work only if one knew the other's needs. That explains the statement in *Ping-fa* that one must know oneself and know the other players in order to have no fear of the consequences of a hundred engagements (III.18).

Ping-fa and the *Tao Te Ching* emerged when the academies got the principles and practices resolved and aligned. With the release of these great works, Qin set itself above and apart from Confucian determinism. Here was a profound statement about the role of government in civilized societies, and the principles and values of enlightened social intercourse. Here too was a new morality that enshrined a new *wu-wei* for correcting deviations from the Way.

Ping-fa was Qin's manual for diplomacy and nation building, built on the new and exciting premise that war was both unnecessary and foolish. A brilliant exposition on strategic planning and change management, *Ping-fa* said that competent organizations achieve success without disrupting the social fabric. That's why *Ping-fa's* value is timeless. It gives us a system for beneficial evolution and change at the least possible cost—to anybody.

When the theory and the practice were assembled, demonstrated and proven workable, the one unanswered question was: why have things not always been seen and managed in this way? There must be, at the bottom of it all, not an equation, but an utterly simple idea. That idea, when we finally discover it, will be so compelling, so inevitable, that we will say to one another, "Oh, how beautiful. How could it have been otherwise?"

(John Archibald Wheeler in *Leadership and the New Sciences*)[42]

The academicians that created *Ping-fa* defined a value framework that showed quite clearly what was helpful and what was not. They realized the healing and sustaining value of benevolence, and the absolute need for both inspired and ethical leadership. These were radical ideas, put into practice with ruthless efficiency.

The work of the Qin academicians came to be summed up in an important new principle: that good observation and analysis leads to good preparation, and appropriate intervention makes for good government. Here was the formula for which the court had been searching. It was bound up in a new philosophical model that would come to be articulated in a new methodology. It was the key to Qin's destiny to become the first empire of China. These were the ideas and practices that propelled Qin from political obscurity to nation builder.

The academies helped turn a whole culture away from defeatism and determinism to proactive management of change. This was without doubt one of the most incredible social transformations ever achieved by a government in the history of the human race.

Neo-Taoism prescribed event management when it was essential, practitioners were instructed to remain strategic and invisible, and often, the proper result could be achieved through strategic inaction. Other times actual intervention would be needed. In these cases, subtlety was the key. Sensitive application of *wu-wei* could cause the course of a river to change without interrupting it and without affecting its final destination. *Thunder in the Sky* says that sages in ancient time would "pressure," which is akin to fishing in deep water and never failing to harvest fish. The *Tao Te Ching* says, "The world is ruled by letting things take their course. It cannot be ruled by interfering."(48)

---

42 Introduction to Cresencio Torres's *The Tao of Teams*

The skilled master of life never tries to change things by asserting himself against them; he yields to their full force and either pushes them slightly out of direct line or else transfers their energy so that it can be used against them. He accepts life positively, and when events must be changed, he negotiates rather than inflicting his will on others. (Norris 1996, 32)

Feng and English (1997) say, "The sage conducts government by guiding his people back to a state of harmony with the Tao." This is the Taoism by which "the soft and the weak overcome the hard and the strong." The Tao is

neither a thing nor an idea. The Tao is followed not by holding what is attained, but by balancing what inevitably must begin and end, come and go, rise and fall, fill and empty. (Grigg 1988)

Now, it is deemed right, and necessary, that the state involve itself in the affairs of people. This involvement is a "profound mutuality, a deep balancing of opposites, a dissolving of the edges so that everything melds into everything else while remaining itself" (Grigg 1988, xxi). Achievement of maximum results with minimum costs comes from exercising control of the self and one's environment.

Water [is] an explanatory analogy for dao [because] it is *wuwei*—literally, water does not 'do' anything, and yet the environment thrives because of its presence. In the Daoist tradition, the function of the sage, like water, is catalytic: to get the most out of the situation. Each participant in the environment maintains its own integrity, while contributing itself fully and without reservation to its nexus of relationships. To accomplish this, the optimum disposition that must obtain among the various participants is one of deference, each allowing the others to be what they are. Coercion is anathema to this goal, and is seen as a wasteful diminution of available creative possibilities. (Lau and Ames 1998, 18)

Qin was not the largest, the wealthiest, or the best armed of the kingdoms. But it certainly met all known standards for being the smartest. Rather than building armies and forging weapons, the kingdom focused on persuading the states of the Middle Kingdom that there was a better way of living and governing. The transformation of a group of self-indulgent, egotistical states into an empire involved more than just marketing. Qin studied its enemies and its allies. And when it knew the players as well as it knew itself, it orchestrated the transition. This was a political change unlike anything that had been seen before or since. It happened in a way that few understood. Most of its causes were invisible.

R. L. Wing (1988, 13) says the purpose of *Ping-fa* was "to outline specific strategies to overcome conflicts while viewing the world as a complete and interdependent system that must be preserved." Importantly, he also criticized translators for "stripping out the significant philosophical context" (1988, 11).

All historians agree that Qin brought the Warring States epoch to a close and ushered in a truly extraordinary time of peace, progress, and social evolution. These histories also declare that the first emperor was a savage despot, worthy of note only for the atrocities he committed, or the absurd monuments of self-aggrandizement he built at huge cost and with extraordinary loss of life. There is no substantiation for any of this, there being only the "histories" of the succeeding Confucian dynasty.

So far explanations for Qin's and its emperor's achievements are based either on pure myth or the writings of the Han's Great Historian, who insisted Qin battled its way to greatness. Time Life's *China Dynasties* video—drawing on these "histories"—says the Qin army of 600,000 was sufficiently strong to capture 450,000 enemies in one battle. Qin was so awesome that the captives waited patiently until all were beheaded.

One writer suggested that Qin owed all its strength and success to occupying an easily defended site (Twitchett and Loewe 1986, 39).[43] Historian Derk Bodde (1967, 5) said,

> China's first, and certainly one of the greatest Emperors was Qin Shih Huangdi who, after twenty years of relentless warfare and Machiavellian intrigue succeeded, in 221, in annihilating the last opposing state.

Bodde, like most historians, insists on placing the accent on warfare while relegating intrigue to a footnote. This scenario is repeated time and again, despite the evident paradox of a relatively small state being able to maintain a mammoth army wielding powerful weapons with an inspired but brutal military leadership. This alleged paradox emanates from the Han mantra that Qin was "hardly civilized," certainly not a part of the great Middle Kingdom.

Ping-fa commentary remains essentially unaware just how Qin learned, and applied much more effective ways of achieving its ends, while making others share

---

43   The Han's Great Historian says Qin was a major military power that consolidated the Warring States by threat and destruction. No other historian of that time endorses that view which to date has not been substantiated. We do not even have archaeological support that the possession of the iron sword was the decisive factor in Qin's success (Watson 1961, 146).

those same ends. Qin's key secret was strength, but this was not the strength of armies or arms. Though a small state, Qin was a major power by 256 BCE yet remained ignored by the rival kingdoms. Its power was not evident to the casual observer. Remaining invisible and of no apparent consequence, Qin grew in stature and size, overcoming its rivals one by one until all were absorbed. Qin achieved the near impossible, creating a unified empire in a decade.

Qin's methods and achievements were shrouded in secrecy. The work on *Ping-fa* required tight security. Its principles and practices, in the wrong hands, could have legitimized and instigated insurrection. Such a situation would have seriously disrupted, if not completely disabled, Qin's strategies.

If Qin's internal enemies had gained access to these "weapons of war," they would need to be dealt with—perhaps severely. Could this be what caused the one and only violence authorization in *Ping-fa*? "If a secret piece of news is divulged by a spy before the time is ripe, he must be put to death together with the man to whom the secret was told" (XIII.19).

The Qin citizenry may have had suspicions, but they could not and would not gain access to the whole truth of the academies. As a result, few understood how Qin achieved its successes. They marveled as the warrior princes of the Middle Kingdom willingly came forward to join Qin. Counterrevolutionaries may have seethed, but the people dared to imagine bright futures with full bellies.

The common folk loved the first emperor. He brought peace and prosperity. There were new job opportunities that had never been open to commoners. The young were no longer conscripted to fight in bloody battles that had no more function than gratifying princely egos. He established and enforced standards in areas as diverse as weights and measures, currency, and Chinese script. He completed important works in roads and transportation.

47

He made extensive tours of his empire to see his people and works.

All of this was of slight interest to the military commanders, members of the displaced aristocracy, and Confucian power brokers who saw, in the space of a lifetime, their whole world come crashing down. For a time they played at intrigue, but as conditions (from their perspective) worsened, they would come to openly challenge the emperor at court.

Matters came to a head when a noble of the former state of Ch'I proclaimed that the emperor should place his own relatives in charge of the new commanderies, in keeping with tradition, respecting the rules of patronage in government appointments. But the emperor refused to appoint even members of his own family to important government positions.

This assertion was rightly recognized as an act of defiance of the emperor, tantamount to denying the will of God. With this act, the Confucians and old feudal knights crossed the line of reason and discussion. Li Ssu studied the issue and recommended greater control of reactionaries. The court agreed that

> there are those who unofficially propagate teachings directed against imperial decrees and orders. When they hear of new instructions, they criticize them in the light of their own teachings. To cast disrepute on their ruler, they look upon as a duty; to adhere to contrary views they consider a virtue. Your servant therefore requests that all persons possessing works of literature and discussions of the philosophers should destroy them. (*Edict on Book Burning*)

While the court acted to control treason at a time when the empire was in its formative years, this decision would be written up in the Han histories as a Qin passion against learning and intelligence—forever immortalized as the "Burning of the Books." The Han declared that alleged act to be an act of literary and cultural destruction. But this was but one of a series of revisionist Han declarations that included the alleged "Burying of the Scholars." These proclamations were intended to discredit the first empire and are nonsensical.[44]

Qin held its scholars and learned academies in great esteem. They had provided the means by which the empire was brought into being. Qin broke with the past and earned the wrath of its enemies. It is ironic that it is the "truth" of those enemies that continues to dominate the commentary. Cottrell, for example, asserts that the book burning (as an official policy) allowed the emperor to

> erect an impassable barrier between the present and the past. History was to begin with Qin Shih Huangdi; everything that had happened before was to be discarded and forgotten. (Cottrell 1962, 139)

The Academy Students

By 240 BCE, the academies had developed the principles and practices of engagement management and *wu-wei*. They would most certainly have "pilot tested" the methodologies in some neighboring states as they evolved and were refined. When it all finally came together, it was found to work so well it was mysterious and possibly frightening. Then, they turned to the needs of the practice and its practitioners.

It may have taken as much as a decade to solve the practical matters of training. The basic building blocks of the *Tao Te Ching,* which gave persuaders their Moral Law and philosophy, and *Ping-fa* which gave them strategic planning, would eventually be supported by

---

44 *The Cambridge History of China* concludes the book-burning allegation was an invention.

many volumes of instructional and procedural material. One such volume was *The Master of Demon Valley* that provided interpersonal tactics (Cleary 1993).[45]

Because the concepts were new and difficult, the academies developed "persuasions" and metaphorical instruments to aid learning. The metaphors made the difficult clear, but also provided practical illustrations of how a wide variety of activities ought to be carried out. This massive collection of work was long in the making and would be very long in the learning.

Qin's engagement practitioners needed expertise in a wide range of fields. Unprecedented situations demanded tact, discretion, and knowledge. They had to know the art of persuasion so well they could act independently in a highly adaptive manner. From these requirements came a new breed of professionals that would carry the academy methodologies into the Warring States. These agents of empire were called "persuaders." Qin persuaders would need to have fully internalized certain new truths: that peace was possible and that they would help achieve it. They would come to understand that winning was all-important. But that winning was not dependent upon another losing.

When the schools were ready, they recruited students. The academicians would be as diligent and thorough in their search for candidates as Qin had been in its search for teachers and analysts. Training was rigorous, as it proved extremely difficult to achieve full competency. Their studies ranged from philosophy and theory to organization and process. Students learned flexibility and adaptability. They were taught to be independent

---

45   Cleary translated this work. He says "In 221 B.C.E., using theories found in (this book) the great Emperor Chin was able to unite China and end its prolonged five-hundred-year brutal civil war" (Cleary 1993, ix). He is quite incorrect. Qin Shih Huangdi won with the *Tao Te Ching* and *Ping-fa*. The persuaders won with *The Master of Demon Valley*.

agents, and when they graduated they knew what had to be done as well as how to do it.

The persuasions that helped them learn were now employed to help them teach. They proved useful in conveying Qin's messages to both the common folk and princes. Many of these ideas and concepts ran counter to common wisdom about the nature of people and order. These were important lessons, not easily learned.

Ping-fa, the manual for engagement management, was crafted using the language and imagery of an army at war. With that device, the obscure became visible and the complex simple. Students were able to envision very complex concepts that they had never imagined before, while learning how one put these concepts to work in the business of achieving peace and unanimity. They learned how to motivate and dissuade, all without the use of force. They learned new roles, dynamics, and processes. They knew the Moral Law, all about competent organizations, leadership, planning, and delivery. They were taught to achieve their objectives while remaining unobtrusive, disinterested and apparently of no consequence. They were to avoid aggression, conflict, and violence at all costs.[46]

Ping-fa's messages made clear that organizations entered into engagements only when they had to, and when engagements were managed appropriately everybody won. Students learned that in the best engagements issues were resolved before they became apparent.

The students were instructed in the principles and practice of *wu-wei*, the techniques of sensitive intervention, and the management of strength. They learned of *qi* (the inner strength of people), *shih* (governing), and *ch'üan* (assessment) of engagement management. They learned how *qi* could be managed,

---

46 Contrast these images with Air Marshal David Evans's 1997 observation that *Ping-fa* is nothing but a work of military tactics—just another Clausewitzian *On War* (1997, 8).

how it could be built and reduced. They discovered that with *qi* management, intervention could be sensitive and invisible. With *ch'üan* they were able to identify both the unhelpful trend, and the essential, minor tweak needed to realign events.

Han-fei Tzu stressed the importance of knowing the mind of the one being persuaded above all other considerations. When the mind was known, the adept was then able to "seize the inclination" of the hearer. This is a practice of *wu-wei*.

Qin's persuaders were infused with the Qin vision of greatness. They were missionaries. Their task was to achieve military demobilization and state capitulation without the use of weapons. They were to convince the rival states that any course of action but that of joining Qin was an act of foolishness. Persuaders were ready for graduation when they could demonstrate full proficiency in "the divine manipulation of the threads," which *Ping-fa* says was "the sovereign's most precious faculty" (XIII.8).

Graduates knew the Way by heart and their place in it. As Cleary put it, "Writings are not real explanations of the Way. When you personally realize the Way, you can dispense with all the writings" (1988b, 131). They were not burdened with forms and manuals. What they knew was in their heads, though it is possible that, as persuaders, they carried a small booklet that looked like a manual for military tactics.

With a new philosophy and methodology, and with people trained in the arts of diplomacy, the movement to found a nation began. It took ten years to end centuries of war and establish the empire. But those ten years had been preceded by centuries of thought, planning, and 140 years of intense preparation.

Persuaders in Engagement Management

Qin had defined its chosen outcomes and the principles and practices by which the outcomes would be realized, and violence was not to be allowed. The Schools of Sun Tzu and Lao Tzu provided the methodologies. The Qin academies converted recruits into professional practitioners of the ways of engagement management. Now, fully competent and infused with a profound sense of mission, Qin's persuaders were filtered out to the states and principalities of the Middle Kingdom. They were the "picked soldiers" referenced in *Ping-fa.*

Persuaders would quote from the Taoist teachings of Han Fei-tzu, empowering the common folk, urging them to take charge of their lives and their countries. Some persuaders became advisors to courts and strategists in member states. In such cases, their training, skills and links to Qin and its mission of empire would have been unknown. As *Ping-fa* says, "All men can see the tactics whereby I conquer, but what none can see is the strategy out of which victory is evolved" (VI.27).

Whatever role they played, their real missions were known to no one. One day they might appear as a peddler—the next as a priest. In the *Tao Te Ching* they are described as "simple people" in appearance:

He knows he makes no fine display,
and wears rough clothes, not finery.
It is not in his expectancy of men
that they should understand his ways,
for he carries his jade within his heart.[47] (70)

Persuaders were diplomats, but these diplomats and the diplomacy they practised was not the formalized international relationship management seen today. While there could be elements of formality and visibility if the need arose, most of Qin's diplomatic achievements

---

47 http://www.clas.ufl.edu/users/gthursby/taoism/ ttcstan3.htm#38

came unobtrusively.[48] But unobtrusive practitioners and practices in no way signified low importance. As *Ping-fa* says, "When a general ... neglects to place picked soldiers in the front rank, the result must be rout (X.19).[49]

Who were these "picked soldiers" that should be in the front ranks? From a military perspective, the idea that one should put the best soldiers in front of the main force is nonsense. To find the meaning of this admonition, one must look elsewhere than in the domain of military strategies and tactics.

With the recent discovery of the terracotta "army" of China's first emperor, we find a remarkable incongruity. There are "soldiers" in civilian dress in the front ranks. But these were not agents of combat, and what weapons they had were knowledge and the skills of engagement management.

Qin's itinerant persuaders roamed the Middle Kingdom, sowing dissent and the prospect of a bright future. They knew many persuasions that could delight children, entertain patrons in a tavern, or demonstrate eloquence before a king. They were masters of disguise, intrigue, and subterfuge. They gathered intelligence in the fields, in the towns, and at court. What was learned was tested against what the persuader knew and understood. With a situation defined, the persuader then applied the tools and techniques of *Ping-fa* and *wu-wei*.

If it was determined that an adjustment or realignment was necessary, it was achieved through *shih*—the exercise of elegant, subtle, and invisible guidance—often from a great distance. Lau and Ames say *shih* is strategic advantage. They deem it the principal learning to be had from *Ping-fa*, as does Sawyer. They say it means achieving one's ends from a distance, just as a crossbow

---

48 *The Emperor and the Assassin* movie contains an intrigue where the voluntary capitulation of the Yan kingdom is to be orchestrated by an agent of Qin Shih Huangdi's court.

49 See the footnotes accompanying X.19.

may strike someone unawares (1996, 86-89).[50] Cleary (1989, 77) spoke of a Confucian story of a court noble that could "stop a thrust from a thousand miles away without leaving the table."

Sawyer (1990, 49) quite correctly understands in *Ping-fa* that *shih* in engagement can exceed the value of numerical strength and terrain advantages. But he fails to see that *shih* is a tool of diplomacy and intrigue, not of military tactics in wartime. Giles wrongly equates *shih* with logistics, while Sawyer further confuses that view by adding the notions of circumstance and shape. Kidder Smith does not add to our understanding by declaring that "we should translate *shih* not as the 'great matter' of the state, but as the 'great services' that the state performs."[51]

With *shih* realignment, the agent's involvement was minimal, achieving *Ping-fa* victory without conflict. They were able to effect "shifts" in position and plans that were undetectable. These techniques are what is meant in the *Tao Te Ching* and *Ping-fa* by "the use of fire and water."

The state of Qin achieved an incredible paradigm shift. In a very short time, the new Taoism and the methods of *wu-wei* had achieved wonders with a gaggle of competitive states that had known only the use of force. The final proof of the brilliance of the academicians came when the last state joined Qin in 221. All objectives had been realized without weaponry. King Cheng had his proof that war could be ended and peace realized without the use of force. Cheng declared water (strength) as the Qin symbolic element. And having proved that Qin had indeed been designated by the gods to realize

---

50   Sun Pin's *shih* was a crossbow killing an unaware enemy from a distance.

51   *Han shu* classified *The Art of War* under the subcategory "*ping ch'üan mou*," meaning roughly "military [imbalance of] power and planning" (1993, 153 note 25).

the Chinese empire, he proclaimed himself Qin Shih Huangdi, first emperor.[52]

With peace across the empire, Cheng took the weapons from the armies of the kings and had them cast into statues. He had a terracotta army constructed as a museum display to remind his citizens of the way things were and would never be again. The famous terracotta army of the first emperor was not a military honor guard for the afterlife, as the anthropologists imagine. They represented the empire's last army, and celebrated competence, control and peace.

The *Shih Chi* tells us that Li Ssu, as senior scribe to the king of Qin, played a key role in the dispatch of Qin's persuaders. Here, as usual, the Great Historian of the Han insists that violence marked all things Qin:

> The King of Qin then appointed Li Ssu Chief of Scribes, listened to his stratagems, and secretly sent strategists, carrying gold and jade, to travel about advising the feudal lords. When the famous knights of the feudal lords could be bribed by material goods, [the strategists] gained their friendship with rich gifts; when [the knights] were unwilling they assassinated them with sharp swords.[53] (Nienhauser 1994b, 336)

Persuasions

Chung Feng-nien's 1939 work *Kuo-ts'e K'an-yen* observed that the *Intrigues of the Warring States* had the look of something that came out of a school. Indeed they did. The *Intrigues* are a fascinating collection of rules, anecdotes, and fables about persuasion, persuaders and

---

52　Qin Shih Huangdi would have been aware of, and may have sought to emulate, the (very likely) mythical Yü the Great, founder of the Hsia dynasty. He took control of the waters and established order throughout the world.
53　These "strategists" are otherwise known as "persuaders."

the foundation of empire. Like *Ping-fa* and the *Tao Te Ching*, they are products of the Qin academies. Liu Hsiang (in the first preface to the *Intrigues*) said they concerned advisers to rulers of the Warring States, who

> were officials of great talent. They estimated the capabilities of rulers of the age, put forward the most amazing plans and manifested uncommon intelligence. They turned peril into security and loss into salvation. (Crump 1964, 41)

Intrigues (69, 14) speaks of Su Tai's rhetorical persuasion of the king of Yen. We see reference to the importance at court of what the king calls "glib deceivers."[54] Of the contemporary *Ping-fa* commentators, only R. D. Sawyer (1996, 18) references Qin's "peripatetic persuaders."[55] But it is a mere mention, with no indication of their role or achievements. J. I. Crump (1964, 1, 30) at least suspects that there was more to Qin's empire building than continual war. He opens his study on the *Intrigues* with the observation that "there is little reason to doubt that much of the *Intrigues* reflects groping toward an administrative apparatus that was to become a true bureaucracy by Han times."

Crump in his study of the *Intrigues* did not see Qin's coordinated, strategic effort. He quotes Ch'ao Kung-wu, a celebrated biographer of the twelfth century, who said that the *Intrigues* were "difficult to take seriously at all [and must be] the product of students of the Vertical-

---

54   Quoted in J. I. Crump (1964, 9).
55   Lei Haizong may have been referring to persuaders when he spoke of "wandering politicians," "itinerant swashbucklers," and "wandering philosophers" in his paper published by the David C. Lam Institute.

Horizontal school of writers."[56] The *Intrigues* were not fantasies written by students. They were well-considered products designed for Qin's persuaders.

There are about four hundred persuasions in the *Intrigues*. They are roughly equivalent to what we might today call "teaching aids." They helped Qin's persuaders learn, and they helped these same people spread the culture and philosophy of empire. These teaching aids were not all that different from what we see in contemporary management practices.

> As we worked on research of our excellent companies, we were struck by the dominant use of story, slogan and legend as people tried to explain the characteristics of their own great institutions. Without exception, the dominance and coherence of culture proved to be an essential quality of the excellent companies. (Peters 1982)

One persuasion concerned the practice of sensitive intervention.[57] It spoke of a young disciple approaching Confucius. He intends to go to Wei, because the prince obviously is in need of advice—the country is so poorly administered. Confucius says, "You will bring disaster on yourself. Tao has no need of your eagerness." The disciple says, "Well then, I will appear there humble and disinterested, doing only what is right."

Confucius says that will achieve nothing. The prince is convinced that only he is right. The disciple then suggests he will then be obedient, accommodate himself

---

56 This area needs research. Some writers speak of the last hundred years of the Warring States period as the "age of alliances" (*ho-tsung* and *lien-heng*), by which they mean interstate treaties. But the alliances were more strategic process than result. The instigators were persuaders, the academies, and the *Intrigues*.
57 See Cleary's "The Human World" in his *Essential Tao* (Cleary 1991b, 84).

to the prince, and revere tradition. "This is still not acceptable," says Confucius, "because you already have plans and you do not know the Prince." Only then is the disciple ready to receive Confucius's direction. He is told he must fast. He must eliminate self-awareness.

> Only then will you be able to go among men in their world without upsetting them. You will not enter into conflict with their ideal image of themselves. If they will listen, sing them a song. If not, keep silent. There is nothing else for you to be but one of them. Then you may have success. (Merton 1965, 50)

Some of the works attributed to the quite likely mythical "Chuang Tzu" are actually persuasions. J. I. Crump, after his thorough analysis of the *Intrigues*, asks,

> Suppose a Chinese rhetorical tradition included ... devices for training men in the art of persuasion, would that not explain much of what is most baffling about the *Intrigues*? [It would explain the many contradictions and aspects of the work] if the training a man underwent ... for political advisor, emissary ... included model advice which *would* or *should* have been offered at certain historic occasions, and somehow found its way into what we now call the *Intrigues of the Warring States*. (Crump 1964, 101–103)

Chuang Tzu's "woodcarver" and "the competent cook" explain sensitive intervention. "The fighting cock" is about maintaining control. The story of "three in the morning" that concerns feeding moneys—on a basis that pleases them rather than the keeper—illustrates *wu-wei*. The message is: "achieve great things with minimum effort" (Merton 1965, 44).

In another persuasion, Master Kuo Wei instructs in the qualities of he who would be emperor. He must, among other things, "live with a teacher, dwell among friends, be hegemon with ministers—while he who will lose his state will dwell among servants" (*Intrigues* 69, 11, in Crump 1964, 65).[58]

Several persuasions follow. They are drawn from a variety of sources, including the *Shih Chi* of Sima Qian, the *Intrigues*, and several Taoist works. They are all very helpful in understanding the *Ping-fa* methodology and its principles, especially the quite difficult *wu-wei* concept.

Training the Imperial Concubines

"Training the Imperial Concubines" is found in the *Shih Chi*.[59] It is alleged to be both "Sun Tzu's biography" and a demonstration of Sun Tzu's ruthlessness before the king of Wu. Some have even gone so far as to suggest that the story "proves" Sun Tzu's brutality, hatred of women, and lack of control. Wee et al. say only that it is "an illustration of the genius and ability of Sun Tzu." They say nothing about how it does that.[60]

This story illustrates the importance of delegation and empowerment in engagement, and the dangers of interfering when delegation has been made. Robin Yates[61] and translator Calthrop both saw that message. No engagement begins until the strategy is conferred and the engagement leader is empowered. *Ping-fa* chapters VII and VIII start with the same instruction: "the general receives his commands from the sovereign."

---

58   This, of course, is exactly what Qin Shih Huangdi did.
59   This rendition is from the *Korea WebWeekly*. It is found at http://kimsoft.com/polwar03.htm.
60   *Sun Tzu: War and Management*
61   Of McGill University. He wrote an insightful introduction to Tsai Chih Chung's *Sunzi Speaks*. I disagree only with his including "insubordination" as one of the messages. (1994, 10–11)

The occupation and sex of the "soldiers" is irrelevant. Their untrained, "civilian" status is not. With the conferral of a commission, the leader had to develop a disciplined team. Teams need the clear instruction and training that is the responsibility of the leader.

The key factor in this persuasion is that when the team is ready to engage, the sovereign withdraws his support as he disagrees with the team's leadership. Here is interference brought about because decisions have been made that seemed inappropriate or unpopular. Despite being set adrift, Sun Tzu carries on as he had been ordered: "there are commands of the sovereign which must not be obeyed" (VIII.3).

Malaysian Business (1 April 1997) referred to the story as a "horror," in the midst of a review of a Khoo Kheng-Hor work on Sun Tzu. Rudnicki (1996, 5–6) says it perfectly illustrates Sun Tzu's "unnecessarily cruel" belief in "the expendability of individual life in the interest of discipline and absolute authority." Though Giles originally had doubts about the legitimacy of the story, he finally says we should not question whether the records consulted by the Han historian Sima Qian were authentic.

> If we admit that the *13 chapters*re the genuine production of a military man living towards the end of the 'Ch'un Ch'iu' period, are we not bound, in spite of the silence of the Tso Chuan, to accept Sima Qian's account in its entirety? In view of his high repute as a sober historian, must we not hesitate to assume that the records he drew upon for Sun Wu's biography were false and untrustworthy? The answer, I fear, must be in the negative. (Giles 1910)

Though Giles believes the source to be authentic, he concludes that the story is "utterly preposterous and incredible." Griffith and Clavell quote the full story without comment. Huang says that it is "no more than a popular Warring States period legend" and that "it is absolutely ridiculous." Griffith (1963, 2) says Yao Ch'i-heng, a seventeenth-century doubter of Sun Tzu's authenticity, believed this story to be "fantastic" and "not worthy of belief." Both Sawyer and Rudnicki consider it apocryphal. Sawyer says,

> Ch'I Ssu-ho, among others, does not believe Sun-tzu would have ever been allowed to commandeer palace women to illustrate his theories of military discipline nor that the execution of the two captains would have been understood as having proved anything. He therefore views the entire episode as an exaggeration. Wu Ju-sung believes that rather than being a lesson about discipline, the incident illustrates Sun-tzu's fundamental teaching that a general—once he is in command of an army—does not accept orders from the ruler; this is in accord with his particular understanding of Sun-tzu's major contribution as having been the isolation and characterization of the professional general. (1993, 152 note 19)

Sawyer misses altogether the distinction between high-level authority and leadership and empowerment in engagement. He also suggests the point of the story is to embolden the king of Wu, showing him how he can build his empire by creating, training, and mobilizing an army and attacking neighboring states (1996, 7). This astonishing statement has no known source in the literature.

The Physician Best Known in the Land

According to an old story, a lord of ancient China once asked his physician, a member of a family of healers, which of them was the most skilled in the art. The physician, whose reputation was such that his name became synonymous with medical science in China, replied,

> My eldest brother sees the spirit of sickness and removes it before it takes shape, so his name does not get out of the house. My elder brother cures sickness when it is still extremely minute, so his name does not get out of the neighborhood. As for me, I puncture veins, prescribe potions, and massage skin, so from time to time my name gets out and is heard among the lords.[62]

The highest medical authority in the land is asked what makes a good doctor. He replies there are three "grades": someone completely unknown, someone who a few people know about, and lastly, one whose "name is heard among the lords." The medical authority says he is one of the famous ones. Is he boasting? No, his point is quite the opposite. He says he is of the lowest order, not the highest. He treats visible ailments and symptoms. Everyone can see what he does and can relate to it. He is successful "according to the rules." But his brother, "whose name does not get out of the house," is the most successful of all. Even his patients may not know how talented he is. He anticipates disease and illness and cures maladies before they even appear.[63]

According to "Chuang Tzu":

The man of Tao
Remains unknown
Perfect virtue
Produces nothing

---

62 http://members.visi.net/~lensim/suntzu.html
63 *The Tao of Negotiation* says, "Preventive medicine is as heretical to the established Western medical profession as mediation is to the legal profession" (Edelman and Crain 1993, 11).

'No-Self
Is 'True-Self.'
And the greatest man
Is Nobody.
(Merton 1965, 92)

The *Tao Te Ching* (77) says, "The sage works without recognition. He achieves what has to be done without dwelling on it" (Feng and English 1997). Says *Thunder in the Sky,*

> Thereby you observe the opening and closing of heaven and earth, discern the creations of myriad things, and see the governance of human affairs. You know the whole world without going out the door, you see the course of heaven without looking through the window, you direct without seeing, arrive without going: this is called the knowledge of the Way. (Cleary 1993, 62)

The *Tao Te Ching* (28) says, "A great tailor cuts little." For a contemporary view of these notions, consider the following. With one exception, it is all very much *Ping-fa* and very much the "Best Known Physician." What is the exception? If things have gone awry, control has been lost.

> Leadership is many things. It is patient, usually boring coalition building. It is the purposeful seeding of cabals that one hopes will result in the appropriate ferment in the bowels of the organization. It is meticulously shifting the attention of the institution through the mundane language of management systems. It is altering agendas so that new priorities get enough attention. It is being visible when things go awry, and invisible when they are working well. (Peters and Waterman, 1982, 82)

The physician story defines standards of competence and incompetence. It gives us a framework of types. *Ping-fa* chapter III.3 suggests the fully competent leader is one who demonstrates the "highest form of generalship." One who is not quite exceptional is "next best." The unacceptable one is the "worst of all." He will "besiege walled cities." From this perspective, chapter III.1 indicates we are not being given a continuum of events, but a classification system for right and wrong. These are not degrees of acceptability but alternates.

Ping-fa says if you seek the truly competent, your measures must reach, and assess, key factors. And when it comes time to reward achievers, pass on those who have become well-known working with superficialities while ignoring those who have quietly achieved miracles.[64] The least-known physician represents "competence." He is invisible, and his name would not get out of the house. He cures disease before it even appears. [65] He would be highly skilled indeed in engagement management.

The Ordeal by Fire[66]

In caring for others and serving heaven, there is nothing like using restraint. (*Tao Te Ching* 59)

One must know when to stop. (*Tao Te Ching* 32)

Of the dangerous faults of a general, the worst is "recklessness that leads to destruction." (*Ping-fa,* VIII.12)

---

64 See IV.7, X.24, XI.35, XII.18–19, and IV.8–9, 12, and 15.
65 "House" or "residence" may be a Taoist metaphor for "beginning" and "life"—to be humble and not filled with oneself.
66 Read VIII.12–13 in conjunction with this story.

When your senior officers are troublesome and they engage others before an assessment has been made, "the result is ruin." (*Ping-fa,* X.17)

Don't engage just for personal gratification or because you are annoyed. (*Ping-fa,* XII.18)

The ordeal by fire (See Annex 1) tells of Pan Ch'ao, a diplomatic envoy to the king of Shan-shan. He decides to exterminate a diplomatic mission from Hsiung-nu as a demonstration of the power of his king. His officers are reluctant, feeling they should gain administrative approval first. Pan Ch'ao does not agree, and Pan Ch'ao is then able to present the mission leader's head to the king.

This event causes widespread fear among the population. But the trouble is only beginning. Ch'ao then, perhaps in retaliation, takes the king's sons hostage. No one knew what this out-of-control leader might do next.

Here a leader acts without authority. He seeks glory and, as a result, disgraces himself and his organization. He is oblivious to the consequences of his actions. Giles tells a similar story about Wu Ch'i in a battle with the Qin state. One of his officers makes what he deems a "successful" preemptory strike. But then he is executed by Wu Ch'i because "he acted without orders" (1994 VII.25).

This story plays counterpoint to the persuasion of the Imperial Concubines (See Annex 2). The message is clear: engagements are undertaken only when essential and authorized. Control is a mission-critical capability, at all times and in all situations. *Ping-fa* says, "The general who advances without coveting fame and retreats without fearing disgrace, whose only thought is to protect his country and do good service for his sovereign, is the jewel of the kingdom" (X.24).

The ordeal by fire illustrates the need for control and the consequences of loss of control.

The Tea Master and the Assassin

A story in the *Tao of Negotiation* conveys very well the use of sensitive intervention in engagement management (Edelman and Crain 1993, 338). A warrior requests an audience with a tea master. He is reported to be dangerous and may have evil intent. His advisers say he should demur, but the tea master refuses to comply. When the warrior entered, the master "saw at a glance the warrior's intention." Offering tea, the tea master intentionally stumbles and spills the tea. This simple device dissipates a potentially explosive situation. The lesson is one of a knowledgeable person anticipating and diffusing a problem before it even occurs. The tea master is a physician whose name never gets out of the house.

Taoists view the universe as the same as, or inseparable from, themselves—so that Lao Tzu could say, "Without leaving my house, I know the whole universe." This implies that the art of life is more like navigation than warfare, for what is important is to understand the winds, the tides, the currents, the seasons, and the principles of growth and decay, so that one's actions may use them and not fight them (Watts 1975, 20–21).

The Monkey King

Cleary's *Ping-fa* translation includes the tale of the "magical monkey" or the "monkey king," who "unwittingly" brings about catastrophe through arms escalation. He says the monkey king was a problem because he "exercised power without wisdom, disrupting the natural order and generally raising hell."

The real meaning is quite different. Monkeys are an ancient Chinese metaphor for unbridled passion, and the monkey king characterizes the ultimate manifestation of this failing. He acts without knowledge and initiates an engagement against an assumed enemy and brings ruin on all. He is released from his imposed confinement only on the condition that he will seek enlightenment (from further thoughtless action). This story illustrates the *Ping-fa* thesis that engagements, if considered at all, must be based on intelligence.

The Competent Cook[67]

The story of the competent cook is attributed to Chuang Tzu and is contained within his so-called "Inner Chapters." It concerns Ting, a cook whose knives are always sharp. He cuts with care and efficiency. One day Ting is cutting up an ox for Lord Wen-hui. The lord observes his elegance, simplicity, and economy in carving and expresses admiration. Ting explains that because of the Tao, he is able to see the essentials of what must be done, and therefore his use of the knife is minimal.

A good butcher changes cleavers every year because of damage, a mediocre butcher changes cleavers every month because of breakage. "I've had this cleaver for nineteen years now, and it has cut up thousands of oxen; yet its blade is as though it had newly come from the whetstone." (Cleary 1988b, 21)(Feng and English 1974, 55)

Lord Wen-hui says, "Excellent! Having heard the words of a butcher, I have found the way to nurture life" (Cleary 1991b, 82). This persuasion explains the process and consequence of practicing sensitive intervention. One accomplishes much through a few deft moves.

---

67   Chuang Tzu section 7, "Fit for Emperors and Kings," translated by Burton Watson

The First Empire of China

With the arrival of Shang Yang, Qin dedicated itself completely to the task of creating the empire of China. Preparations were arduous and lasted generations. When all was in readiness, the final execution of the "battle plan" was precise, swift, and sure. Says *Ping-fa*, "Let your plans be dark and impenetrable as night, and when you move, fall like a thunderbolt" (VII.19).

Ping-fa gave King Cheng the techniques he needed for ending war and building an empire. His methods were unobtrusive yet effective, elegant, and inexpensive.[68] Where war had failed to end war, and force had failed to create a Chinese nation, Qin realized both through intelligence, patience, and its talents in sensitive intervention.

There is a great deal of mystique, and error, regarding the founding of the first empire. This is because of the secrecy that surrounded the achievement at the time, subsequent revisionism, and the inability of the commentary to consider the heretical notion that war was ended and the first empire established by peaceful means.

The second empire Han created a paradigm of belief around the Qin, the empire, and the first emperor, which seems to have remained essentially impenetrable. There are also linguistic and cultural issues: the Chinese of today is not the language that was spoken and written before the empire came into being. In addition, the meaning of pre-China literature and records is difficult to understand, often dealing with very complex concepts

---

68   Lei Haizong says Qin achieved victory by "wiping out" its opponents until it was "the only state still standing," even though "Qin liked nothing better than victory without war" (http://www.cic.sfu.ca/nacrp/articles/leihaizong/leihaizong.html).

and processes in a language replete with metaphor and other literary devices.[69]

What we can reasonably surmise is that Qin undertook arduous preparatory work before it launched its peacemaking and empire-building initiatives. From the time those initiatives were launched, it took only ten years to end war and lay the foundation for empire. The execution was flawless. Qin deployed its new moral code, sound methodologies, a dynamic diplomatic machine, and a government of genius. In the two hundred years preceding the death of Qin Shih Huangdi, Qin did not make a mistake. The great mystery of the ages is just how this remarkable state could have been so unprepared for the emperor's death. Despite having covered all bases in its long hard road to empire, the dynasty collapsed with his demise. Qin Shih Huangdi did not have a succession plan. It may have been his only failing.

Despite his untimely end, Qin Shih Huangdi left the world an unequalled, though as yet unappreciated legacy of ideas and ideals. His central programs and standards, revolutionary and progressive as they were, are now found almost everywhere today. Now, people do not seriously challenge the role of government in leadership, standards setting, and management of the social agenda. Such was more than revolutionary 2200 years ago. It was heretical.

Today there is only grudging recognition of Qin achievement. The commentary focuses on trade and commerce incidentals—such as standard measures— and even these not insignificant innovations are attributed to a "despotic government." Sadly this golden age is dim compared with the glitter of the much later

---

69 As Stanley Herman observed about the *Tao Te Ching*, "the nature of Chinese character writing [which] can represent a large number of things and ideas, makes it literally impossible to translate verses without interpreting them" (1994, 2).

T'ang dynasty (618–907 CE), now considered China's "age of enlightenment."

Confucian hatred of all things Qin had smoldered throughout the state's ascendancy. Their chance came with the demise of the emperor and the absence of a strong successor. They moved quickly, liquidating Qin Shih Huangdi's dynasty and installing a puppet at the head of the second dynasty. They commandeered the bureaucracy, ridding the administration of Legalists.

The Han tinkered with the rules and practices of the first empire and even considered a return to feudalism. But they quickly discovered that the empire was not broken, and there was more danger than gain in going backward. Because of that seminal realization China today retains much of the government principles, practices, and structures of Qin Shih Huangdi. The nation he built is still called "Qin," though "Han" is the word the people use to refer to themselves.

To measure the first emperor, look at what he was and what he achieved. He was a master strategist who brought an end to the epoch of the Warring States. He built an empire from a group of principalities ruined by war. He put in place a structure and system that has survived—essentially intact—for two thousand years.

Qin defined the shape and size of China and set in motion a process for defining what China would be.[70] The last Qin army was cast in terracotta, and all weaponry was cast into statues as an everlasting testament to the first emperor's achievement. These were powerful symbols.

The royal crypt that we are told contains the first emperor's remains will not be explored until it is certain that no loss will ensue from opening the tomb. When that

---

70   Clutching the theme of the emperor's alleged superstitions, Cottrell says Qin Shih Huangdi established thirty-six commanderies because it was six times six, and six was the emperor's lucky number (1962, 132).

happens, China will find the answer to many riddles, including how their nation really came about.

Though the Han did no more than maintain Qin Shih Huangdi's organization, policies, and plans, they achieved something that the first emperor could not. They succeeded in having themselves remembered as the founders of China.

The Second (Han) Empire and Its Revisionism

The victors write the histories. And when Qin fell in 206 BCE the victors were the Confucians and other conservatives who had opposed Qin Shih Huangdi and the Legalists. Their first task was to explain to the people why Qin failed. Then, they had to legitimize the new empire—an empire that would be run by what the Qin court had called "vermin." One theme permeated all these messages—that denial of Confucianism was a direct cause of Qin's fall. Lu Wen-Shu, in the first century BCE, said that

> under the Qin, he who spoke out the truth was stigmatized as a slanderer. All who acted up to the precepts of the ancient [Confucian] code found themselves out of place. And so the rod of empire fell from their grasp for ever. (Giles 1965, 87)

The Han were faced with a real challenge. There was a great deal of residual awe for the first empire and its emperor. He had, after all, created the greatest nation on earth, as had been foretold. It was a tall order indeed to reestablish Confucianism and ensure all the teachings of Neo-Taoism and the academies were discredited and obliterated where possible. These changes were essential if they were to effectively reestablish the old "benevolence" with its privilege, patronage, and favoritism.

The Han Confucians knew they had to replace the people's awe for Qin Shih Huangdi with respect, if not adoration, for the new dynasty. The evidence of Qin dynasty invention and success was everywhere: in the coinage, in the national system of roads, in language and literature. How could they cast such an administration in a poor light while allowing their own to shine with radiance? The Han decision to build a general belief that the Legalists and their awful empire had been insane and an affront to heaven, while only Confucianism had relevance for people, was a significant turning point in Chinese history.

Sima Qian recorded an invented dialogue between the Han emperor and his chief minister. The emperor said, "It is precisely because the fate of the empire is not yet settled that we need to build palaces and halls" (Ebrey 1996, 67). The commentary imagines the subject of that conversation was building construction, but the message is: we need to redefine Qin in order to stabilize our administration.

To change what the people knew and what they thought to be true demanded a thorough and highly successful rewriting of history. The artifacts of the Qin were debased, reinterpreted, and destroyed – but only if they were ornamental and not essential. A policy and program of disinformation was crafted and implemented. The evil and arrogant Legalists, the Han insisted, had disallowed independent thought and enforced brainwashing.

Han revisionism reached far back in history to the Warring States period. Qin was declared a backward and remote place where even the music was raw and uncultured. Sima Qian says Shang Yang, one of pre-China's greatest government theoreticians and administrative practitioners, was apparently of a "cruel nature ... guilty of dishonesty, guile, and the inability to heed the views of others." And if that wasn't enough, he is alleged to have been a poor administrator (but wealthy), and utterly devoid of ethics and honor. Despite clear evidence that Qin was an intellectual powerhouse, we still see this sort of thing:

The Qin tried to efface cultural differences from the minds of the inhabitants, but they offered no substitute, no positive new ideal of rallying the best minds. (Pirazzoli-t'Serstevens 1982, 15)

When all was said and done, the first dynasty became an insignificant blip, a mere interregnum—and an evil one at that. The losses resulting from this pogrom are incalculable.

Though the glory of Qin was largely forgotten, there were nagging reminders of its brilliance. The works of Qin were everywhere. There were buildings and bridges, canals and castles. And there were writings—thousands of them, some in thousands of copies. The Han attempted to recover and destroy all these artifacts, but they were unsuccessful.

What could never be fully eradicated was dismissed as Legalist foolishness, evil or of no relevance to a modern state. *Ping-fa* and the *Tao Te Ching* were classified as such and (officially) devalued. Thomas Cleary could not imagine that the *Tao Te Ching* came from the Qin, not from the Han.

The versions of the *Tao Te Ching* ordinarily used by Taoists and general readers derive from oral traditions written down after the Qin dynasty, for the purpose of reviving literary and historical traditions suppressed by the militant Qin legalists. (Cleary 1991b, 129)

The Han ensured the *Tao Te Ching's* and *Ping-fa's* (official) association with the Legalists and Qin was broken, and their messages obfuscated.[71] It would not do if the common people continued to believe that they ought to be taking charge of their lives and disobeying the ruler if the ruler was not behaving properly. But copies of

71   See Zi-Chang 1969, 144.

documents and memories of the people were not entirely eradicated. The "Chuang Tzu" writings, a key device developed and used by Qin in its march to empire, were kept hidden by Taoists for about two hundred years after the fall of Qin (Cleary 1991b, 129). This is a remarkable achievement, given that Confucians likely considered the works traitorous, despite "his" alleged Confucianism.

The revisionists seized on the great palaces of Qin Shih Huangdi, his monuments and memorials, and "his" Great Wall as testimony to his wickedness and waste. They created highly effective symbols of the Qin regime to strike at the hearts of the common people. Burning books and burying scholars were two of their inventions.

In 2002 Robert Kaplan gave the Han credit for ending the Warring States period and founding the Chinese empire (Kaplan 2002, 40). In 1957, Yang Shih-Chan of the Chinese Communist Party said,

[The Communist Party's] massacre of intellectuals and the mass burying alive of the *literati* by the tyrant, Qin Shih Huangdi, will go down in China's history as two ineradicable stigma. This cannot but make us feel utterly heartbroken."[72]

Another invention was "Meng Chiang-nü." Her tragic life, as the widow of a man who died during forced labor on the Great Wall, is an immortal Chinese folktale (Waldron 1990, 195).[73] To this day, she is believed to have been a real person, but she was real only as a factor in Han revisionism. (See Annex 3).

Today few question the allegation that Qin fell to a peasant revolt that was driven by the harsh policies and practices of the first emperor. But it was in fact "the vermin"—the disenfranchised soldiers and princes and

---

72   In a letter quoted in *Mao Tse-Tung: Emperor of the Blue Ants* (1962, 322).
73   See http://www.sh.com/culture/legend/meng.htm.

the Confucian philosophers—who engineered the fall. The vermin and their agent, Sima Qian, would have us believe the absurd tale of field laborer Chen She. He is said to have caused the eventual "toppling" of the first empire. Armed with "hoes and tree branches," a ragtag band that was delayed in their transport of prisoners— and knowing they would be executed for it—took on the empire. They were talented enough to find Liu Pang to lead the military assault on Qin. He is reported to have "overcome" the great military might of the empire.

It is far more likely that the "destruction" of Qin was a change in government. When Liu Pang arrived in the capital, he wanted to leave everything intact. But that was not to be. In 206 his superior, Hsiang Yü, "sacked the city, burned the palaces with a resulting loss of literature that was possibly even greater than that caused by the earlier official burning of the books" (Twitchett and Loewe 1986, 84).

Much of the physical glory of the Qin disappeared at that time. Such wasteful destruction can only have been retribution. The Confucians, landed gentry, and the rest of the Five Vermin had won back their feudal rights, and in their view, heaven and earth would not rest until "appropriate" conditions were restored.

The Han published an "analysis" of the failure of the first empire. Titled *The Faults of Qin*, it was pure propaganda. It was written by Jia Yi, who tells us the warlike Qin knew combat and destruction, but they knew nothing about good government.[74] "Qin failed to realize there is a difference between the power to attack and the power to consolidate."

We are told:

---

74 Apparently a common charge made against defeated administrations, it was likewise said that those who ruled the Spartans knew only how to govern in a time of war (Cotterell 1988, 57).

1. That everything about the person of the first emperor was contemptuous: his low birth and illegitimacy, his superstitious beliefs, his draconian practices, and his evident insanity in later life;
2. That what the first emperor achieved he did by force, that his administration was violent, and that his people as well as his enemies suffered horribly at his hand;
3. That his administration was rule-bound and vicious, driven by Legalist fanatics who cared for nothing but the state and procedural perfection;
4. That his monumental constructs, except those in current public use, should be condemned as vainglory that cost horridly in human lives and misery;
5. That the state of Qin, rather than being proclaimed by heaven to found the empire of China, was destroyed because it violated that will. The will of heaven is entrusted to, and represented by, the Confucians.

Main stream histories of the first empire do not question Qin Shih Huangdi's "religious lunacy," including his alleged frantic search for the elixir of everlasting life. He is deemed a tyrannical despot who built hundreds of castles (allegedly, and perhaps incorrectly as many as three hundred in Qin alone) and many other works, all on the backs of the peasants. He has been criticized for wasting lives and resources on works of self-aggrandisement. Cottrell (1962, 124) says he was "probably a megalomaniac monster."

The so-called "Great Wall" appears often in the list of the first emperor's "megalomaniac" enterprises, despite the known fact that Qin's involvement was limited to joining several wall segments. Time Life's video on the

Chinese dynasties has Qin Shih Huangdi building it all in ten years.[75]

The Han's "Great Historian" Sima Qian was an important agent of the revision. He divided the story of Qin into two *Annals*: one on the state and one on the first emperor. Nienhauser (1994a, 124) says that

> Ch'eng Yü-ch'ing believes [this was done] to show that those kings prior to the First Emperor were legitimate [scions of the Ying clan], but the First Emperor himself was illegitimate [the bastard son of Lü Pu-wei].

Herbert A. Giles, duped by revisionism, sums up the "ten great follies that helped bring about the overthrow of the Qin dynasty"(1965, 87):

1. Abolition of the feudal system
2. Melting down all weapons
3. Building the Great Wall
4. Building a "great pleasaunce"
5. Burning of the Books
6. Massacre of the Literati
7. Building a vast mausoleum
8. Searching for the elixir of life
9. Appointing the heir apparent to be commander in chief
10. Maladministration of justice

This list is illogical, largely unfounded, and analytically invalid save the reference to the issue of succession. Giles is most off the mark in helping perpetuate the view about the "injustice" of the Qin administration. The Legalists, and the empire they helped craft, were procedurally rigorous. The court was unequivocally fair in its political

---

75 See Waldron (1990) for a comprehensive challenge to these notions.

and legal administration. Even the emperor would not exempt himself from the equality demands of the law.

The Cambridge History of China notes that a "recent survey of the attitudes of traditional and modern Chinese historians toward Qin, cites only two pre-modern scholars as strongly favorable" (Twitchett and Lowe 1986, 93). The "evidence" accepted by the keepers of this shallow accord is far below the intellectual rigor they demand elsewhere. Consider Zhang Wenli's (1996, 14) assertion that "two assassination attempts [on Qin Shih Huangdi] attest to his unpopularity."

Later Chinese historians decreed him to be "cruel, arbitrary, impetuous, suspicious, and a superstitious megalomaniac" (Ebrey 1996, 61). Other words used to describe him include "overzealous, exploitive, despotic, autocratic and tyrannical; an enslaver of the common people." He is recorded as having established harsh laws and forced work. C. P. Fitzgerald (1986, 138) declares Qin Shih Huangdi "one of the great destroyers of history."[76]

It would be closer to the truth to say that the death of Qin Shih Huangdi would have been seen at the time as an extraordinary tragedy. The survival of the emperor's tomb without disturbance, among other proofs, is evidence of this. It is reported that work continued on the tomb for thirty-eight years after his death (Wenli 1996, 14). It had survived the capital's sacking by Hsiang Yü, who had been sent by the Han to demolish all remnants of the first empire. That signifies reverence, not contempt.

Qin Shih Huangdi was a brilliant strategist in the arts of diplomacy. He was also the founder of fundamental principles and practices of good government. When he cast the weapons of the Warring States into statues, he proclaimed his abhorrence of war and his love of peace. When he fashioned an army of terracotta soldiers and installed them in rows near his tomb, he was telling his

---

76 Fitzgerald does not reconcile this view with his later statement that the first emperor achieved his primary goal of creating a unified empire, which was his "true legacy."

subjects that was the last army they would ever see. The devious Han Confucians have convinced all there could be no other intent for the terracotta soldiers than "protecting" the emperor in his journey to the afterlife.

The first emperor was a thorough researcher and gifted communicator. He used images and models that all could understand. When he told his subjects how much work he had to do, he reported on the weight of the documents he had to read. What an inspired way this was to explain to an illiterate peasantry how hard he was working for them. *Ping-fa* said, "Fighting with a large army under your command is nowise different from fighting with a small one: it is merely a question of instituting signs and signals" (V.2).

But Qin Shih Huangdi was not without fault. As he advanced closer and closer to death, he shared his state responsibilities less and less. He buried himself in his work. While the emperor reviewed and administered, his court seethed with intrigue. Qin Shih Huangdi is alleged to have believed in his own immortality, but more likely he believed in the immortality of his empire. He died without a named and trained successor.

After his death, the knives came out. They killed Li Ssu in 208 BCE, as it was said "he would not be silent."[77] Whether they were unwilling or unable to understand the "magic" of Qin Shih Huangdi we may never know. But when the enemies of Qin eliminated his advisers and ensured that a competent successor did not come to power, they began writing a vision of history that would last two thousand years.

The Confucians of the Han dynasty achieved a remarkable propaganda victory. Their evident skills at truth management have perhaps never been equaled. They effectively delivered a complete denial of the facts around China's founding.

---

77   Li Si may have declared himself a traitor to the fierce second emperor when he presented a paper at court on the subject of "supervising and responsibility."

Part III: The Ping-fa Methodology

Introduction

Few commentators dispute the Great Historian's story about the origin of *Ping-fa*: that about 500 BCE in the land we now know as China an army general named Sun Tzu (or Sun Wu) wrote a little treatise called *Thirteen Chapters*. It was of little consequence, focusing entirely on military tactics.

The *Shih Chi* of the Han's Great Historian says

> The oldest three treatises on war, Sun Tzu, Wu Tzu and Ssu-Ma Fa, are, generally speaking, only concerned with things strictly military: the art of producing, collecting, training and drilling troops, and the correct theory with regard to measures of expediency, laying plans, transport of goods and the handling of soldiers. [This is] in strong contrast to later works, in which the science of war is usually blended with metaphysics, divination and magical arts in general. (*Ssū K'u Ch'üan Shu* (ch. 99, f. 1)

Li Yu-ning (1977) speaks of a "noted military expert" who may have guided Shang Yang's victory over Wei. This could have been the author of the *Thirteen Chapters* of antiquity. But historical records from then on make no reference to *Thirteen Chapters, Sun Tzu: The Art of War*, or "General Sun Tzu." That omission includes the fourth century BCE *Commentary of Master Tso*, which focused on the military and war. Nor is it in *Ancient Dynasties*, a record of major works of philosophy.

Consider Kidder Smith (1990, 52) on the dating of the work: "One might conclude from Sun Tzu's use of *yin-yang* that the Sun Tzu, or such elements of it, are later than 300 BCE. Evidence in the text proves it is earlier than 300 BCE." The "evidence in the text" are references to people and places from ancient times. But they appear not because they reflect the time of writing, rather they represent a long-standing literary tradition. Authors wanted their work "grounded" in antiquity to give the appearance of wisdom.

Because the commentary does not question the origin or function of *Ping-fa*, it remains relegated to the military canon. Its philosophy and import remain unseen and unappreciated. *Ping-fa* can't be found in *Chinese Thought: From Confucius to Mao Tse-tung*. Herbert Giles's *Gems of Chinese Literature*, published in 1922, only twelve years after the release of Lionel Giles's translation of *Ping-fa*, makes no reference to it.[78] His *A History of Chinese Literature*, published in 1901, listed "Sun Tzu" as a "miscellaneous writer." The otherwise prestigious *Cambridge Encyclopedia of China*, commenting on the classification of ancient Chinese works, says some are certainly in the wrong place. There are authors with "no obvious connection with any sort of Taoism whatsoever, such as the Sun-tzu, a military treatise" (Hook 1982, 316).

The commentary holds that *Ping-fa* "appeared" within an "experience of war that was often savage, cruel and deadly serious" in the "vastly different context" of "military operations in China during the period of the Warring States" (Teck and Grinyer 1994, 289). While ceaseless war was indeed a contextual factor in bringing about *Ping-fa*, we need to recognize it was also a time of glory. *Ancient Dynasties* says the period gave us Confucius, Mencius, Xun Zi (whose work led to the School of Law), the school of *yin-yang* and the five elements, and Mo Zi. It was a time that

> witnessed unprecedented cultural prosperity. [It was] the "golden age"' of China. So many different philosophies developed that the era [produced] many of the great classical writings on which

---

78   Giles published his *Ping-fa* in 1910. He was with the British Museum department of oriental books and manuscripts.

Chinese practices were to be based for the next two and one-half millennia.[79]

It was also the time when the Chinese nation was being born. Despite the grave importance of this time to China, comparatively little study has been undertaken of what happened then, why, and how. Little is known of the state of Qin and the empire it founded, in comparison with the much better documented Han dynasty. The histories and commentary have accepted what the Han had to say, whether it conformed to logic and common sense or not. Precious few have challenged hallowed assumptions or conducted original research that was not bound by convention. *The School of Sun Tzu* has made use of that very approach.

An immersion in the Warring States intrigues and a thorough study of the *Tao Te Ching* will prove very beneficial before looking at *Ping-fa*. Without that preparation, *Ping-fa* looks pedestrian, pedantic, and obscure. Preparation is needed for dealing with its military vocabulary, the quite amazing fluidity of the Chinese language, and the highly condensed nature of ancient China's metaphorical works.

To "know" *Ping-fa*, one must do two things: one must start by discarding what is assumed about the work, and focus on what is known. Then, apply tests of logic and coherence to the text. These applications expose evidence so consistent that certain conclusions are unavoidable. *Ping-fa* is not about the management of war. It is about managing to ensure there is no war. It is high-level theory and principle. It is strategic, and comprehensive. It is both knowledge and the path to knowledge.

J. H. Huang says, "Ping-fa's position is that the purpose of strategy is not conflict, but advantage: conflict serves as no more than one of the strategic

79 *The Ancient Dynasties: The Hundred Schools of Thought* (http://www-chaos.umd.edu/history/ancient2.html)

tools. Therefore conflict is a tactical choice rather than a certitude" (Huang 1993, 23).

And Jacques Gernet, very likely speaking of *Ping-fa* as an engagement methodology, as we do here, said,

> In the Han kingdom in the mid-fourth century [BCE] a reformer [we do not know if his advice was taken] told a prince of the advantages of having his intentions and political decisions shrouded in the greatest secrecy, and recommended a severe control over officials with strictly defined duties. (Gernet 1968, 94)

Ping-fa does not give up its secrets easily. One learns *Ping-fa* the same way Alan Watts says you should learn Zen: by not trying to learn it overnight or from only one experience. The same rules apply to Confucius and other writers from antiquity. Donald Bishop (1985, 16) says the only way to learn Confucius is to read it again and again and again. Consider this quote from Giles:

> When Confucius held office under the Duke of Lu, and a meeting was convened at Chia-ku, he said: "If pacific negotiations are in progress, warlike preparations should have been made beforehand." (Giles 1910, p. xlvii)

Though one might wish to see an admonition for armament here, logic dictates that "pacific" demands a different understanding of "warlike." This "warlike" means something other than weapons and soldiers. It too is *ping-fa*, and it refers to the practice of diplomacy. "Confucius"—or at least this admonition attributed to him—says you should not go into negotiations without having gathered facts and prepared the ground and your strategy. If you are ready for the engagement, you will win it.

When reading *Ping-fa*, look to redundancies for key messages. And there are riddles. When you locate a riddle, you know you have your mental work cut out for you. But the work is worth it: the riddles prove what *Ping-fa* is all about. And the erroneous ways certain passages have been linked[80]in the commentaries is proof that the commentary has missed *Ping-fa's* meaning.

To understand *Ping-fa*, move slowly.

It is only when there is no goal and no rush that the human senses are fully open to receive the world. The difficulty of describing these things for Western ears is that people in a hurry cannot feel. (Watts 1957, 176)

Ping-fa is a very clever, interactive exercise. It engages readers in a learning dialogue. Every reading brings new information or new understandings. *Ping-fa* facilitates a transforming experience that leads to perceptual and comprehension change. This is a powerful work.

Ping-fa gave expression to the *Tao Te Ching's* higher abstractions concerning objectives, purposes, and values, while providing a guidebook for organization, management, and control. It sets out, for example, how government, as an important social institution, could be proactive, identifying emerging issues and subtly influencing events as a normal part of business.[81]

Ping-fa is the tool of a new social order, where objectives are defined systematically and achieved strategically. Analysis includes assessment of effort, cost, and the consequences of error. If costs outweigh benefits, activity should stop. Responsibility for organizational well-being and appropriate engagement management rests squarely on the shoulders of officials. If matters are out of hand, the organization has no one to blame but itself.[82] Rather

---

80 See XI.51–59 for example.

81 Professor Robert Bedeski speaks of "Peacefare."

82 The *Tao Te Ching* says, "To be restless is to lose one's control" (26).

than a treatise on war, it is a methodology for the management of organizations in complex environments, and the management of engagements when warranted, according to strict rules. Conflict is a choice, and war is the supreme demonstration of failure.

Ping-fa Language and Metaphors

Imagine Qin in 245 BCE. It was led by a learned and progressive king. He appointed professionals to his administrative posts and governed by law. The economy was booming. People were at peace, working, and well fed. In the court were the best intellects the pre-Chinese world had to offer. The king, his advisers, and intellectuals had established academies of learning that brought highly competent teachers and students together to examine and plan for the realization of Qin's destiny.

Imagine what had to be learned and resolved. Imagine the volumes of theory and practice that would have been necessary to formulate all the strategies and plans required to end war and establish an empire!

What of Qin's civilian "picked soldiers," forever immortalized in the terracotta army?

Qin's peripatetic persuaders had to know the why and how of political analysis, sensitive intervention, and intrigue. They had to be competent orators and able to effect disguises of all kinds. Only then would they be equally comfortable in the courts of kings and the gathering places of working people. Here was a not-easily delivered requirement for both content and pedagogy. Qin could not afford to spend decades realizing its destiny. It had to find ways of creating competent persuaders in a minimal time.

Among the curriculum texts was a small volume called *Ping-fa*. The academicians had created a mechanism for conveying very difficult concepts in leadership, communication, teamwork, strength management, and sensitive intervention. They wrote it up as a manual of war, perhaps drawing on the very ancient *Book of Changes,* where "combat and armament are used to symbolize all manner of internal and external struggle and conflict" (Cleary 1992b, 170).

This was a format appropriate for both training and memorizing. Practitioners of the engagement art had to know how it was done. And that knowing was part memorization, part intuitive understanding. The military language provided a familiar context for a very difficult subject. Poetry and imagery served as memory aids.

Ping-fa's authors had another useful technique. They approached the same issue from different perspectives so that one might see it from many angles and therefore achieve a comprehensive understanding. That was especially useful in situations where the "truth" and the "right" might have to be situationally determined.

Because *Ping-fa* uses language strong in imagery and metaphor, it fosters exploration and learning. It offers subtle twists and turns that force readers to exercise their minds. Persuaders were expected to use their heads, not follow specific instructions. As Cleary (1988b, 131) says, "What ancient adepts set up as truths were mostly in the form of indirect allusions." The academicians trained their students to reach and therefore learn. And they learned best through exploration and discovery.

Ping-fa solved a whole host of communication and comprehension challenges with one remarkable solution. Physical representation of armies in opposition was intended to convey complex concepts on organization, strength, control, relationships, communications, leadership, and success.

Roger Ames (1993, 35, 40–41, 73) shows insight when he tells us that "military strategy can be used as a source of metaphors to shape philosophical distinctions and categories." He says teaching practices in ancient China "grounded" theory and philosophy in experiences and "evocative metaphors." These devices were intended to aid learning and the development of knowledge, not through rote but through cognitive processes.[83] This is all very good, but then he says, "The place of [*Ping-fa*] as the fundamental work in classical military literature is unassailable."

It *is* an attractive trap to wander in *Ping-fa's* tactile, tactical world of fires, floods, armies, battles, and different types of ground. *Ping-fa* takes us over mountains, through valleys, onto plains, and into the woods. But you can get lost in those woods. The *Ping-fa* authors did not intend this to be a guide to cross-country travel. This is metaphor—the vehicle whereby the physical world illustrates and guides us through the treacherous terrain of principle, practice, and value.

The commentary has seen only the physical, while missing the conceptual. This shallow analysis disregards the *Ping-fa* content, its having been written at a time of transition from war to peace, the emergence of empire, and the fact that it was an era of brilliance in philosophy, science, engineering, and statesmanship. *Ping-fa* no more intends that we should study woodlands and marshes than Stephen Covey (1990) thinks we should use a box compass to find the "True North" he speaks of.

Here is Michael Handel (1992, 43-76), an authority on military strategy, on III.3, *Ping-fa's* critical position on "the highest form of generalship." Mr. Handel exposes *Ping-fa* as something far different and greater than the military work of Carl von Clausewitz. But unfortunately, he suggests *Ping-fa* is "greater" only in that its obscurity makes its readers think.

> *Sun Tzu's* brevity and reliance on the less precise development of a similar idea is also the source of his argument's strength. The ambiguity of his statement that "the supreme excellence in war is to attack the enemy's plans" forces the reader

---

83 Similar conditions and motives could have led to the veiling of *The Masters of Huainan* and Zhang's *Understanding Reality* (Cleary 1989b, xxvii).

to reflect in greater depth and work harder on deciphering meaning of his statement. Instead of providing his readers with manual-like advice, it is Sun Tzu and not Clausewitz who here presents his readers with an inspiring metaphor rather than with a formula for strategic and operational planning.

Handel concludes that while it is an entertaining read, there is no strategy or planning in *Ping-fa*. Then, in a bizarre demonstration of insight without understanding, he says the messages are about "defeating the enemy before war breaks out, preferably by nonviolent means." One should "attack the strategy" and "disrupt alliances." All of this is on the mark, but then he concludes that *Ping-fa* is saying that destroying armies is of only secondary importance. He says, "after a war has begun, it is reasonable to assume [such] would become a higher priority even for Sun Tzu." Handel does not think for one minute that *Ping-fa* is concerned with anything but war. For him, the metaphor is the message.

James Clavell (1983, 7) is the author of a *Ping-fa* version that a *Globe and Mail* reviewer called "slapdash,"

I would like to make *The Art of War* obligatory study for all our serving officers and men, as well as for all politicians and all people in government and all high schools and universities in the free world. If I were a commander in chief or president or prime minister I would go further. I would have written into law that all officers, *particularly all generals,* take a yearly oral and written examination on these thirteen chapters, the passing group being 95 percent—any general failing to achieve a pass to be automatically and summarily dismissed without appeal, and all other officers to have automatic demotion.

A refusal or inability to move away from a militaristic perspective and see that *Ping-fa* is a Taoist work, combined with centuries of commentator rivalry, have meant that none has addressed the key themes explored in *The School of Sun Tzu*.

Some commentators have made a valiant effort to escape the clutches of militarism. So far none have fully succeeded. Cleary had doubts about the war focus, being not quite sure why someone had attached *Art of War* to *Sun Tzu*. Lau and Ames said *Ping-fa's* imagery "naturalizes the military culture, by bringing together military detail and philosophical ideas" (1996, 41).

> Contemporary scholars who work on classical Chinese military thought [consider Sun Tzu to be] a philosophical text. In a highly conceptual and even philosophical way, Sun-tzu addresses the issues of warfare, the operations of the military, its strategy, tactics, and so on. It is, in their view, the fact that Sun Tzu is philosophical, that has assured it a place in the world's literature, while the *Sun Pin* has been 'lost to posterity.' (Lau and Ames 1996, 57)

While the *Ping-fa* military metaphor has certainly been a factor in frustrating penetration to the real messages, there have been linguistic blocks as well. We need to look at the excellent work by J. H. Huang. His knowledge of the epoch, culture, language, philosophy, and writing style, and his focus on the Linyi text have enabled him to examine *Ping-fa* from a fresh perspective. He followed the same linguistic analysis process as Paul Lin used with the *Tao Te Ching*, achieving a high level of coherence as a result. His conclusion: the persistent war context and application of *Ping-fa* is highly suspect.

Ping-fa's refusal to acknowledge war's inevitability, and its assertion that conflict is caused by incompetence, must trouble the military. *Ping-fa* says that success and winning are never achieved at the cost of someone else. When another—significant to you or your organization—loses, your loss will be equal to, or greater than, theirs. This scenario is of course anathema to those domains that concern themselves with conflict and competition.

The military canon most often links *Ping-fa* to the *On War* of military strategist Carl von Clausewitz. But there is little real connection between them. The editors of *On War* say that "Clausewitz was ... less concerned with establishing a formal system or doctrine than with achieving understanding and clarity of expression" (Howard and Paret 1976, Introduction). Bernard Brodie says Clausewitz had a "pronounced disinclination to provide formulas or axioms as guides to action." In contrast, *Ping-fa* is comprehensive, logical, consistent, and methodological.

For a really trite reason; that is the military metaphor used in *Ping-fa*, they have assigned this work a pedigree that is shared with military writers Machiavelli, Clausewitz, and Antoine Henri, Baron de Jomini. Consider Clausewitz, whose subject is not in doubt, as he defines "war" is

> of two kinds. Either the objective is to *overthrow the enemy* —to render him politically helpless or militarily impotent, thus forcing him to sign whatever peace we please, or *merely to occupy some of his frontier-districts* so that we can annex them or use them for bargaining at the peace negotiations. (Howard and Paret 1976, 69)

Commentator intransigence on the war metaphor has denied an important work the benefits that would accrue from free analysis and dialogue. For a century Western debate has focused on the margins and on terminology incidentals. Today, the range in translation and interpretation exceeds even the most liberal allowances for the inherent ambiguities of Chinese script.

Because one commentator, or several acting in unison, decided *"Ping-fa* means the "Art of War," the war metaphor—a simple pedagogical device—came to be seen as the substance of the work. Since then, only one or two commentators have challenged that notion. Consequently, the world has missed *Ping-fa's* key message: that conflict is not inevitable, that organizations can achieve all they desire while acting for the common good, that such happens with the proper development and application of intelligence, and that managing all of this requires the use of a new methodology—a methodology we call *Ping-fa*.

Laure Paquette (1989), who did her Queen's University master's thesis on Clausewitz and *Ping-fa*, offers a rare understanding of the difference between these strategists:

> [Comparing Clausewitz to Sun Tzu] reveals some striking differences. In *On War*, instant conception, prolonged engagements, restricted flexibility and knowledge, emphasis on tactics over strategy, and difficulties created by surprise all characterize strategy. In *The Art of War*, strategy is conceived over a longer period of time and constantly revised, engagements are quick when they are absolutely unavoidable.

Most of the commentary sees the military metaphor as the painting instead of as the frame. They praise *Ping-fa's* attention to detail while criticizing their colleagues for failing to understand what it is really all about.

> Sun Wu loved brevity of diction, but his meaning is always deep. Whether the subject be marching an army, or handling soldiers, or estimating the enemy, or controlling the forces of victory, it is always systematically treated; the sayings are bound together in strict logical sequence, though

this has been obscured by commentators who have probably failed to grasp their meaning. (Mei Yao-Ch'en [1002–1060], quoted by Lionel Giles)

A thousand years ago, Mei Yao-Ch'en failed to see for what this "systematic treatment" was intended for, as the war smoke screen is difficult to penetrate. Only when one grasps the true import of *Ping-fa* is one able to see that it was necessary to use a real-world metaphor, because there was just no language for the terms and concepts it revealed.

Because *Ping-fa* is intentionally, and delightfully, metaphorical, the messages need to be ferreted out, tasted, and tested. Searching for military meaning in salt marshes, swollen rivers, and ways to spread fire will not prove useful. *Ping-fa* is not written in such "very specific and operational terms," as one commentator has it (Teck and Grinyer 1994, 289). This makes it useless as a military manual in the view of Machell-Cox (1943, 6). He believes it a waste of time and energy for the military strategist to read anything non-tactile. "Really sound knowledge of topography, movement and supply are the foundations of military knowledge, not tactics and strategy as most people think."

Ping-fa is deemed tactile and tactical rather than metaphorical in the military commentary. As a consequence, the land-based tactics are accepted at face value and crowbarred into meanings and categories so it can link to the canon. This often brings bizarre results.

Consider this illustration. *Ping-fa* Chapter X is concerned with six kinds of "terrain." The first thirteen lines speak of "accessible ground; entangling ground; temporizing ground; narrow passes; precipitous heights; and positions at a great distance from the enemy." In most of the commentary, terrain means "land, " so chapter X then becomes a system for classifying geographic land types. But this is nonsense. Only when you replace "terrain" with "ground" do you get an inkling that what is being discussed is position, not place. But even with that leap we are still not at the point of full understanding.

Engagement management is all about gaining, maintaining, and protecting "ground." And in the management of engagements, one starts with a system for the classification of "situations." We see there are nine types, and we have appropriate engagement action associated with each. The system exposed here is comprehensive and its value immediately evident.

But there is still a problem. The system contains a riddle to be solved. *Ping-fa* also specifies six "conditions." We see appropriate action for five of them, but none for "positions at a great distance from the enemy." We know that terrain is not about geography, so this is not physical distance.

Here we must go to *wu-wei* for understanding. "A great distance" means the parties are polarized. The issues are visible, and resolution is unlikely. Here we have no engagement instructions, because engagement is not appropriate. The parties are too far removed from one another to assure success.

Now, consider "strength," which in the *Ping-fa* methodology is a critical factor. This concept is a particular challenge, viewed from a great geographical or historical distance, or from a radically different conceptual framework.[84] Military commentators always read "strength" as "numerical strength" or "combat force." Sawyer says strength is "weapons and masses."

Another troublesome term is "force," which Wing (1988, 91, 11) considers a synonym for "troops." But Ping-fa teaches us that "force," "strength" and "order" are near equivalent. And none of them necessitate action. We need to look to other sources than the "traditional" commentary for insight and understanding. The Master of the Hidden Storehouse said,

---

84   Kwok *et al.* (1993, 22) ran into this problem in their work with the *Tao Te Ching*.

The best militias esteemed order. When order is strong and trustworthy, adversaries are weak and humbled. When you achieve this, it says, how could an other even be worth beating? (Cleary 1993, 159)

Giles (1994, I.5) says, with some accuracy, that an army's "strength" can be measured both "morally as well as physically." Huang says,

We can see possible relationships between the terms *bing* or the 'force of people' and *qi* as the 'strength of people.' 'Which side has the stronger weapons and people?,' in the Chinese text reads, *bing zhong shu qiang. Bing zhong* indicates 'weapons' and 'people.' Some scholars have mistakenly believed *bing'zhong'* indicates 'troops.' The term 'combat power' is an interpreter's guess of the meaning of the term *shi,* which in the time of *Ping-fa*'s creation meant only 'power.' (1993, 132)

Huang says we should not assume "military affairs" translates as, or even implies, armed force or armed forces.

'Military affairs' in the Chinese text reads *bing.* Since *bing* is modified by 'a country's vital political concerns', we thus know its meaning is 'military affairs.' Only in present times [have] interpreters of Ping-fa tried to define *bing* as 'war' (*zhanzheng*). Their source for this definition is unknown.

Huang says *bing* is a part of "the affairs of a government." Confucius once said that governing was about "sufficient food and sufficient *bing.*" He says *bing* may mean variously "people" or "force" or "military strategy." "The *Ciyuan* incorrectly gives 'war' as the third definition of *bing*. Forcing the definition of war on the character *bing* here goes way beyond its original meaning." R. L. Wing agrees. He translates *bing* as "strategy" and says "force" comes from an ideogram that can be translated as "military," "corps," or "national defense."

Kidder Smith says that the "fa" of *Ping-fa* certainly refers to models, but also to methods, standards, and in a military context, regulations. Whichever English word we choose for *fa* pulls us toward a particular Warring States philosophical tradition (1990, 47-48).

"*Zhan*," says Huang, "may usually mean war today," but "in pre-Qin writings, it generally indicates 'battles.' The earliest instance where the term *zhanzheng* (war) can be found is from the Qin dynasty, but this was [*sic*] more than two hundred years after Sun Tzu." And later, "the actual meaning of the term *zhengzhan* is to employ *zhen* in contending with someone." Huang (1993, 121, 141) suggests the subject of the thesis was "engagement," not "war."

Says Huang:

> "The enemy," which is how *diren* has been translated by Giles, among others, really means "adversaries in conflict." In modern Chinese this term means "enemy," but in Sun Tzu an enemy is referred to simply as *di*. "Generals" in the Chinese text reads *jiang*. In the pre-Qin era, *jiang* had such official positions as civilian governors or district chiefs. So, at any time, *jiang* were civilian administrators of both people and military affairs. There is no exact English equivalent for *jiang* so we loosely interpret it as "generals." (1993, 131, 225)

Agreeing, Giles says that from the Zhou dynasty to the Spring and Autumn, all military commanders were statesmen as well. But that dual role did not end with the Qin ascendancy; rather, it blossomed at that time. Then, Qin's persuaders learned that "strength," which they had always equated with "force," now meant something different.

Consider the persuasion involving Chiang Yi and the state of Ch'u. In that story, a fox is represented as the most powerful animal in the forest because all other animals run from him. But it is because the fox is followed by a tiger that he is powerful (Crump 1964, 47).

The Tao of *Ping-fa*[85]

China's ancient traditions included a practical guide for personal behavior that we now call "Confucianism," as well as a conceptual guide for social behavior that we refer to as "Taoism." Confucianism, very generally, tended to look to the past for guidance. Ancestor worship was an element, as were admonitions, metaphors, and anecdotes.

In its earliest iteration Taoism was philosophy and perhaps religion. But it was most certainly not what we would call political science. Meddling in human affairs was discouraged, if not prohibited. The social order was "natural." It was ordained. People were individually responsible for their lives, and the notion of people directing the affairs of other people was troublesome.

Should one wish to be "successful," he could seek to become more learned. Then, no social condition was intrinsically more worthy than any other. One might explore the cosmos and one's place in it, but one did not strive to make the cosmos fit the self. The *Lun-yü (Analects) of Confucius* show how "the exemplary person" reinforces harmony. Confucius said that good people

85   Victor Harris, translator of *The Book of Five Rings*, says, "Way is equivalent to the Chinese 'Tao' and means the whole life of the warrior, his devotion to the sword" (1974, 34:1). This may be Japanese *Michi*, but it is not Chinese *Tao*.

strengthen themselves ceaselessly and support others with enriched virtue. Resistance to events would have been deemed illogical, if not insane. For one to seek to cause a change of state or condition was to tamper with the will of heaven.

Cleary (1992b, 171) said Confucianism "valued practical application rather than mere theoretical philosophy." One might envision a better or worse condition for himself, but people were hesitant to suggest that what worked for one could work for all. One could not assume to know the Way better than another or assume the right to adjust the Way—to declare his or her way as *the* Way. People of good intent and honor might collaboratively resolve issues among themselves, but the very idea of proclaiming or enforcing order was unconscionable.

Handel quotes Fairbank in his *Chinese Ways in Warfare*, saying, "For the emperor to resort to violence was an admission he had failed in his own conduct as a sage pursuing the art of government. The resort to warfare (*wu*) was an admission of bankruptcy in the pursuit of *wen* (the arts of peace)" (Handel 1992, 77). Giles says, "Our Master Confucius said: 'I have never studied matters connected with armies and battalions'." With equal disdain, he is also reported to have said, "I have not been instructed about buff-coats and weapons."

In times of antiquity Taoism opposed all things artificial, including government, which should be kept to the most minimal level possible. Nevertheless, Confucius recognized that from time to time punishment was just as necessary at the state level as it was in the home. He said, "Those whose paths are not the same do not consult one another" (15:40). It follows that those whose paths are or may become the same ought to consult. But he did not go so far as to suggest societies should institutionalize mechanisms for order and control.

Management and intervention were not, in the time of Confucius, of "grave importance for the state."

Confucius said, "Was it not [the emperor] Shun who did nothing (*wu-wei*) and yet ruled well? What did he do? He merely corrected his person and took his proper position as ruler." Watts says emperors did not then involve themselves in the "fussy details of government" (Watts 1975, 77).

Governed by the Way, people were unencumbered by regulation. They also knew that without the Tao, they faced the prospect of living in a society that was authoritarian, rule-bound, and restrained by complex systems of rewards and punishments. Such a society might also be warlike and troublesome. Disruptions in the social fabric were, for a very long time, infrequent and of limited consequence. Events, however, were recognized to have a yin and a yang side. They flowed from good to bad, from peace to war. This too was as things should be. *The Way of Zen* says yin and yang manifest opposites that are "relational and fundamentally harmonious." Communities recognized that dissidence and deviance had to be handled on a case-by-case basis by reasonable people.

According to Alan Watts (1975, 19-20), to define war as bad and peace as good, or to try to eradicate a condition, such as the state of war as against the assumed higher value of the state of peace would be "as incomprehensible as an electric current without positive and negative poles ... and the disappearance of either of them would be the disappearance of the system."

The elegance of society's yin-and-yang relationships came to an end when war became the norm in the Middle Kingdom. No one could see its end or how that end might come about on its own. Clearly, the natural balance of the world was in disarray.

> At first [the ancients] did not yet know that there were things. This is the most perfect knowledge; nothing can be added. Next they knew that there were things, but they did not yet make distinctions

between them. Next they made distinctions between them, but they did not yet pass judgments upon them. When judgments were passed, *Tao* was destroyed. With the destruction of the *Tao*, individual preferences came into being. (Fung Yu-Lan 1995, 15)

The heretical notion of social intervention emerged when certain people came to realize that they could no longer trust their lives to fate. Those certain people were officials in the state of Qin. Qin concluded, at the height of the Warring States period, that something had to be done, or society would come crashing down. And if that doing something was inconsistent with the Way, then the Way was also in disarray and would require adjustment. Qin's leaders were brash Legalists who believed that almost anything could be achieved if you planned it well enough.

Qin studied the world and the nature of war and peace. It studied what people thought and how they managed their lives and their communities. It studied the values that people had and the philosophies they subscribed to. Qin concluded that war was unending because people were allowing it to continue. And for war to end, people had to do what was necessary to bring that end about. Such an intervention, by individuals or states, would have to be done in a way consistent with the will of heaven.

As Qin unfolds its plans for empire, stories circulate throughout the Middle Kingdom. One speaks of Confucius visiting Lao Tzu. During that visit, Lao Tzu tells Confucius that he was of the past and no longer in step with society's needs. Lao Tzu says the old ones are long gone—that only their words exist: "Let go, Sir, your proud airs, your many wishes, your affectation and exaggerated plans. All this is of no use to you Sir" (Carus 1964, 70).

This was a Qin persuasion, intended for wide retelling, its message direct. Don't look to history to solve your problems; you have to solve them yourselves. This persuasion is indicative of an emerging schism in Chinese belief. It represented a transition point between a Confucian dominated Middle Kingdom and the ascendency of Legalism and a new Taoism. Driven by need, the new Taoism was evolving from a philosophical worldview that traced its origins from the *I Ching* of antiquity with an almost dogmatic belief system, to one that was more fluid than fixed. It ebbed and flowed as it related to new and changing circumstances, new ideas and new perspectives. As a consequence, it developed an amazing vitality.

"Chuang Tzu," an alleged but fictional wise person, said,

> Thus, those who say that they would have right without its correlate, wrong, or good government without its correlate, misrule, do not apprehend the great principles of the universe, nor the nature of all creation. One might as well talk of the existence of heaven without that of earth, or of the negative principle without the positive, which is clearly impossible. Yet people keep on discussing it without stop; such people must be either fools or knaves. (Watts 1975, 26)

The emerging new Taoism claimed that war was not inevitable (or even appropriate) and that people with good intent could bring about peace. New concepts and values ushered in new methods. Such was the birth of the *Tao Te Ching* and *Ping-fa*, emerging from a worldview shaped to new individual and social requirements. This "Neo-Taoism" involved a dramatic movement away from absolute fatalism. *Wu-wei* was transformed from a tenet of monastic social isolation to a tenet of pragmatic social intervention and nonintervention.

Taoism assumes that nonaction can lead to the reduction of conflicts and changing behavior in the desired direction only when the actor understands how to use nonaction according to the operations of the three systems, each of which specifies a situation related to the other that the actor must be aware of in order to unravel conflicts. (Key Sun 1995)

The *Tao Te Ching* says, "The sage avoids extremes, excesses *and* complacency" (29). It became recognized that "adaptation and change are inevitable and necessary in government and law" (Cleary 1993, 80). "The ruler needs to govern a state as one cooks a small fish—that is, don't turn it so often in the pan so that it disintegrates" (Watts 1975, 78). While the commentary usually imagines this is an admonition against big government, the message is really about the need for appropriate intervention. To cook the fish, you have to turn it now and then. The truly benevolent leader of people accommodates himself to the Way.

The Tao of Leadership says, "The Tao does not preach sermons or dictate behavior. What people do is their own responsibility. No one can decide for you what to do in a given situation" (Heider 1988, 145).

Therefore the sage says:

I take no action, and the people become civilized;
I wage no war, and the people become just;
I transact no business, and the people become wealthy;
I have no desire, and the people become innocent.
(*Tao Te Ching* 57)

Wu-wei is also "the concept of doing for no reward—of being beyond any personal interest in anything" (Kwok et al. 1993, 18).[86]

But here we must be very careful. Having no personal interest does not mean we do not have a social interest. Kaltenmark (1965, 99) is quite wrong in suggesting, "In everyday life, contacts with others are dangerous unless both parties are utterly disinterested." How can there be contact without interest? How can mere contact be dangerous? More thoughtful views are gained from Ray Grigg who speaks of care, caution, and attention in the affairs of the world. Donald Bishop (1985, 50) says one should do only what is "appropriate" with "maximum efficiency through minimum work." The *Tao Te Ching* says, "A nation is best governed by innocence; a war is best waged by treachery; the world is best controlled by inaction" (57) and even more directly, "A perfect war is not warlike." (68)

This "war" is really engagement (*bing*), and "treachery" means the tactics of engagement management, such as the use of deception. Here is Watts (1975, 75) in *Watercourse Way*:

The Tao does nothing, and yet nothing is left undone. These famous words of Lao Tzu obviously cannot be taken in their literal sense, for the principle of "non action" (*wu-wei*) is not to be considered inertia, laziness, *laissez-faire*, or mere passivity. In the context of Taoist writings it quite clearly means forcing, meddling, and artifice—in other words, trying to act against the grain of *li*.

The Chuang Tzu writings brought the new philosophies to the populace through poetry, analogy, and allegory.

---

86   Clare Hollingworth imagines that Taoism was of minor import. These "mystics ... had little influence on matters of government," but did have some effect on poetry and painting (1985, 3).

They challenged the Confucian belief that one could only gain the "secret of the Way" by being virtuous. The secret of the Way was to be found in the practice of *wu-wei*, the

> non-doing, or non-action, which is not intent upon results and is not concerned with consciously laid plans or deliberately organized endeavors. If one is in harmony with Tao—the cosmic Tao, "Great Tao,"—the answer will make itself clear when the time comes to act, for then one will act not according to the human and self-conscious mode of deliberation, but according to the divine and spontaneous mode of *wu-wei*. (Merton 1965, 24)

Among the key messages of Chuang Tzu was the importance of naturalness over artificiality. Of birds and fish, "Chuang Tzu" said changing their nature would bring pain and suffering. "In dealing with other men and other things, we should let them alone without interfering with them." Cutting off the legs of an animal to make it shorter is to interfere with the natural way of things. But Chuang Tzu makes it clear that change can be achieved without force or attacking the inherent nature of things. Attacking means meddling. D. C. Lau's (1963, 55) *Tao Te Ching* says the empire is won through not meddling.

Chuang Tzu tells of the rulers of the northern and southern oceans. They tried to repay a kindness to Chaos by boring a hole into him (because more holes would obviously be better). But this kills the ruler of Chaos (Fung Yu-Lan 1995, 9). Change must be handled in a sensitive manner. One needs to know both cause and effect. Here, Kaltenmark provides a useful clarification of his remarks on noninvolvement:

> We can see why the Holy Man's *wu-wei* is such a superior form of government: it consists of leaving

all men, creatures and things to order themselves spontaneously in accordance with natural harmony, and not perturbing the order of the Tao through intervening artificially. (Kaltenmark 1965, 60)

Chuang Tzu says that people who are to achieve greatness do not *seek* office, but they may be known by the frequency of the appeals for them to assume one. They are sought after because they are tranquil: they have achieved union of the Tao with appropriate action and nonaction. They accommodate themselves to the Way and become persons of "obscurity and solitude," within whom "the Tao acts without impediment." Chuang Tzu ridiculed the old idea that *wu-wei* meant "do nothing." He said, "Hearing the theory of nonaction, some people think that lying is better than walking."

Good leaders do the minimum and achieve the maximum. Bad leaders seek glory. An assertive *wu-wei* driven by the need for social order is the key link between the *Tao Te Ching* and *Ping-fa*. The *Tao Te Ching* sets out the principles and philosophy for an ordered society, and *Ping-fa* delivers the strategy that provides, in excruciating detail, how that social order is to be created and maintained. Says the *Tao Te Ching* (17)

The best government is one of which people know nothing more than its mere existence. The second best is one loved and praised by people. The next is one that they fear. And the last is one which people despised.

Sima Qian recognized the *wu-wei* transformation when he said it should not be thought of as isolation and withdrawal, but rather alertness and action (Kaltenmark 1969, 21). Cleary's (1992a, ix) *The Book of Leadership and Strategy,* a selection of classical Taoist works, speaks of healthy societies in terms of balance and harmony on each level of being, from the way the individual human body-mind complex experiences itself to the way it experiences interaction with the natural and social worlds. The masters also deal with larger questions of sociopolitical morale in terms of its relations to conflict and reconciliation.

Neo-Taoism authorized managed change. It redefined the roles of statesmen and set down the conditions under which change could be initiated and carried out. It told princes and kings that if they truly seek to achieve greatness they must rule with benevolence,[87] and they must manage relations with their fellow princes in the same way. Therefore, we see the *Tao Te Ching* speak of sages who offer advice on "military cunning, political maneuvering and inter-state diplomatic policies" (Kwok et al. 1993, 10).

The *Tao Te Ching's* essential nature, like that of *Ping-fa*, is complex but integrated. Both are theoretical and practical, artistic and scientific. They are solidly related in their purpose, basic values, methods, and key messages. They both rest on *qi*, on *wu-wei*, and on the absolute need for achieving benevolent solutions by inspired leaders. Without understanding these meanings and relationships, the *Tao Te Ching* appears to be obscure poetry. For many *Ping-fa* remains a book on how to cross rivers and move through forests.

The Art of ***Ping-fa***

When Qin introduced *Ping-fa* it was not as visible an occasion as it was auspicious. There was certainly no "official release," as the book was never intended for

---

87 "Benevolence" does not equate with "kindness" but with "knowledge of the whole."

public consumption. It was a "most secret" and powerful Qin tool for nation building.

The academicians of the Sun Tzu School who delivered the strategy for empire were passionate about the challenge that had been given them. They had to solve a number of tricky philosophical questions in Taoist thought and belief, and they had to build—from the ground up—a comprehensive methodology for bringing the Warring States together and ending the long-standing hostilities. Conflict was an evil that had to be brought under control, but equally important, humankind had to find more beneficial ways of conducting their affairs.

It's certain the Sun Tzu School was well versed and experienced in the arts and sciences of politics and government; in philosophy, theory, and religion; and with the will and nature of the people. Their knowledge would have taken in all classes, the military, and the literati. Though filled with excitement and expectation, they deeply understood the grave need for care and control. They moved cautiously.

Their studies would have doubtless noted that conflict often came about because of people driven by self-interest who had little concern about consequences. Why, they wondered, did the many have to suffer because of the whims of a few? They asked whether it was natural— "human nature"—that people should always be in conflict. They asked if competition must always lead to conflict. They speculated on social models where competition was not honored, and conflict was discouraged. They asked whether, in the midst of competing interests, individuals and organizations might peacefully coexist.

The academicians concluded that in earlier times life may well have been simpler and people could pursue their individual comforts and enlightenment. Now, conditions were different. And these conditions were demanding new institutions founded on new understandings. Everyone would have to give up something so that everyone would in turn benefit. These were revolutionary notions.

In time the academicians delivered a change and control methodology solidly grounded in a refined Taoism. It ushered in new principles for social living, where the needs of the many overtook the needs of the individual. Here was a philosophy and practice for maintaining harmony in a world of complexity and competition. The new methods dictated that government play a key role in both identification of need and maintenance of order. Government activity should be based on a polished body of law, guided by what was learned through a sophisticated system of intelligence gathering. As *Ping-fa* says, "foreknowledge cannot be elicited from spirits" (XIII.4). Qin had to know when action (engagement) was essential and when action was the worst thing that could happen.

With the home state in hand, Qin took its methods for organization and engagement management on the road. They applied their skills to arrogant states that soon became convinced that the world had to work in a new way. The tools of Neo-Taoism, applied within the community of Warring States, ended centuries of conflict—in less than a decade.

Says Cleary,

In a military action embodying the Way, the war chariots are not launched, the horses are not saddled, the drums do not thunder, and the banners are not unfurled. (1992a, 62)

Ping-fa is a remarkable, timeless document. It opens with a series of pronouncements: "What I am about to say to you is of vital importance. Wise organizations are controlled organizations. They know themselves, and they know the environment they are part of. They understand activity and trends so that they will know when trouble is on the horizon. When they determine a need to intercede they do so strategically, and minimally."

Organizations do only what must be done, using only those resources that must be used. Action, when necessitated, is delivered quietly and unobtrusively and is mutually beneficial. They "win" by achieving essential change without high cost. They win through the management of "strength." Well managed, well advised, and continually on the alert, these organizations are in control. When control is lost, failure ensues.

The Tao of Negotiation speaks of a "Conflict Continuum," in which events range (and move) from order to disorder, harmony to chaos. They say,

> Events happen. The real test is how events are handled. The *Tao of Negotiation* is intended to show how you can prevent conflicts from occurring in your life. We learn to stop, look and listen before we act, even before we think. (Edelman and Crain 1993, xii, xiii, 35, 344)

Control of the time and place of commencement of an engagement is essential. *Ping-fa* says, "Knowing the place and the time of the coming battle, we may concentrate from the greatest distances in order to fight" (VI.19). There are two brilliant illuminations here. Consider that there is only one way that you can *know* the place and time of the coming engagement. You decide. The second phrase means, because you are in control, you are influencing events without being visibly, or physically, involved. Your mind is clear and your strategy is uninfluenced by situational noise. You intervene strategically.[88]

---

88 US Marine Corps documentation on Command and Control says, "The enemy is unpredictable and beyond our capacity to 'control'." Nevertheless the Corps will "strive to operate in a manner which makes our own actions unpredictable to the enemy." Both are strategically important.

The fundamental meaning of *Ping-fa* remains unimagined in the traditional commentary. Handel says that the philosophy of *Ping-fa*

> clearly recognizes the supremacy of *raison d'etat* over all other considerations. War is a rational activity of the last resort (the *ultimo ratio*) that correlates ends and means to enhance the vital interests of the state. It is a political activity, as we understand it today. (1992, 43–76)

But *Ping-fa's* central message is that war is an irrational act undertaken by incompetent organizations when relationship management fails. Competent organizations have sophisticated intelligence networks. They know when to remain aloof, and when a tweak will avoid trouble. Leaders achieve wonders by "the divine manipulation of the threads." *The Tao of Leadership* says,

> If you are conscious of what is happening you will recognize emerging situations long before they have gotten out of hand. Neither avoid nor seek encounters, but be open and when an encounter arises, respond to it while it is still manageable. (Heider 1988, 125)

"Still manageable" is a key phrase. When conflict breaks out, regaining control is difficult.

> When force is used, conflict and argument follow. The group field degenerates. The climate is hostile, neither open nor nourishing. (Heider 1988, 59)

There are other complications. The rules change. Ethics and morality take second place to survival. *Just and Unjust Wars* says,

War is a world apart, where life itself is at stake, where human nature is reduced to its elemental forms, where self-interest and necessity prevail. Here men and women do what they must to save themselves and their communities, and morality and law have no place. *Inter arma silent leges*: In time of war the law is silent. (Walzer 1977, 3)

Ping-fa was written to provide a set of instructions to ensure that harmony is maintained, and conflict does not emerge. These methods indicate an understanding of the importance of managing the very challenging and troublesome organizational environment. *Ping-fa* tells us that the best managers in the land manage what is impacting on their organizations and also what their intelligence tells them could become an issue in time. Such strategically managed organizations are continually and fully aware, studying activities and trends and potential intersections of interest. They are of the sort that Jay Galbraith spoke of when he described "organizations created in order to execute business strategies" (Hesselbeing et al. 1997, 88). When they act, they achieve victory not on the backs of real or potential opponents, but in mutually beneficial ways.

Competent organizations are always "engaged," even though they are rarely in engagement. The fully competent organizational leader chooses his interventions wisely and infrequently. Organizations in management mode subtly influence or diligently avoid encountering others. To be successful in these treacherous waters, good managers need to be expert in organizational relations. An organization may engage when it senses a real or apparent convergence of interests. The well-disciplined organization will shift itself or shift the other so that the other never learns that it was on a collision course. Such engagements are sensitive and unobtrusive.

Engagements may involve competitors, associates, "bystanders," or constituents—indeed they could be any person or group whose interests pose a challenge to harmony. There are other requirements. Engagements must be short, incisive, and of minimum cost and maximum return for all players. *Ping-fa* says when engagement is indicated, role and responsibility definition are mission critical. We are told: "Let there be no misunderstanding about what needs to be done and who does what."

In the truly elegant engagement, the other does not know an engagement is under way. If the engagement results in a "shift" of the other, that other either is unaware of the shift or deems the shift beneficial. Under no circumstances is the other to perceive the organization as an aggressor or an enemy. The most competent organizations bring others into their fold, or ensure distance is maintained, without effort.

The more competent leader achieves full awareness and greater strength before others are ready. They commence engagements only when the strength situation is favorable. As they are fully prepared and their strength is greater, they prevail.

The Qin academy *Ping-fa* definitions of "leadership" and "teamwork" are far removed from what we understand these to be today. "Teams" were a new construct, with tightly defined rules, competencies, and processes. They were guided by trained professionals who were fully empowered to achieve their mission. These teams, when fully competent, are rarely surprised. They process great volumes of information before and as they move. They are a hotbed of innovation and experimentation, continually testing new strategies and tactics, and developing and testing hypotheses to determine what may be beneficial and what may be harmful. Competent organizations win—for everyone.

Being continually prepared, the organization ensures balance is maintained. Costly disruptions and destabilization that emerge from loss of control and order are avoided or minimized. "Hence the saying: The enlightened ruler lays his plans well ahead; the good general cultivates his resources" (XII.16).

Objectives are realized cheaply, quickly, and without the waste of unproductive and distracting conflict. When the environment is managed, organizations glide past one another or perhaps even constructively involve one another. This sort of "relationship management" takes intelligence, planning, and the right people.

Capable leaders know what to do and what not to do. Sometimes doing nothing at all is the right thing to do. *Wu-wei* can be intelligent inaction as well as minimal action. For example, one can reduce or eliminate possible difficulties by studied disinterest. The leader may use deception to suggest his attention is elsewhere. But when these or other techniques do not work, engagement may be necessitated. In engagement, the organization uses "sensitive intervention," which is the least possible level of activity needed to achieve a desired course change. When handled appropriately, nobody knows that it has happened.

Wing (1988, 19, 54) says,

> Only unskilled leaders work out their conflicts in courtrooms and on battlefields. [They achieve their objectives] through tactical positioning. For a skilled strategist, triumph is effortless and confrontation is finally an unnecessary exercise to prove the point.

Engagements come in many sizes and shapes, depending on the situation being addressed. An engagement strategy may involve a gentle, undetectable "tweak" by the organization head or his representative. It may require additional resources, up to the level of an engagement team that would be directed by a trained team leader.

Whatever form the engagement takes, sensitive intervention and strength management are guided by thorough analysis and superb planning, and they are carried out by trusted professionals. Agents respect the *Tao Te Ching's* injunction to "seek the simple in the complex, and achieve greatness in small things." They "nip problems in the bud," to use LaTorra's terminology (1993, 63–64).

The leader's first task is to determine where strength (*qi*) is found and where it is not. When he knows the disposition of strength, he is able to carry out his strategy successfully. He conducts a though gathering and analysis of intelligence so he knows where strength is, and where weakness may be found. "In respect of military method, we have, firstly, Measurement; secondly, Estimation of quantity; thirdly, Calculation; fourthly, Balancing of chances; fifthly, Victory" (IV.17) The leader divulges nothing. "Carefully study the well-being of your men. Keep your army continually on the move, and devise unfathomable plans" (XI.22).

The leader manages strength (*qi*) of his team members and the strengths of other parties. This "strength" is not the numerical strength of troops and armaments. It is the "vitality" of ancestor Lü:

In heaven, vitality is the Milky Way, it is the light of the sun, moon and stars, it is rain and dew, sleet and hail, snow and frost. On earth it is water, streams, rivers, oceans, springs, wells, ponds, and marshes. In people it is vitality, the root of essence and life, the body of blood and flesh. (Cleary 1988b, 81)

Leaders ensure "plans are unfathomable" to everyone, including one's own team. They convey information only when there is good reason to do so. "Confront your soldiers with the deed itself; never let them know your design" (XI.57). At other times, the leader will lie outright to the team members. "He must be able to mystify his officers and men by false reports and appearances, and thus keep them in total ignorance" (XI.36).

Conventional management wisdom holds that managers should be "fully open." That a leader would intentionally lie to his charges is, on the face of it, troublesome and illogical. But even the best trained and disciplined team might betray something quite unintentionally. When team strength has been brought to an operational level and they are fully prepared to engage, they must betray nothing. Engagement teams work on a need-to-know basis.

What they do not know, they cannot divulge. And leaders will ensure that some of what the team "knows" is disinformation. Giles says, "The treacherous and underhand nature of war necessitates the use of guile and stratagem suited to the occasion." He refers to "the infinite pains which Stonewall Jackson sought to conceal, even from his trusted staff officers, his movements, his intentions and his thoughts." When teams are at full strength, they may believe they are invincible. They have the capacity for rash action and may move before they are ordered to or brag about their achievements.

General Tao Hanzhang disagrees. In his view, these notions involve "looking down upon the laboring people." Such "backward or even reactionary views [are the result of] the limitations of the times and the author's class status" (1987, 91, 93). Kidder-Smith's (1990, 51) objections focus on *Ping-fa's* leadership model:

In particular circumstances the skillful general will be obeyed even without training his troops: He does not give orders yet they trust him. For Sun Tzu orders are an interactive phenomenon. They involve the meeting of two forces or states of mind, not simply the imposition of one person's will on another.

Orders are not "interactive" in *Ping-fa*. There is no democracy in team management. Engagement orders are adjusted only by the leader and then only when intelligence indicates an adjustment is required.

Engagement strategies are crafted in the context of the Moral Law: What is being done is the best for all concerned. There is no ambiguity in this. A beneficial objective for all must be delivered. Strategies are based on the known situation, contain clearly articulated objectives, and define authorities, resources, and broad parameters for the team leader. But as engagements unfold, new intelligence is gathered. As the teams of *Ping-fa* are fully empowered they make changes according to what they learn. They are creative, adaptive, and mobile.

While engagement teams are most effective when they are unseen, they sometimes must act in the open. Visible teams in engagement must work even harder to ensure their activities are unclear and the intents indiscernible. Here they must be truly creative in their discretion and deployment of deception, and their use of varied techniques.

Open engagements are not always amicable, and they are not always easily resolved. In such cases, organizational and team leaders will be tested to the limits of their abilities. None can lose sight of the needs for issue resolution with minimum cost, no conflict, and with benefit for all.

An analysis of the conditions leading to conflict, and the range of possible responses to those situations, is of benefit to fully appreciate the *Ping-fa* model and methodology. Are there conditions so intolerable that any action whatsoever is justified to bring it to an end? Are there circumstances where conflict is unavoidable and appropriate, such as when one is attacked and defense is mandatory for survival? Many have asked these very questions, including Vladimir Vassin (*The Eleventh Commandment* 1995), Nicholas Fotion (*Military*

Ethics 1990), and Martin van Creveld (*Transformation of War* 1991).

Churchill said, "War is horrible, slavery is worse." Walzer said, "A just war is one that is morally urgent to win. Critical values are at stake: political independence, communal liberty, and human life. Other means failing [an important qualification], wars to defend these values are justified" (1977, 110).

Newt Gingrich notes,

> Contrary to American tradition, there are some people who are actually evil. There was no reasoning with either Hitler or Stalin; both were men who respected only strength and had nothing but contempt for weakness. (1984, 227)

The Master of the Hidden Storehouse says war may be necessary when the cause is "truly just, when it is used to eliminate brutal rulers and rescue those in misery" (Cleary 1993, 159). According to Griffith (1963, Ch. IV), in *War in Sun Tzu's Age,*

> the human-hearted ruler did not "massacre cities," "ambush armies," or "keep the army over the season," nor did a righteous prince stoop to deceit; he did not take unfair advantage of his adversary. Philosophers and kings distinguished between righteous and unrighteous war; an enlightened prince was morally justified in attacking "a darkened and rustic country," in civilizing barbarians, in punishing the willfully blind, or in dealing summarily with a state going to ruin.

The need for social care and control, and methods for ensuring same is no less evident today than it was when *Ping-fa* came into being. Look at Rosabeth Moss

Kanter's "social contract," Max DePree's "covenant,"[89] Peter Drucker's "Manager's Letter," Stephen Covey's "Performance Agreement," and sportswriter Pat Riley's "Core Covenant" for very similar concerns and applications for resonance with *Ping-fa*.[90] While politicians and philosophers may well conclude that there are circumstances where war is justifiable (and control is by definition lost), we need to ensure that control in engagement is retained. Without control, management is difficult, if not impossible. Leo Tolstoy said, "Every great battle is a meaningless and undirected chaos ... entirely lacking in intelligently coordinated direction." (Gallie 1979, 105)

Ping-fa says organizations need to manage their affairs, and they need to manage the environments within which those organizations operate. In this way competent organization leaders have already won before engagements begin. "In war the victorious strategist only seeks battle after the victory has been won, whereas he who is destined to defeat first fights and afterwards looks for victory" (IV.15). When the organization is focused on the right, when an effective strategy has been crafted, when a competent leader is involved, engagement—when necessary—is a formality. The outcome has already been decided. It is a beneficial conclusion for all.

Because the competent teams of *Ping-fa* conclude (their rarely necessary) engagements readily and inexpensively, they demonstrate "excellence in engagement." They ensure effective, productive, and peaceful interorganizational relations that are governed by benevolence and directed towards shared outcomes.

---

89   He is CEO of Herman Miller. Quoted in Thomas A. Stewart's *Intellectual Capital*.
90   Riley speaks of a NUMMI and UAW covenant, which was a simply worded fifteen-page letter of intent that focused on values, goals, and principles.

Part IV: The Principles and Practices of Engagement

Peace is easily maintained; trouble is easily overcome before it starts. (*Tao Te Ching* 64)

Those who aid the ruler with Tao do not use
military force to conquer the world
The good man stops after getting results
Without daring to conquer
He achieves results without bragging
Achieves results without exalting
Achieves results without arrogance
Achieves results with reluctance
Achieves results without conquering.
(*Tao Te Ching* 30)

Ping-fa contains both "admonitions" and "instructions." The former are warnings to organization leaders: "Pay attention. This is important." The latter are techniques for organization and engagement management. The *Ping-fa* framework for analysis and action management can be applied to a very wide range of interests.

In this section I will explore, explain, and expand upon the key themes in *Ping-fa,* linking these themes and associated issues to recent thought in the management, military, and other domains.

These are "discussion papers" that can function as dialogue facilitators. *Ping-fa* and the *Tao Te Ching* raise many questions and many fascinating propositions. Can we really define quality management? Are the indicators of failure really as evident as they seem here? Do we really benefit from competition and conflict? Could we ever have a shared process for solving interorganizational and international issues before they emerge into public view?

Admonitions

Follow the Moral Law

The Art of War, then, is governed by five constant factors, the first of which is The Moral Law (I.3).

The Moral Law causes the people to be in complete accord with their ruler, so that they will follow him regardless of their lives, undismayed by any danger (I.5).

The consummate leader cultivates the Moral Law, and strictly adheres to method and discipline; thus it is in his power to control success (IV. 16).

In pre-China, shared values were known as the "Moral Law." *Ping-fa* says Moral Law "causes a people to be in accord." It is the socially binding higher truths and principles that define nations and societies. It energizes and gives purpose and direction. Moral Laws are the values for which people die, literally and figuratively. It is of heaven. It is solidly before and over all the people.

Moral Law conveys the absolute necessity for integrity, honesty, and benevolence in relationships and *Ping-fa* engagement management. Moral Law is enabled when there is a highly ethical relationship between the players in engagement. Leaders follow the Moral Law,[91] bound to their organizations through a complex web of beliefs and values that guide their decision-making, planning, and direction. These are the intransigent values that mold, guide and control. There is no confusion, no ambiguity. When we see commentators accuse *Ping-fa* of not adhering to the "code of a feudal warrior," as was

---

91   Confucius said, "The armed forces may be deprived of their commander, but a man cannot be deprived of his will" (9:26).

historically demonstrated by Duke Hsiang of Sung,[92] what we are seeing is their own non-comprehension:

> War to Sun Tzu was neither a duel nor a sportlike contest. Rather, it represented one way, and a rather undesirable way, of settling disputes between social and political groups. For [Sun Tzu] it was a question not of honorably meeting an opponent face to face, but of settling the dispute with the least possible disturbance of cosmic harmony, or *dao*. (van Creveld 1989, 72)

Do organization heads establish Moral Law and then proclaim it? No, says *Ping-fa*, "the Moral Law causes, etc." Therefore everyone is equally subject to it. Moral Law is the source of strength of a people. Organization leaders personify and nurture it. Translator Brian Bruya says,

> Establishing a moral cause means that there must be a common conviction shared by both the people and the government. The people must agree with the goals of the government before they will be willing to sacrifice themselves for the sake of the country. (Chung 1994, 25)

This "common conviction" explains another curious riddle: why in *Ping-fa* is there no reference to disloyalty and insubordination? Whether the subject is warfare of peaceful engagement, surely discontent and dissonance can be expected. *Ping-fa* does not provide for these circumstances because the mandate, the mission, and the shared values of the Moral Law preclude self-interest.

William A. Levinson provides a useful interpretation from the military perspective. He says *Ping-fa's* "commitment" means

---

92   See Walzer 1977, Chapter 14, "Asinine Ethics."

people will put the organization's welfare before their own, and willingly endure hardships and sacrifices. When Moral Law prevailed, soldiers would follow their leader willingly, obey his orders cheerfully, and die with him if necessary.[93]

Engagement strategies and tactics may vary by conditions, but the Moral Law is a constant. "An organization must be prepared to change everything about itself except those beliefs as it moves through corporate life" (Pascale and Athos 1981, 184). Covey (1991, 165) says the single most chronic problem in organizations is the absence of shared vision and values: "... either the organization has no mission statement or there is no deep understanding of and commitment to the mission at all levels of the organization." Covey's second "chronic problem" is the absence of a "strategic path."

Leaders apply their strong sense of values to the goals and processes of the organization. Art McNeil (1987, 16) said, "When the vitality of an organization's people is focused and combined, almost anything can be accomplished." Tom Watson said, "I firmly believe that any organization, in order to survive and achieve success must have a sound set of beliefs on which it premises all its policies and actions."[94] Leigh D'Orso says that his formula for successful sports negotiations requires a "focus on value identification, clarification and prioritization" (Steinberg 1998, 21).

Peters and Waterman (1982, 26) say, "The real role of the chief executive is to manage the values of the organization." Steven Covey, in thinking highly

---

93 "Mutual Commitment" in *Executive Excellence*, Vol. 16, No. 6, p. 19 Provo, June 1999. W. A. Levinson is the author of *The Way of Strategy.*
94 At his McKinsey Foundation lectures at Columbia University in 1962

reminiscent of *Ping-fa*, says organizations need alignment of values, visions, and strategies.

> The strategy should be congruent with the professed mission, with available resources, and with market conditions. Moreover the strategy should be monitored and changed to reflect shifts in the wind. (1991, 186)

Ethics in Practice, a Canadian Defence Department publication, says soldiers need to be guided by ethical considerations. Quoting *Ping-fa*, they say, "When you see the correct course, act; do not wait for orders." In engagement there is precious little room for consultation and consensus-building. One needs to know what is right.

Ethics in Practice goes on to say that, "Our [military] rank and uniform do not excuse us from the responsibilities of behaving like civilized, respectable, and responsible members of Canadian society. In all our actions we must be guided by common sense."[95] I would argue that that "common sense" emanates from "Moral Law" and military training.

The *Ping-fa* commentary has made Moral Law complex and elusive. Some think it is "morale," others "loyalty." Martin van Creveld assumes "heaven" is "religion," and that adherence to a "Moral Law" has something to do with "piety." He says,

> Sun Tzu listed the "favor of heaven" as the first condition for success. The idea that war [would] be considered exclusively as a problem in power-politics would have struck him as both impious and stupid. (1991, 126)

---

95 "Proceedings of the Conference on Ethics in Canadian Defence" (Canada, Department of National Defence. October 1997)

General Tao Hanzhang (1987, 14) translates Moral Law as "politics." He says *Ping-fa* "meant that the sovereign should use political pressure or other means to bring the people into harmony with him."

Giles (1994, 1.4) does much better. He explains that a ruler "imbued with the Moral Law" (I.13) is the same as one who is in "complete accord" (I. 5) and "in harmony with his subjects." Though he does not see Moral Law as a "binding force," he does understand it to be a "principle of harmony not unlike the Tao." It would equate to morale "were it not considered as an attribute of the ruler."

Ping-fa says victory is achieved when the commander stands for "the virtues of wisdom, sincerity, benevolence, courage and strictness" (I.8). For these reasons, *Ping-fa* was quite clear that organizations in engagement must be guided by the Moral Law. The practice of benevolence is a fundamental requirement for action. "Success in warfare is gained by carefully accommodating ourselves to the enemy's purpose" (XI.60).

The welfare of others is as important as your own. *Ping-fa* warns us in no uncertain terms that nobody should suffer loss in engagement. The Moral Law's central place in *Ping-fa* is acute testimony to the humanity of the Legalists of Qin.

The commentary from time to time suggests *Ping-fa* suffers from a dearth of ethics. Robert Kaplan (2002, 42, 44), who thinks it is only about "cold-blooded self-interest," says Chinese philosophy "combines icy, morally detached observation."

Cleary says humanity can get in the way of achieving objectives, as it did when the duke of Sung lost a battle because he refused to engage until the opponent was ready. But the issue with the Sung battle was not good manners, but rigid adherence to obsolete methods. Mao Tse-tung was very clear on this when, during his *On Protracted War* lecture, he proclaimed, "We are not the Duke of Sung, and we have no use for his asinine ethics" (Walzer 1977, 226).

Mao was not advocating neglect of humanity—only that there was no place for absurd, anachronistic conventions in the life-and-death circumstances of war. His military conduct was anything but brutal when it came to dealing with the enemy and his prisoners (Marrin 1989, 82).[96]

In 1997 Christopher Andrews, a Canadian medical student, visited the site of the 1994 Tutsi genocide in Rwanda. Horrified, he wondered why we could not be better at "primary prevention," so these sorts of incidents did not happen. We need a strategy, he said, such as was "summed up perfectly by Lao-tzu [sic] in The Art of War: 'To win without fighting is best.'"

To some extent, military ethics has little or no relevance for Ping-fa, and vice-versa. Considerations of wartime justice, rightness, fair play, and logic are extraneous in a methodology that defines open conflict as proof of failure. Ping-fa has only one thing to say about engagement leaders who lose control and cause conflict: "Let them be dismissed" (I.13).[97]

The practice of engagement management, with its intelligence gathering and covert operations, is solidly dependent upon a sound code of ethics. Sensitive intervention and strength management do involve "influencing" others, which is why the Qin academies took such pains to ensure that Ping-fa was guided by the Tao Te Ching.

---

96 It is known that Qin Shih Huangdi was a role model for Mao. But to what model was Mao subscribing? Salisbury (1992, 190) says Mao's "role model was the terrible emperor Qin" but observed before that on page 144 that when others spoke of the hated first emperor, Mao would note the first emperor's positive achievements in government and nation building.

97 In an observation interesting to the field of ethics, Business Line (July 23, 1997) made this remark: "There are indeed no fixed codes in any warfare. Marketing warfare too falls in this realm, where almost everyone is both a customer and a victim of industrial espionage."

Win without Conflict

Ping-fa says, "Supreme excellence means breaking resistance without fighting" (III.2).

"Thus the highest form of generalship is to balk the enemy's plans; the next best is to prevent the junction of the enemy's forces; the next in order is to attack the enemy's army in the field; and the worst policy of all is to besiege walled cities (III.3).

Star Trek VI: The Undiscovered Country has Spock saying, "What do you suggest, Lieutenant? Opening fire won't retrieve the Captain, and armed engagement was precisely what he wished to avoid." [98]

Ping-fa Chapter II defines failure: if there is conflict, management has failed. Its admonition against conflict is, "Therefore the skillful leader subdues the enemy's troops without any fighting,"

Make no mistake concerning *Ping-fa*'s message. There is no ambiguity, only relentless admonition. It says, "Don't fight." Find ways to accomplish your goals that do not involve damaging anyone (including yourself). Even minor interventions must be undertaken only when it is evident that difficulties will ensue without involvement.

Much of the commentary on *Ping-fa* has yet to uncover its passionate opposition to conflict. In that regard, it resonates more with the innocence of Qin's academy students than with its graduate persuaders. The untrained are unable to see *Ping-fa*'s inspired methodology for conflict prevention, and sensitive issue

---

98   The theme of the *Star Trek* book called *Rules of Engagement* is quite similar to *The Sun Tzu School.*

resolution. And without enlightenment, they believe conflict is a natural and unavoidable—some even think beneficial—fact of life. "All men can see the tactics whereby I conquer, but what none can see is the strategy out of which victory is evolved" (VI.27).

Two thousand years after Qin's stunning dismissal of fatalistic determinism, commentators still insist that war is a natural, unavoidable result of interpersonal and interstate relations. Some analysts of the human condition go so far as to say that conflict is fundamentally beneficial because, among other things, it brings about a lot of progressive innovation and invention.

When Qin embarked on its quite incredible journey to build the Chinese empire, it had to shatter as many beliefs as it built. Paupers and princes had to be convinced that life could be better, that war is not ineluctable, and that it is right and good that people should work to make such things happen. Qin understood that change could not come about as long as people believed that things could not be managed differently.

Conflict is as well institutionalized today as it was during the Warring States period. Most, if not all, nations have military and police forces whose role is alleged to be maintenance of peace and safety. But that peace and safety is achieved often through the use of force[99] and usually after events have "gone public." Much more money goes into preparing, equipping, waiting, and reacting than into watching, analyzing, intervening (sensitively), and resolving. The use of strategic avoidance appears to be both unknown and unpractised.

Is society ready, even now, for *Ping-fa's* ancient declarations about winning without conflict? As Leung and Tzosvold (1998, 336) say, "There is no realistic alternative to conflict management." Machiavelli told us that resistance is futile: "For a war is never avoided, but

---

99   Here, "force" is not the force of *Ping-fa* that comes from *qi*, but physical force.

is only deferred to one's own disadvantage" (*The Prince,* chapter 3).

General Tao Hanzhang (1987, 83) says that rulers might yearn for a society that is humane, just, and virtuous—the very model of civility. But this, he says, has been found to be impossible. "One has to solve certain problems by force." And worse yet, Fotion says, "There may be times when the actual use of nuclear weapons, poison gas, and other generally admitted immoral weapons is morally permitted" (1990, 107).

Immanuel Kant said war emanated from "the natural egoism in human nature."

> I have argued that when two or more minds meet, conflict exists. I can't imagine two people meeting and being together for any amount of time without finding themselves in conflict. (Hofffman 1993, 24)

Clausewitz saw war as "permanently rooted in the competitiveness of human groups" (Gallie 1979, 21, 63). Michael Walzer believes wars to be quite natural. They "break out" from time to time—meaning causes can't be determined—but "usually wars are more like arson [than an accidental fire]" (1977, 31). Emerich de Vattel (1714–1767) saw war as an

> inescapable fact and tool of political life, but one which governments should be persuaded to use with ever greater moderation, ever more rarely, although not in the credulous hope that it could ever be entirely dispensed with. (Gallie 1979, 19)

Donald Krause says that in the business world, "conflict is inevitable [and] we cannot learn too much about how to compete." He says if conflict isn't happening, we should be making it happen. "Competition should occur when we have something important to gain or when we are in danger"(1995, 109). Carolyn Dickson's *Creating Balance* says there is a "natural order" to conflict.[100] It is "inevitable" when people work and live together. "Sooner or later we're going to find ourselves in conflict with somebody else" (1997, 11). Manwaring and Fishel say the

> anarchical nature of the international security system [means that] there is nothing to check a world political actor except the power of other actors. The hard evidence over time and throughout the world indicates that violence is all too often considered an acceptable option in attempting to achieve personal, subnational, transnational, and national goals as well as international objectives. (1998, 198)

Carolyn Dickson speaks of "social scientists [who theorize] that no significant social change can take place without the struggle that occurs when interests/needs collide" (Dickson 1997, 11). Winston Churchill said in *The River War* that societies without conflict face inevitable decay.[101] Then, we have Robert Kaplan asserting that "as Machiavelli cruelly but accurately puts it, progress often comes from hurting others. While virtue is good, outstanding virtue can be dangerous (Kaplan 2002, 77).

Robert Kaplan, who likes both *Ping-fa* and Machiavelli, is only thirteen pages into his *Warrior Politics* when he asserts, "It takes a shallow grasp of history to believe that solutions exist to most international problems" (Kaplan 2002, 13, 18). Handel has no patience for those

---

100   As does Hoffman. "Collaborative competition" is his way of driving conflict solutions through our "natural competitive instincts" (1993, 5).
101   (Kaplan 2002, 26)

who think serious matters may be peacefully resolved. His chapter 9[102] opens with a quote from *On War*

> Kindhearted people might of course think there was some ingenious way to disarm or defeat an enemy without too much bloodshed, and might imagine this is the true goal of the art of war. Pleasant as it sounds, it is a fallacy that must be exposed. (1992, 32–75)

Wing's (1988, 12) sense is that *Ping-fa* is all about efficiency—"tactical positioning ... so that the moment of triumph is effortless and destructive conflict is averted." Wing's "averting of destructive conflict" means that in a good war you destroy only what you must, and no more. "Surgical bombing" with "precision guided munitions" in the Gulf War instructed forces to get in, destroy only what you must, and get out.

Here is Handel on the consequences of trying to "win without going to battle," which is how he reads *Ping-fa's* "victory

> [*Ping-fa*] recommends victory without bloodshed as an ideal, yet disregards the fact [which Clausewitz accepts as central to his theory] that reluctance to shed blood may cause one side to play into the opponent's hands: for an awareness of the other nation's reticence to 'come to blows' might cause such an opponent to bluff, by either pretending that he is willing to make a greater sacrifice, or applying even more force to bring about a decisive victory. (Handel 1992, 7–8)

Sounding like militarist Clausewitz, Newt Gingrich said that diplomacy should be backed by force and "generals [should be] masters of the art of war instead

---

102   Titled *The Ideal and the Real: Victory Without Bloodshed and the Search for the Decisive Battle*

of bureaucrats in procurement and paperwork" (1984, 238). US Under Secretary of State for Political Affairs Thomas R. Pickering had the same message:[103]

> Diplomacy backed by force has been a large factor in U.S. leadership in this century. Diplomacy is our first line of defense in almost all cases, yet [sometimes] force becomes indispensable to effective diplomacy. As Sun Tzu put it a thousand years ago [sic]; 'If you are prepared to use force you may subdue the enemy without fighting.'[sic]

Ping-fa's framework is much broader than that of Clausewitz, who wrote a treatise on the art of waging war itself, not on the working of diplomacy before, during, and after war. Clausewitz's analysis begins at the point where diplomacy has failed and war has become unavoidable. *Ping-fa*, on the other hand, views the political, diplomatic, and logistical preparations for war as well as fighting to be integral parts of the same activity. Consequently, it devotes as much attention to the environment in which an engagement takes place as to the engagement itself.

Before such messages will be heard, however, we will have to overcome our axemaker minds.[104] Consider the "visioning" exercise conducted by General R. R. Fogleman, USAF chief of staff at the Air University. He instructed his people to "look 30 years into the future to identify the concepts, capabilities and technologies the United States will require to remain the dominant air and space force in the 21st century" "Project 2025" used something called the "alternate futures procedure"

---

103   Under Secretary for Political Affairs address at Supreme Allied Commander Atlantic symposium in Norfolk, Virginia, October 30, 1998 (http://www.usia.gov/topical/pol/eap/pickcol8.htm)
104   See Burke and Ornstein, *The Axemaker's Gift*

to describe "various plausible future worlds." Here's what they came up with:

1. The United States's military might is constrained by many world players with other forms of power.
2. This is a future dominated by multinational corporate giants.
3. Information and biogenetic technology is dispersed, giving individuals and small groups untold power.
4. The United States loses its status as a superpower to an Asian colossus.
5. World experiences fundamental changes in the social structure, environment, and international security system, making it difficult for the United States to determine how best to exert its power and influence.[105]

Though the participants felt option three was pretty scary, the methodology may be the scariest part of this whole exercise. The only option is "dominance." Peace is deemed "unrealistic."

Paul A. Strassmann says that in the American expedition to Haiti, *Ping-fa* certainly applied.[106] "There were no American casualties. These days, the superior warrior wins without fighting because the superior warrior is part of an enterprise that applies knowledge."[107] The most heavily armed country on the planet taking a defenseless small island without loss of life is no demonstration of *Ping-fa's* methods.

---

105   http://tuvok.au.af.mil/au/2025/
106   Former director of defense information at the DoD. Now professor in the School of Information Warfare at the National Defense University in Washington.
107   *CIO Magazine* (August 1, 1997). See http://www.cio.com/archive/080197_learn_content.html.

In warspeak, "invasion" can mean "not fighting." F. W. Rustmann Jr. says, "The military advice that Sun Tzu espoused so long ago applies equally to today's business. Know yourself, know your enemy and know your battlefield. Armed with this knowledge, you cannot lose. *The worst that can happen* is that you decide not to engage."[108] In actual fact, the Taoist *Ping-fa* says the *very best* thing that can happen is that you decide not to engage.

After he completed his extensive work on Baron von Clausewitz, W. B. Gallie said he wished that someone would work on the issue of war's inevitability.

Clausewitz spoke of war, "not as independent phenomena, but the continuation of politics by different means" (Howard and Paret 1976, 7). Seabury and Codevilla (1989, 184) say—evidently without any sense of horror—that "war" and "peace" are delivery mechanisms, the choice of which rests with an official.

> Clausewitz's famous dictum, that "war is a continuation of politics by other means," which refers to war itself, is quite compatible with Sun Tzu's political vision. The practical meaning of all this was perhaps best summed up by a Soviet theoretician: 'A state official is offered a choice—to attain this or that political aim, whether to act along lines of peace or with the help of armed violence.... what is important is to select the means which is the most suitable under the given conditions.'

Clausewitz encountered a formidable adversary in Peter F. Drucker (1982, 17). His novel *The Last of all Possible Worlds,* offered a full-frontal challenge to

---

108 With a "worldwide business intelligence organization," he wrote *Sun Tzu and the Art of (Business) War*. See: http://www.ctcintl.com/CTC_Rustmann_Sun_Tzu.html.

Clausewitzian "diplomacy" and the alleged inevitability of war:

> "No, General," he had answered, "I am not a pacifist, but war is much too risky to be taken lightly. I do not subscribe to the famous Clausewitz epigram always spouted in your General staff schools: 'War is the continuation of diplomacy by other means.' I see it as the failure of diplomacy."

Tackling the inevitably (and rightness) of war means going up against a long and tall hoarding of assumptions and beliefs. It also means going against economies, business, and wealth.

War is big business. *How to Make War* asks, "Can the world afford peace?" At the end of the Cold War the annual US munitions budget alone was about $12 billion. The 1992 US Defense budget was $242.7 billion.[109] But high military spending is not limited to the United States, and it has been going on for a very long time. Major General J. F. C. Fuller, speaking of the Third Battle of Ypres (1917), said that the preliminary British bombardment was over four million shells that cost $110 million ($US).[110] Dunnigan says worldwide defense spending today accounts for 5 percent of global GNP. A major war would consume 30 percent to 50 percent of GNP for as long as the war lasts (Dunnigan 1993, 522).[111]

National economies are made and broken by the defense industry. The issue, however, is also about

---

109   Other countries for the same year, according to the International Institute for Strategic Studies (in 1985 US dollars): Russia ($39.6), China ($22.3), France ($21.8), UK ($20.7), Germany ($19.2), and Japan ($16.9)—all in billions
110   Noted by Colonel P. S. Meilinger, USAF, in a paper titled "Ten Propositions Regarding Airpower"
111   We don't have data, but the cost impact of the so-called "war on terror" has been quite incredible.

human currency. Toffler's *War and Anti-war* notes that "since 'peace' broke out in 1945, an estimated 7,200,000 soldiers [have been] slaughtered. That is the figure for deaths alone—not for the wounded, tortured or mutilated. When civilian deaths are added the total reaches an astronomical 33 to 40 million—again, not counting the wounded, raped, dislocated, diseased or impoverished" (Toffler 1993, 13).[112]

With all our technological advances and increased globalization, we are yet to make real strides in countering a very serious trend. Gabriel Kolko (1994, 470) says in *Century of War*, "The technology and firepower that warfare relies upon has intensified enormously, even exponentially. It has increasing engulfed far greater sectors of the civilian population, and become vastly more destructive of their lives, as well as more costly." For a time it looked like we were about to add outer space to the world's battlefields, establishing a whole new meaning for the term "cold war."

The 20th century, which had a series of wars (World Wars I and II, the Cold War) that saw Britain as the principal naval power at the beginning, finds the USN holding that position at the end. The planet has gotten a lot smaller during that period. In the future, "Victory at Sea" will lose its meaning as future fleets head for orbital space. (Dunnigan 1993, 608)

We have then, widely divergent views on war and its alleged inevitability, peace and whether we shall ever see it in our lifetimes. *Ping-fa* as practical philosophy defines a methodology that carries profound promises for society. With increasing global relations, consider how beneficial it would be if our thinkers, leaders, and each and every one of us at least considered the possibility that conflict

112 "Mutual Assured Destruction," otherwise known as "MAD," was, and maybe still is, US military policy.

is not a fundamental, irrevocable aspect of life. We accept as a truth that man is innately competitive and combative, and there will therefore always be wars. As Galtung (1995) says, we are both beastly and spiritual under the surface; we choose what to emphasize. "The human being is constructed as a vessel, seething with more or less tamed desires. The question is: 'how tight is the lid'?" In other words, how good are the controls?

Ping-fa says, "Only one thoroughly acquainted with the evils of war can thoroughly understand the profitable way of carrying it on."[113] Military analysts think this "acquainted one" is a "wise general." But *Ping-fa* means something else altogether. The message is: Control is essential. Unnecessary engagement is the "evil of war." It is the "height of inhumanity." Contemporary analysts recognize the seriousness of the control issue.

> Once soldiers are actually engaged, a steady pressure builds up against the war convention. And then, the rules are broken. Just wars turn into crusades. The statesmen and soldiers who fight them seek the only victory appropriate to their cause: total victory, unconditional surrender. They fight too brutally and too long. They sow justice and reap death. (Walzer 1977, 110, 227)

To offer concluding arguments, here are Michael Handel and J.G. Merrills. Commentator Handel (1992, 156) believes *Ping-fa* is the stuff of dreams:

> At times, differences more apparent than genuine have emerged when Sun Tzu's observations were taken too literally; that is, when his statement of an ideal was thought to be an unrealistic prescription for practicing the art of war. For example, although Sun Tzu states that the greatest victory one can achieve is that which (ideally)

---

113   Read in conjunction with II.8-10, II.15, and II.17

involves no fighting and minimal cost, this does not necessarily mean that Sun Tzu believed this feat could be accomplished frequently.

And here is J. G. Merrills, author of *International Dispute Settlement*:

It is clear that the destructiveness of modern warfare is such as to inflict suffering on an unprecedented scale. I have tried to show how the intelligence and resourcefulness that have produced contemporary weapons have also developed methods of dispute settlement that can make the use of force unnecessary. The present situation can and must be improved. The tools are already at hand. (Merrills 1998, 311)

Manage Your World

Gentle interventions overcome rigid resistances. Few leaders realize how much how little will do. (*The Tao of Leadership*, 85)

It has been understood since the first community was established that the prime objective of organizations has been to ensure their own welfare and continuance. *Ping-fa* made forty separate references to the grave need for managing organizations, and engagements when they were required. *Ping-fa* adds a major condition: you do not benefit your organization when you cause loss to another. With this injunction *Ping-fa* redefined long-standing notions of "right" and "just."

Interaction (or "engagement") is a normal and healthy part of organizational life. These engagements need to be managed economically, efficiently, and effectively. When we manage with regard for all concerned we don't waste our time and resources in conflict.

Ping-fa is about the management of organizations in a universe of risk and opportunity populated by others with real or impending conflicting interests. Its focus is on the grave importance of observation and learning, of knowing what must be done, in ensuring that the needs of the organization are realized in as effective a way as possible.

The methodology is primarily intended for important organizations that involve and affect many people. When these organizations fail, there is loss of position, of possessions, of life. Their importance justifies the effort and expense involved. Engagements are healthy and jointly beneficial encounters, interventions, and interactions. Engaged organizations have defined what they want, and they strategically advance to their defined objectives. *Ping-fa* teams do not defend. They advance. But that advance is not into conflict and "overpowering" opponents.

One *Ping-fa* strategy is to seek to have others join you solely on the attraction of your evident strength. Those who advocate withdrawal—or cannot even confront an issue—"dwell in the depths of the earth." *Ping-fa* says be forthright and in the forefront in engagement management and in the use of sensitive intervention.

Making progress and ensuring safety in a world guided by a complex web of intersecting forces demands care and control. When care and control are elusive or threatened, the aware organization needs to assess the situation, develop a strategy and charter a team should an engagement requirement be identified. Organization engagement teams rise above subjective and petty detail, and fully understand the management of strength in engagement.

Managing strength is not at all about destruction. Wing (1988, 13, 9:III) assumes—like most commentators—that *Ping-fa's* strategy follows "a direct path that escalates until victory is assured, from analysis and projection, through planning and positioning and on to confrontation." This is the path to loss of control. Handel (1992, 108), who barely finds *Ping-fa* credible, says the text conveys an "apparent belief that it is possible to exert at least a modicum of control over events on the battlefield."

The *Ping-fa* methodology was an absolutely brilliant breakthrough in the field of interorganization relations management. It challenged the inevitability of conflict and defined it as a failure indicator. The *Ping-fa* concepts and its integrated principles and practices were and are revolutionary.

Ping-fa provides the structure and process for organizations and engagements of all sorts. They may involve a few or many people, one or many issues. Deployed, we have the means by which one achieves personal and organizational objectives without cost to other parties. In other words, this is all about wins without losses. Strategic issue management and resolution require high-quality analysis and planning, deployment and resolution effectiveness, and efficiency. With sound management and planning, this instrument can help break the deadly and endless repetition of failure that characterizes relations between organizations that have similar or competing interests.

With *Ping-fa* we have the yin and yang—the hit side and the flip side of policies and practices. We are told the costs and consequences of failure. We are warned repeatedly against losing control. Relaxation and slippage are not permitted. There is no scaling the castle walls as a last resort when we have failed to achieve our objectives peacefully.[114] When control is lost, the engagement is lost. Ping-fa is about the prevention – or minimalization – of the failure that is conflict.

Edward de Bono (1985) brings special insight to the problem of "how." He says, "The existing structures for conflict resolution at best are inadequate, at worst they are positively dangerous and may actually exacerbate

114   See "The Physician Best Known in the Land" for the meaning of "options" in *Ping-fa*.

conflicts. In structure and in idiom, they are part of our crude, primitive and antiquated approaches to conflict." Clearly, we need new, and perhaps rediscovered, models. "Our ways of resolving conflict tend to rely on the argument mode, which is a continuation of the conflict. We need to move towards a 'designed outcome' mode which consists of exploratory mapping followed by creative design."

Corporate executives, policy leaders, and strategists from many disciplines are seeking solutions in a dynamically changing world. *The Financial Times* (6 June 1998) observed that CEOs were reading everything they could get their hands on—from Socrates to Machiavelli to *Ping-fa*:

> Cynics may think company managers are deeply insecure and are being exploited [but they are] searching for sure-fire success and moral guidance in a world of shifting values.

Executives who are looking for a new value regime might consider the wisdom of the *Tao Te Ching*. It says to be "alert to problems and opportunities, addressing them with prudence and calm. [Be] solid in principle and fluid in execution; open to ever-changing possibilities; generous and considerate" (Herman, 1994, 32).

Other authors and subjects can bring insight. Consider *Leadership Secrets of Attila the Hun*. It concerns an apparently much misunderstood military and social campaigner who had a good deal to say about how to do good things. Author Wess Roberts says Attila "symbolizes single-minded determination and concern for his followers." He describes Attila's leadership in words similar to what we find in *Ping-fa*. Roberts says building great organizations is not that difficult. They simply need to focus on effective recruitment, training, rewards, and direction within an environment that both cares for and challenges its people (Roberts 1993, xv).

143

Our worldviews tend to link diversity with complexity and complexity with difficulty. We are convinced that in a diverse world, simple solutions are a naive idea. But many people—recognizing our many social, workplace, and international problems—are ready to look at new approaches.

We can look to the old for some of these new solutions. Consider *Ping-fa's* brash suggestion that real results can be achieved effectively, and unobtrusively, sometimes without even the awareness of some of the players. *Ping-fa's* "engagement management" methodology is concerned with engagements that are more like a couple becoming engaged than the sort of engagements that military forces undertake.

But unlike couples "engaged," *Ping-fa* engagements are of very short duration; they last only as long as they must. Effectiveness is defined by goal achievement with low or no cost to others or ourselves. These principles and practices challenge us to determine whether we are truly managing the relationship between tectonic plates, or we are only creating friction and resistance that will someday cause a real shake-up.

Ping-fa's minimalism is the application—only when absolutely essential—of a small (economic) tweak in the social fabric. For contrast, consider Air Marshal David Evans's view of what "economic engagement" means. He says he is guided by *Ping-fa*:

> Another factor pertinent to the use of precision guided munitions is that it has never been economical or preferable in war to destroy the enemy's civil infrastructure, beyond the extent to which it is supporting his military operations. (1997, 84)

This is not economical management. This is managing the deployment of weapons of mass destruction. *Ping-fa's* "economy, efficiency and effectiveness" are all about preventing loss, not maximizing loss in order to "win" an engagement. These goals are realized through the use of *Ping-fa's* carefully detailed instructions concerning engagement roles, rules, and processes. Key among these processes is "sensitive intervention" involving "other parties." *Ping-fa* defines success and failure, the qualities and faults of key players, and definitions for what must be done and what must never be done.

Ping-fa offers a theoretical and practical framework for change. Appropriate change demands competent, ethical people working in the interests of their own organizations and others. Organizations and their officials must be part of the solution, not part of the problem.

> The general that hearkens to my counsel and acts upon it, will conquer: let such a one be retained in command! The general that hearkens not to my counsel nor acts upon it, will suffer defeat. Let such a one be dismissed! (I.15)

The School of Sun Tzu is not the place to find guidance on the management of conflict. We have set out, drawing from the words of *Ping-fa*, what an organization must do and how, if it wants to be the best that it can be. With time and talent, such an organization could be the Best of Breed. But as a *Ping-fa* Best of Breed, the prize ribbon will never appear in the head office lobby. Organizations that follow the rules of *Ping-fa* are like the "hidden champions" of Hermann Simon. They are successful but they are not well-known. They want to stay that way (Simon 1996).

Instructions

Be Prepared

The "Taoist Wizardry" - ancient field of alchemy - that is spoken of in *The Secret of the Golden Flower* is the first stage of engagement preparedness; that is, strength (*qi*) assessment. In *Ping-fa* Chapter IV we see: "In respect of military method, we have, firstly, Measurement; secondly, Estimation of quantity; thirdly, Calculation; fourthly, Balancing of chances; fifthly, Victory."[115] When *Ping-fa* says "prepare," it means build "organizational strength." And strength must grow to the point where another believes you are completely invulnerable and all-powerful. Strong organizations do not *proclaim* their strength, they *radiate* it.[116] When an organization is "prepared," it is full of strength and the leader is full of knowledge.[117] A strategy has been prepared and the team is ready to engage. Strong teams are unconquerable. When they are ready, they will prevail.

Giles makes the argument that preparedness is about *qi* when he records that "Chang Yu (1994, VII.21) quotes Wei Liao Tzu saying we must not break camp until we have gained the resisting power of the enemy." His understanding is not well shared. The commentary almost always interprets "measurement" as arithmetic comparisons of soldiers and armaments. They draw this from VIII.II and IV.I, which indicate only that attack from without is unlikely when *qi* is at its peak. This is one of several serious misunderstandings the military has about *Ping-fa*.

The Giles *Ping-fa* translation, introduced just before the First World War, quoted a letter that was written by Lord Roberts. In it, he said, "Many of Sun Wu's maxims are perfectly applicable to the present day, and no. 11 is one that the people of this country would do well to take

---

115   At the time of Lu Yen, "the alchemist signs became symbols of psychological processes" (Wilhelm 1954, 6).

116   The Lau and Ames *Weighing with the Lever Scales* (1996, 89) is the only proper assessment of the issue I have found.

117   Machiavelli said the greatest "armament" was knowledge—"coupled with the will and the ability to use that knowledge to your own advantage" (McAlpine 1998, 14).

to heart." *Ping-fa* XI speaks of the importance of *qi* in engagement. Lord Roberts thought it advocated buying guns.

Doubtless much time, energy, and wealth has been spent on military (and civilian) preparation in what has likely been a futile effort to forestall unfriendly acts. The argument goes: "if we are 'better prepared' than they are—then they 'wouldn't dare' challenge or attack us." In this line of argument, being "better prepared" means having more troops, more and bigger bombs, and the best technologies. Nicholas Fotion (1990, 108) says, "My position insists on a strong and healthy military establishment when danger is present, and even when it is on the horizon."

History and research have yet to prove "preventative armament" is a valid proposition. The "Cold War," for example, which allegedly maintained "peace," was a fiscal and environmental nightmare that kept the world on edge for decades. Such facts don't restrain the military. Captain Roger F. Cavazos, of the US Army at Fort Benning, Georgia, says all we learn from Sun Tzu and Sun Pin is that "the Chinese view warfare as the most important thing they do. Thus they will make every effort to be prepared for war. We must not only match but exceed their efforts."[118]

Ping-fa decried the costs incurred by both parties in military engagement, suggesting the chances of benefits equaling costs as remote. Arming for defense is inconsistent with *Ping-fa* on two fronts. First, buying and building armaments means that the organization is losing or has already lost. It may be a matter of simply wasted expenditure. Secondly, while strategic planning should include an assessment of vulnerabilities, organizations do not win when their focus is defense.[119] As Huang says (1993, 23), *Ping-fa* has no content on

---

118   http://www.airpower.maxwell.af.mil/airchronicles/
bookrev/cavazos1.html
119   IV.7 is critical to understanding this admonition.

defensive tactics because in Sun Wu's opinion, strategy requires a dynamically assertive spirit."

Chang Yu (1994, III.17-18, IV.7) says able commanders know when to attack and when to defend. Giles says this capability (attack and defense) defines "the epitome of the root-principle of war." He says that generals who are skilled in defense will hide themselves well, "ensuring the enemy may not know his whereabouts."

Handel (1992, 98) quite rightly wonders how one can win solely through defensive tactics, as defense "cannot in and of itself enable one to triumph over the enemy. Sooner or later, the defender who aspires to victory must move over to the attack." But he somehow hears *Ping-fa* say, "Defense is the stronger form of warfare."

Defense preparations not only contribute to polarization, but also escalation that can precipitate eventual conflict. And they—quite paradoxically—telegraph inadequacy. *Ping-fa* says that parading soldiers and armaments communicate more weakness than strength.

Use Intelligence

Overseeing by knowledge is appropriate for a great leader. Attentive overseeing is auspicious and impeccable." (*The Book of Changes*)

There is no substitute for knowing how things happen and for acting accordingly. Everything, like it or not, is bound by this principle. (*Tao of Leadership*)

Knowledge allows "unraveling and coordinating the patterns of continuity that emerge and persist in the natural, social, and cultural flux around us." (Lau and Ames 1998, 21)

"The effective CEO develops numerous sources of information, so you should be seeking out not only facts but informed opinion." (*The CEO Paradox*)

Use knowledge and keep your cool. That's Sun Tzu's message. (*The Winner Within*)

If we see exasperation in *Ping-fa*, it concerns leaders who don't keep themselves informed and continue mindlessly on with plans that have been overtaken by events. In such cases, they expend resources uselessly or they run the risk of loss of control. Loss of control signifies failure.

Intelligence is a fundamental requirement in organizational and engagement management. In *Ping-fa* nothing happens without knowledge, and one can't manage strength (water) without it. *Ping-fa* says, "Spies are a most important element in water, because on them depends an army's ability to move" (XIII.26).[120]

It is not inconsequential that this is the last line in *Ping-fa*. Intelligence is mission critical, and its strategic importance causes it to receive the one and only admonition for violence in *Ping-fa*. XIII.19 says, "If a secret piece of news is divulged by a spy before the time is ripe, he must be put to death together with the man to whom the secret was told."[121]

Intelligence helps ensure benevolent management. If one does not know the plans and interests of others, how could one possibly manage yourself and the environment effectively, in the best interests of all concerned? *Ping-*

---

120   The Pentagon calls intelligence "Dominant Battlefield Knowledge."

121   If this admonition is original and legitimate, it can only have been intended to underscore the critical nature of intelligence in engagement. But this is an anomaly in *Ping-fa*, being the only approval for causing physical harm in the entire work. The admonition, or its phrasing, may be a later addition.

fa says, "It is the height of inhumanity" to remain oblivious of others because it might cost a little to gather intelligence.

The persuaders' tactics manual, *The Master of Demon Valley* says

> When affairs are handled unskillfully, this is called ignorance of feelings and loss of the Way. When you have thoroughly clarified matters yourself, and have determined measures whereby it is possible to govern others, and yet you reveal no obvious form, so that no one can see into your privacy, this is called genius. (Cleary 1993, 13)

One of the key talents of the chief is an ability to manage an intelligence network: "… divine manipulation of the threads … is the sovereign's most precious faculty" (XIII.8).[122] Intelligence leads to clarity. When you have complete intelligence you know what is happening and what must be done. You know the consequences of action and nonaction.

Philosopher J. Krishnamurti cautioned people to do a "mental wobble." He said they should hesitate before deciding (Watts 1997, 82). *Sun Tzu: War and Management* gets it partially right in observing that "Sun Tzu generally favors caution and measured calculation more than reliance on the commander's intuition" (Wee et al. 1996, 134). Edelman and Crain say, "Instead of concentrating on the other person in a defensive or offensive manner, we stop, grown calm, look inward."

> Knowing others is wisdom
> Knowing the self is enlightenment
> Mastering others requires force.

---

122   Secret service authorities Faligot and Kauffer imagine *Ping-fa's* "divine web" involves a "network of agents who would lie dormant sometime for decades before being activated" (1987, 130).

Mastering the self requires strength.
(1993, xiii)

And when the potential for an unhelpful organization encounter becomes known, intelligence will suggest if and when an engagement is appropriate and how it should be conducted. In the midst of engagement, intelligence shows how the strategy should be modified.

Flowing from its source it becomes a gushing spring,
What was empty slowly becomes full;
First turbid and then surging forward,
What was murky slowly becomes clear.
(Lau and Ames 1998, 13)

Sometimes, however, there is simply too much complexity to enable effective analysis. Water rushing, gushing, and overflowing its banks is how *Ping-fa* describes a condition of being overwhelmed. In such circumstances, don't move when there is too much data, the situation is confused, or there are knowledge conflicts (IX.14). Wait till things settle down and you may then conduct a proper assessment of the situation.

When you are puzzled by what you see or hear, do not strive to figure things out. Stand back for a moment and become calm. When a person is calm, complex events appear simple. (Heider 1988, 27)

In general, the commentators seem unsure about this whole intelligence thing. Clausewitz, Handel, and Bevin Alexander (*How Great Generals Win*) aren't convinced that intelligence can be trusted or that it has military application. General George Marshall believed intelligence was always incomplete and too late to be useful (Kaplan 2002, 14).

As Handel puts it, agents and spies are

notoriously unreliable and may do more harm than good. Sun Tzu's confidence in espionage as an effective means of obtaining useful information is therefore rather exaggerated if not misplaced, and must be viewed as part of his quest for less costly, indirect methods of winning in war. (1992, 112)

Some commentators think intelligence, like deception, is beneath them. Griffith believed that using intelligence, subversion, and deception made for unethical war. *The Handbook of Espionage* calls *Ping-fa* "the father of espionage," assuming it advocates a "permanent espionage service spying on both neighbors and enemies to wage war economically and defend the state against others" (Deacon 1988, 5, 147).[123] Other commentators are convinced if you are doing it, so is the enemy, so there is no net value.

Clausewitz, who considered intelligence unimportant, gave it all of one and one-half pages in *On War*.

Many intelligence reports are contradictory, even more are false, and most are uncertain. What one can reasonably ask of an officer is that he should possess a standard of judgment, which he can gain only from knowledge of men and affairs and from common sense. He should be guided by the laws of probability. (Howard and Paret, 1976, 117, 227)

---

123 The intelligence community to date has been unable to sever Ping-fa's intelligence function from the conduct of war. Roger Faligot and Remi Kauffer deliver an "exhaustive study" of the secret service in China since "its inception in the 1920's." Qin Shih Huangdi, who championed what was probably the first secret service on the planet, is mentioned only as the "builder of the Great Wall."

Teck and Grinyer (1994, vii, 1, 289) ask what possible use can be made of *Ping-fa* instructions on using spies and interpreting "the significance of the flight of birds, taking the high ground, [and] dealing with emperors?" J. H. Huang considers chapter XIII (on spies) to be "additional discussion" (1993, 22).

Military and management literature to date suggests that only a minority of authors and practitioners don't follow this path of denial. Peter Perla and the Israeli Army suggest that "military power is composed of human beings, weapons and wisdom, of which wisdom is the dominant force" (Perla 1990, 156).

Handel thought Clausewitz's followers might have been more successful if they had used intelligence.

> Sun Tzu's insistence on obtaining the highest quality intelligence must be seen as an ideal that contributes to the educational value of his work. Even if reliable intelligence could be obtained only on rare occasions, and uncertainty never eradicated, Sun Tzu's positive attitude toward intelligence would still be important. In contrast, Clausewitz's negative, if not antagonistic, opinion regarding the utility of intelligence has probably been responsible for many of the costly failures of his more dogmatic followers. (Handel 1992, 111)

But now it appears that organizations are rediscovering the importance of information and intelligence. Some are looking to *Ping-fa* for insight into how that ought to be handled. In a televised news story on corporate intelligence, Katherine Hobson said,

> 2000 years after Sun Tzu, corporate America is applying the information-gathering and analytical skills first developed on ancient battlefields to size up business rivals' strategies, products and services.

Ms. Hobson says a 1997 survey by The Futures Group stated that 82 percent of major companies "now have an organized intelligence unit."[124] Thomas Horton (1992, 30) says, "Good planning starts with an information base composed of what Harold Geneen, former chief executive of ITT, called unshakeable facts."

But those who would venture into using intelligence need to study both its methods, and the ethics underlying it as did the Qin academies. Lau and Ames, who are clear on what intelligence is, can't see its use beyond serving self-interest:

> the ability to read a situation, to transform information into meaning, and then to anticipate and manipulate the unpredictable factors as a way of reconfiguring the circumstances to one's own advantage. (1996, 75, 74)

Ping-fa was adamant that the "Moral Law" came before all. In other words, the management of organizations and their engagements had to be ethically based. And too, the Qin academies challenged hallowed truths about placing competition before collaboration, while stressing the overwhelming benefits of ensuring harmony is maintained in the organizational environment.

The terracotta soldiers of China are now so familiar to the world that they are an iconic image; however those who would develop and build their intelligence capabilities ought to consider just what that icon represents.

Zhang Wenli, in his study called *The Qin Terracotta Army,* noted that the soldiers in front were in robes. The ones behind were in armor. He could not fathom a reason for this alignment. But that's just what one would expect, if the Qin "army" had been constituted as *Ping-fa* instructed—with persuaders way out front, gathering intelligence and manipulating the threads. They were

---

124   ABC News report (1998-09-24) found at ABCNEWS. com.

Qin's "picked troops in the front rank." The author of one of the most popular *Art of War* versions imagines that "picked troops" were "highly mobile and well-trained shock and *elite* troops." [125]

Assign, Delegate, and Empower

There are ... commands of the sovereign which must not be obeyed (VIII.3).

Ping-fa has perhaps more content on roles than any other issue. *Ping-fa* instructs us on the role of chiefs (princes), leaders (generals), and teams (armies), among others. Role ambiguity is not tolerated. Along with role definition, we are instructed in how relationships need to be managed, including delegation of authority and empowerment. While flexibility and initiative are operational and engagement requirements, there is to be no negotiation or compromise in separation of functions.

Organizational chiefs decide when an intervention is required, based on their ongoing situational analysis. When doing nothing is not the appropriate action, the chief will craft a strategy and deliver it to an engagement leader. With that done, the chief has no further role to play in carrying it out. The team leader has responsibility for carrying out the strategy and amending it according to conditions, and accountability for project delivery. He cannot perform effectively if he must suffer political interference.

These strident and powerful instructions are neither seen, nor understood in the commentary. When Giles studied *Ping-fa* he did not see "empowerment," but only leader "expectations." Calthrop, who wrote about *Ping-fa* and (the militarist) Watzu, did not carry out an effective comparison between the two. Had he done so, he would have found significant differences in delegation and field authority. For example, where *Ping-fa* instructs

---

125   See X.19.

leaders to learn through the engagement and amend strategies accordingly, Watzu is a "command and control" authoritarian, who believes in strict punishment for "disobedience."

Ames (1993, 87) says that the "fundamental question" in *Ping-fa* was to figure out how an "enlightened ruler achieved victory at minimum cost." The answer, he says, was to "give free rein to the consummate military commander." Calthrop was plainly confused about the leader's authority in engagement. His chapter I says if a general "differ from my plans, he will be defeated and dismissed from my service." But he has the immediate next line reading, "The plan must be modified according to circumstances."

Griffith (1963, 112) feels "commands of the sovereign which must not be obeyed" is just a summary statement, "a catchall which covers the variable circumstances previously enumerated." R. L. Wing agrees (1988, 29.VIII).

Wee et al. give the matter no special attention, but later they do recognize the somewhat, but remotely related, issue of "battlefield initiative."[126] Though they document *Ping-fa's* critical message about "non interference" between chief and leader, and they evidently recognize that field officers are likely capable of assessing situations better than the far-removed chief, they ask if the passage could be "advocating disloyalty."

Adding even more mystery, they tell us, "Loyalty to the Chinese historically refers to loyalty to the state and not necessarily to the emperor" (1996, 111, 147, 280). Perhaps they were thinking along the same lines as Huang who said, "If a lord's order is to be rejected, it should not be an act of defiance with regard to the planned strategic goals." It should, he says, be based on "the facts" (1993, 202).

---

126 Which they understand to be something a leader might do only when the end is apparent.

Handel (1992, 7-8) feels both Clausewitz and Sun Tzu dropped the ball on the issue of field authority by not providing any guidelines.

> Both Sun Tzu and Clausewitz insist that for war to be conducted on a rational basis, politics must be in command; at the same time, however, they also emphasize that the field commander must be afforded sufficient freedom of action to exploit local opportunities to the greatest advantage. Nevertheless, neither strategist develops any criteria to indicate in what circumstances the field commander is justified in disregarding orders. Admittedly, it would be impossible to establish unequivocal criteria applicable to every type of situation, but this does not obviate the necessity of attempting to do so.

Handel says principles that could aid field decision-making would be valuable, but they are unachievable.

> The art of command in war is to make creative choices in the midst of ambiguity. Those seeking to extract simple, unalterable and universally applicable scientific principles from the complexity of war are bound to be disappointed when they encounter its inevitable paradoxes, contradictions and tensions.

The issue of "conception of command" is variable and troublesome for military authorities. During World War I, Douglas Haig, who was commander in chief of British forces in France, allowed negligible field authority. On the opposite side, the Germans who practiced *Weisungsfuhrung* (or "leadership by directive") balanced this hierarchical control model with *Vollmacht* (or "delegated authority") to general staff.

British military remoteness came under attack by Major General J. F. C. Fuller in 1933. He and such military notables as General the Earl of Cavan, General George C. Marshall, and the secretary of the US Navy John F. Lehman[127] became the modern era's advocates of leadership and adaptation in engagement. But, say Cohen and Gooch, "the Rickover Way, which he tackled head-on, survived his onslaught" (1990, 243).

The issue is also troubling for military think tanks. Clausewitz editor Michael Howard (1976) says,

> The Korean conflict caused a resurgence in Clausewitz studies due to the issue of field command ("the relationship between the civil and military powers"), and how to handle limited engagements ("not aimed at the total overthrow of the enemy").

There is significant debate concerning separation of authority. Some analysts have thought it either unworkable or impractical. And politics, technology, and/or incidents of "field excess" may be complicating the issue. General Tao Hanzhang (1987, 92) says that modern technology means "supreme command has every small change at its fingertips. A commander is in no way allowed to disobey orders from the supreme command for local interest."

The US Joint Chiefs of Staff Command and Control (C2) speaks of command over subordinates; use of resources; planning, organizing, coordinating, and controlling; and personnel responsibilities. But there is nothing about assessing conditions in the field and making changes as one gathers new information. And certainly there is nothing here about defying the orders of the commander in chief when they are deemed inappropriate. These regulations do not encourage the

---

127   Accorded the victory of having ousted centralist hard liner Admiral Hyman Rickover

situational decision-making needed when events are moving at light speed.[128]

At the Institute for National Strategic Studies, Colonel Adolf Carlson says, "Surprisingly little has been written about how a commander modifies a plan when circumstances do not permit the formal command and staff actions associated with deliberate planning."[129]

In Carlson's view, a new methodology for field decision-making is needed, but evidently it will not emerge from studying *Ping-fa*. He says, "The use of nonspecific or metaphoric language carries with it the greater risk that the image [sent] will not match with the image [received]." *Ping-fa's* metaphoric but hardly ambiguous instructions to field officers in engagement are based on principles, not strict practices. In fast-moving situations calling for rapid, appropriate judgment, it can't work any other way.

The Institute needs to listen to General Peter Schoomaker.[130] He says that whatever the domain (military or civilian), creative solutions are needed.[131]

We must have the intellectual agility to conceptualize creative, useful solutions to ambiguous problems and provide a coherent set of choices to the supported CinC or joint force commander—more often like Sun Tzu, less like Clausewitz This means training and educating people how to think, not just what to think.[132]

---

128   http://www.dodccrp.org/capoKEYCNCPT.HTM
129   "Information Management and the Challenge of Battle Command"
130   Commander, US Special Operations Command
131   From an article that appeared in *Fast Company*, Issue 27, p. 278
132   *Defense Issues*: Volume 13, Number 10. "Special Operations Forces: The Way Ahead." See: http://www. defenselink.mil/speeches/1998/s19980201-schoomaker. html.

Look to General C. C. Krulak's *Beyond C2: A Concept for Comprehensive Command and Coordination of the Marine Air-Ground Task Force*[133] for new perspectives for "coordination" in engagement. The commandant of the Marine Corps says, "We must envision the day when mechanistic control will be replaced by broad coordination." According to the Marine Corps these changes were being driven by "a dynamic, volatile world characterized by inherent complexity and unprecedented levels of global interaction and connectivity. *Beyond C2* is a transformational departure from traditional notions of command and control."

Beyond C2 quoted *Ping-fa* four times.

Practice *Wu-wei*[134]

The *Tao Te Ching* says everyone knows the elements of issue resolution, but no one seems capable of putting them together.

Use weakness to overcome strength
Use softness to overcome hardness
None in the world do not know this
But none can practice it.
(*Tao Te Ching* 43)

In the practice of *wu-wei*, when judicious noninvolvement doesn't work, an organization may intervene in accordance with a defined strategy. Here, the intervention must be sensitive and, if possible, invisible. Effecting change is a time-consuming and costly business even when the other party is unaware of your existence. But if the other party does become aware, management is a great deal more difficult. As the costs go up, so too do the risks. New, unexpected dangers emerge. The pace of activity quickens. Ensuring control

---

133   http://www.concepts.quantico.usmc.mil/bc2.htm
134   It is more properly *wei wu-wei*.

and focus demands more and more time. Only the very skilled are able to perform with excellence under such circumstances. For these reasons, *Ping-fa* says that if engagement is warranted, do it quickly and quietly.

The *Tao Te Ching* (57) says, "Become master of the universe without striving." A master practices *wu-wei*, or sensitive intervention, in the management of strength in engagement. This is the underlying thesis of *Ping-fa*, yet we read that "great captains ... have sought to follow the *Ping-fa* axiom that 'supreme excellence consists of breaking the enemy's resistance without fighting.' This, of course, is an ideal, seldom attained in practice" (Alexander 1993, 305).

> The wise man, then, when he must govern, knows how to do nothing. Letting things alone, he rests in his original nature. Let him sit like a corpse, with the dragon power alive all around him. In complete silence, his voice will be like thunder. His movements will be invisible, like those of a spirit, but the powers of heaven will go with them. Unconcerned, doing nothing, he will see all things grow ripe around him. Where will he find time to govern? (Merton 1965, 71)

Qin's Neo-Taoism provided the foundation for the "engagement" needed to address and resolve the threat to pre-China's social fabric due to ceaseless war. This was not to be military engagement, but in accordance with the *Tao Te Ching*, "instinctive activity" within a state of "naturalness." *Ping-fa* defined the method by which one could gain the world without taking it. Order was achieved by the means of "noncontrivance," where one acts unobtrusively and without self-awareness. In this manner, the Way prevailed.

Through noncontrivance, organizations manage their affairs and their environments through judicious avoidance or sensitive intervention.

Noncontrivance means not musing or mulling. Though you may act in the midst of love, desire, anger, accumulation, gain, and loss be always uncontrived.[135] (Cleary 2000, 110)

Noncontrivance does not mean stagnant inaction. It means nothing comes from the ego. [It] means that personal will cannot enter the public Way. Likings and desires cannot warp the true arts of leadership, and you forward the spontaneous momentum of nature so that no twisted intentions can get in.[136] (Cleary 1992, 44, 83)

Manage Strength

So the sage controls people by:
Emptying their hearts,
Filling their bellies,
Weakening their ambitions,
And strengthening their bodies.
(*Tao Te Ching* 3)

Strength management is *the* critical function and factor in engagement management. With thirty-eight references in *Ping-fa*, it is the second most frequently referenced issue.

The "fire" and "water" referenced throughout *Ping-fa* are symbolic representations of "*qi*" or "strength."

---

135   Cleary sees applied Taoism coming only much later with, or after, the Buddhist entry into China in the third century CE (1991b).

136   Cleary quotes a mystic named Chuang Tzu, alleged to have lived from 399 to 295 BCE. He says he wrote "allegorical fiction" (1991b, 125). But these writings are neither mystical nor allegorical, and Chuang Tzu was no more real than Sun Tzu. "Chuang Tzu" was a device for propagating Qin's messages concerning peace, empire, engagement management and *wu-wei*.

Qi is not "power" or "force" in the sense of assertion or domination. It is the invisible strength that resides within the individual. Though it cannot be seen, its "levels" and its effects are evident to the adept.

According to Kenneth Cohen, *qi* is the Chinese word for "life energy." It is "the animating power that flows through all living things." Mr. Cohen studied the history of Chinese pictographs and found one of the earliest characters for *qi* consists of the word for "sun" and "fire," suggesting that *qi*, like sunlight, is a source of warmth and is essential for life. But it is not only "inner strength" of the individual either. While *qi* infuses the body, it also affects those with whom the body comes in contact.

> The concept of *qi* is both integral and fundamental to many aspects of Chinese thought. One popular view holds that the character originally represented the vapors rising from cooking rice and is thus symbolic of nourishment in every sense. Unfortunately, this critical concept lacks any comprehensive or systematic Western language study. (Sawyer 1993, 428 note 35)

Engagements are won by whoever best manages strength. This is not physical strength, but strength of conviction, purpose and energy. It is strength that can be nurtured and grown, but it is also the strength that can be reduced. When *Ping-fa* says strong organizations "disable" others by their superior force, it portrays a condition where you *appear* so strong that another would be foolish to get in your way. The application of force in engagement is counterproductive. It can reduce your strength and build that of others (*Tao Te Ching* 30).

Brilliant leaders ensure that their team strength is as "a pound's weight placed in the scale against a single grain" or as "a grindstone dashed against an egg" (Giles 1994, IV.19, V.4). This is the same metaphor we see in *Thunder in the Sky*. It says, "Take the empty by solidity,

163

take the lacking by having, like using pounds to weigh against ounces; then movements will surely be followed, initiatives will surely find cooperation."

Ping-fa I.19–25 is about strength management in engagement. We are told that when you are fully knowledgeable, you are able to use water and fire to manage strength. Water builds strength, and fire reduces it. *Ping-fa* VI.18, VI.21–22 and IX.40 are instructions, not on numbers as we see in the commentary again and again, but on the management of *qi*. "If sovereign and subject are in accord, put division between them" (I.23). The instruction is repeated in III.3: "Prevent the junction of the enemy's forces." Chapter XII can be read (sensibly) no other way than as a methodology for strength reduction. Reading "incendiary tactics" as "the use of a blazing fire" is quite incorrect in the context of Taoism. The *Tao Te Ching* says,

> Harsh laws and severe punishments are not practices that will perpetuate hegemony or kingship, and the repeated use of a horsewhip is not the way to get to a distant destination. (Lau and Ames 1998, 79, 93)

Ping-fa's qi and *wu-wei* management techniques include the use of emotion. "Now in order to kill the enemy, our men must be roused to anger" (II.16) Then, he says, "If your opponent is of choleric temper, seek to irritate him. Pretend to be weak, that he may grow arrogant" (I.22). The commentary—perhaps because it does not see *Ping-fa's* instructions on control—sees here only heat in support of aggression: "soldiers" must be "angry enough to attack." But the meaning is just as it says: feign anger in your team, while driving real anger in others to gain advantage.

Only by understanding the meaning of *qi* and its management do two of *Ping-fa's* more famous quotes make any sense:

He wins his battles by making no mistakes. Making no mistakes is what establishes the certainty of victory, for it means conquering an enemy that is already defeated. (IV.3)

And:

Thus it is that in war the victorious strategist only seeks battle after the victory has been won, whereas he who is destined to defeat first fights and afterwards looks for victory. (IV.15)

It is only from the perspective of *qi* that we can understand "if you are careful of your men, and camp on hard ground, the army will be free from disease of every kind, and this will spell victory" (IX.12). "Being careful" means caring for hygiene, diet, exercise, thought, and emotions. Ming-Dao Deng says, "Control your environment and make sure that you do what is necessary to keep it free of disease." *Qi* means that your immune system is strong, and you will have longevity and stamina. "The Scholar Warrior remedies deficiencies of *qi* and stores energy through the art of *qigong*, which can gradually increase *qi* and bring it under conscious control" (Ming-Dao Deng 1990, 23).

J. H. Huang sees *qi* in *Ping-fa* IX 27-28: "When there is much running about and the soldiers fall into rank, it means that the critical moment has come." Strength is at its peak. Huang gives the Chinese text as *benzou zhenbing, ch'i ye*. "Ch'i means an engagement. When all troops are engaged, this indicates a large action is being conducted." We might see this as a "gathering of *qi*" as focus emerges and activity is about to begin. Cao Kuai says, concerning battle, that "with the first drum roll, *qi* is raised." Huang says the term "morale" is represented in Chinese today as *"shiqi"* (Huang 1993, 195, 213).

Thunder in the Sky speaks of "internal *qi*" and *qi* between "opposing" parties in engagement. This is strength management at work.

So if there is outward friendliness but inward estrangement, reconcile the inner relationship. If there is inward friendliness but outward estrangement, reconcile the outward relationship. Thus you change others based on their doubts, affirm them based on their views, make pacts with them based on what they say, reinforce them based on what they do, assess them based on what they dislike, fend them off by what distresses them. Frighten them by pressure, stir them by excitement, prove them by surrounding, confuse them by disturbance—these are called tactical strategies (Cleary 1993, 46).

Lau and Ames tell us, "Water in many ways is a synecdoche for *qi*, the sea of vital energy that is both constitutive of the world and an expression of its activities. Water is transformative." They say that water is also

an analogy for *dao* and *yin-yang*: at once the weakest and the strongest of things, the most pliant and the hardest, the most nourishing and the most destructive, the most unselfish and the most self-inclined, the most unsubstantial and the most concrete. It is described as the most exalted of all things. (1998, 17–18)

Water is the Taoist symbol for and illustration of the Way. Water is growth. It benefits. Water is "a pattern and example to the ten thousand things." Fire brings things downward. Water brings things upward.[137]

---

137   See: http://alt.venus.co.uk/weed/laotzu/laotzu08. html.

In the *Tao Te Ching,* the word *te* literally means virtue/power. It means to come into accord with the universe (*The Tao*) and thus to have a selfless sense of power that comes not from opposing things but by flowing with them. (Grigg 1988)

The *Tao Te Ching* (78) says, "Under heaven nothing is more soft and yielding than water. Yet for attacking the solid and strong, nothing is better" (Feng and English 1997). "Water freely and fearlessly goes deep beneath the surface of things; water is fluid and responsive; water follows the law freely" (Heider 1988, 15). Cohen (1997, 30) suggests that fire and water may come together; therefore *qi* can be defined as the "energy produced when complementary, polar opposites are harmonized."

Water also conveys movement, formlessness, depth, and flexibility. In IX.4, 5, and 14, it suggests uncertainty. In IX.3 and XI.30 it suggests achieving clarity. Fire and water do not burn and drown; they lower and raise. The *I Ching* says,

> Water over fire: the image of the condition
> In After Completion
> Thus the superior man
> Takes thought of misfortune
> And arms himself against it in advance.

> Heaven together with fire:
> The image of Fellowship with Men.
> Thus the superior man organizes the clans
> And makes distinctions between things.

Water nourishes and overcomes. Alan Watts notes,

> The Taoist mentality makes, or forces, nothing but "grows" everything. When human reason is seen to be an expression of the same spontaneous balance of *yin* and *yang* as the natural universe,

man's action upon his environment is not felt as a conflict, an action from outside. (Watts 1957, 176)

Morihei Ueshiba says that "The Art of Peace" is based on four great virtues: bravery, wisdom, love, and friendship, symbolized by fire, heaven, earth, and water.[138]

'Grow' strength through water and reduce strength through fire. Use fire and water as the principle means by which reduction is managed and destruction prevented. The highest excellence is like [that of] water. Among things that can be delineated, none occupies a position more exalted than water. (Lau and Ames 1998, 105)

Tsou Yen speaks of "the five elements or energies" (*wu hsing*). They are (1) *wood*, which as fuel gives rise to (2) *fire*, which creates ash and gives rise to (3) *earth*, which in its mines contains (4) *metal*, which (as on the surface of a metal mirror) attracts dew and so gives rise to (5) *water*, and this in turn nourishes (1) *wood*. This is called the *hsiang sheng*, or "mutually arising" order of the forces.

The forces were also arranged in the order of "mutual conquest" (*hsiang sheng*). (1) *Wood*, in the form of a plow, overcomes (2) *earth*, which, by damming and constraint, conquers (3) *water*, which, by quenching, overcomes (4) *fire*, which by melting, liquefies (5) *metal*, which, in turn, cuts (1) *wood* (Watts 1957, 33). Recognize here that water nurtures; fire reduces. Water and fire are full of meaning. Cleary says they can be represented as wood and metal, named woman and man, paired as wife and husband (1989b, 106).

---

138   See: http://www.gojuryukaratedo.com/artofpeace.asp.

Strength management is inextricably related to *wu-wei*. Opponents in martial arts are not overcome by your physical strength, but by the strength of your position. When they approach you, they are already defeated. Chuck Norris says,

> The basic philosophy of all martial arts is not winning. In point of fact, most of the arts are designed to skillfully control conflict and win-lose situations. (Norris 1996, 35)

Martin van Creveld, speaking of "effective fighting organizations," says that mobs are dispersed by teams with strength, like "chaff before the wind" (1991, 125). Watts says that in judo and aikido, the ultimate is

> winning without doing anything. The [aikido] art reaches such heights of skill that I have seen an attacker thrown to the floor without even being touched. In *judo*, for example, one uses muscle— but only at the right moment, when the opponent is off balance or overextended. (Watts 1975, 76)

Dr. Chester W. Richards developed a war "paradigm" that blends the mental and the physical. He thanks the late US Air Force colonel, John Boyd, "of the Sun Tzu school, and by far the most influential strategist of our generation," for his help in establishing a "modern paradigm for winning in armed conflict by destroying morale with quick and painless tactics." The paradigm he calls "rapid OODA speed"[139] was applied with success, he says, in the Gulf War. Richards summarizes *Ping-fa* as "an uncompromised indictment of generals whose only ideas of strategy are frontal assaults and battles of attrition."[140]

---

139 *Riding The Tiger: What You Really Do With Ooda Loops*
140 See: http://www.belisarius.com/ for this and similar material.

Sawyer is likely quite correct in his ideas about *Ping-fa's* relative weighing of the factors due to variable importance. He says, "Estimations means the sense of objectively estimating the relative strength and weakness of oneself and the enemy for a series of factors." But he is incorrect in suggesting that the analysis took place in the "ancestral temple." Estimation of strength was a scientific procedure (1993, 156–159).

Mihaly Csikszentmihalyi approaches understanding with his use of "flow."[141] Calthrop's chapter XII offers tantalizingly, "the fire must be unquenchable, the flood must be overwhelming" (1908, 68). Cleary grasped the correct meaning of chapter VI. "Be filled with energy while at the same time draining opponents" (1988, 21). But he incorrectly sees "draining" as simply preparatory activity, rather than a fundamental engagement process. Cleary adheres to the common commentator view that you attack when the other is vulnerable, failing to grasp that in a successful engagement all *qi* is managed. *Ping-fa* says that when strength has been appropriately managed, the battle is already won. A team with superior *qi* will win over a team with inferior *qi*. There can be no other way to read this line intelligently:

> Thus it is that in war the victorious strategist only seeks battle after the victory has been won, whereas he who is destined to defeat first fights and afterwards looks for victory. (IV.15)

Giles recognizes there is something in *Ping-fa* about energy. He says, "The way of water is near that of the Way of Tao." But it is all "mysterious East" to him: "Though Chia Lin illustrates some useful techniques for using water, some would only occur to the Oriental mind" (1994, VIII.10). His note 1.VI.ss.21 proves his "strength" equates with "force" and "numbers." Cleary could find no Taoism in "fire." To him, fire is fire. And because

---

141 In *The Psychology of Optimal Experience*

fire is such a "vicious form of martial art," he says Sun Tzu makes his "most impassioned plea for humanity" on this subject (Cleary 1988a, 26, 29). Huang says the Linyi V.12 reads "the strength of water." But he says this is not "sensible" and uses the translation of other commentators. Oddly, he later refers to "a correct method for handling water" (1993, 175).

In related domains of study we are finding interesting, odd and incorrect demonstrations of emerging interest in personal and organizational strength. Art McNeil says, "The hurricane is like a nuclear breeder reactor. It can go on forever, unleashing enormous amounts of energy, as long as it keeps in touch with its source—the water and warmth" (1987, 50). Robert Ringer's *Winning Through Intimidation* speaks of "abstract power," where he equates strength with "image." Of his methodology (of intimidation), he says it is not "brutal," just a matter of dealing with the world as it is (1974, 129). A less troubling examination of *qi* can be found in *The Winner Within*, a book primarily about sports and teamwork.

Says van Creveld, "In war there comes a point where what is needed is not strategy but a steamroller" (1991, 119). Robert Greene, who says he bases his "theories" on *Ping-fa*, sees nothing more to "strength" than raw power. Don't give your enemies an option, he says—"annihilate them, and their territory is yours to carve. You cannot afford to go halfway. Negotiation is the insidious viper that will eat away at your victory" (Greene 1998, xxii, 112).

Wee et al believe *Ping-fa* speaks both of sheer numbers and the skill with which troops are deployed.

> When Master Sun says defend when you cannot win (your forces are inadequate) and attack when you can (your forces are abundant), he refers to 'the need to have numerical superiority in force before launching an attack.' The strength of an army does not depend on large forces. Do

not advance basing on sheer numbers. Rather, one must concentrate the forces and anticipate correctly the enemy's movements in order to capture him. (Wee et al. 1996, 287–289)

In his chapter on "Numerical Superiority and Victory," Handel says,

Once Sun Tzu turns his attention to strategy in practice, his views on the art of war do not differ as much as previously thought from those of Clausewitz. Like Clausewitz, Sun Tzu is searching for the quickest and most decisive victory. This can be achieved most directly by absolute numerical superiority in general or relative superiority at the decisive point of contact. (1992, 91)

Some military analysts recognize the concept of strength management but aren't sure how it would work. *War: Ends and Means* says,:

The conduct of war ... depends substantially on knowledge of the enemy. The purpose of war is to convince the enemy to abandon the aims for which he fights and to place himself at the winner's mercy. But what would bring about such a development in the enemy's mind is not self-evident. Fighting without good intelligence consists, at best, of mindless campaigns of destruction conducted in the hope that indiscriminate damage to the other side's arms and body will somehow affect vital but unknown pressure points. (Seabury and Codevilla 1989, 186)

There have been a good number of tries at figuring out how you could deliver *Ping-fa* winning without fighting. Unhelpfully, *Transformation of War* gives us a solely physical model based on attrition:

From Moltke through Schlieffen to Liddell Hart, the shining goal of strategy has been to outflank the enemy, encircle him, cut him off, deprive him of supplies, and bring about his surrender without actually having to fight. (van Creveld 1991, 125)

Others, such as John Keegan, think the answer is to be found in the Chinese military mind, with its (alleged) predisposition to avoid risk, be patient, and worry the enemy into submission. This comes across as strategic avoidance.

Sun Tzu drew on an existing corpus of ideas and practices in formalizing his theory; it would not have otherwise recommended itself to the Chinese mind. In its emphasis on avoiding battle except with the assurance of victory, of disfavoring risk, of seeking to overawe an enemy by psychological means, and of using time rather than force to wear an invader down (all profoundly anti-Clausewitzian concepts) his *Art of War* encouraged the integration of Chinese military with political theory in an intellectual whole. (Keegan 1993, 202)

To see the effects of *qi*, look to where strength can be found and where it is being managed. Look to the Swiss head of state, who is little known on the world stage. He governs as a sage and enlightened ruler. He is "the physician" who "sees the spirit of sickness and removes it before it takes shape, so his name does not get out of the house."[142]

Switzerland is a very powerful organization. It may even be indestructible. But in a military engagement against a modern army, Switzerland would not survive

---

142   See the persuasion: "The Physician Best Known in the Land"

173

a day. If the international banking and business community decided that it didn't need Switzerland, it would revert to a cheese- and chocolate-based economy overnight. Switzerland's position is a lesson in strength management and survival.

The country endures and is internationally successful and important because of its strategic brilliance. It fills a key niche in international relations. Countries depend on Switzerland. And to prove it is not at all a threat, it maintains only a voluntary citizen army. *Ping-fa* says, "Pretend to be weak, that he may grow arrogant." The *Tao Te Ching* says, "A great nation needs more people; a small country needs to serve" (Feng and English 1997). Stanley Herman notes that "power is most secure when not displayed" (1994, 60).

Switzerland has extraordinary skill at anticipating world needs in financial and commercial transaction management. It is powerful without the expression of power.[143] It is a force to be reckoned with, without any indication of force. This is "strength," as *Ping-fa* understood it. It is the strength of *qi* and the "power" of Stephen Covey (1991, 23).

Strength can maintain the peace and prevent war as well as win engagements. Will Ferguson speaks of peacekeeping in Cyprus in a manner reminiscent of a *Ping-fa*-managed engagement.[144] He calls Cyprus a

> touchstone of the Canadian Way, just as surely as Vietnam remains an indictment of the American Way. The odds are you haven't heard much about Cyprus lately. There was no napalm, no gory

---

143   IV.6, VI.22, VI.27, VI.30, IX.18, XI.55, and XIII.9 are evident in Swiss government.
144   But the vocabulary and models of peacekeeping bear watching. "Peace enforcement" would seem to go far beyond sensitive intervention. See Fishel (1998).

escalation, no Hollywood mythmaking. Cyprus is a standoff, not a showdown.[145]

This is the achievement of peaceful objectives through the exercise of control and sensitive intervention. We hear similar themes from the US World Special Operations Forces, where, under the direction of General Schoomaker, "warrior diplomats" and "quiet professionals" are applying *Ping-fa* sensitively in the international affairs domain.[146]

Canada's Professor Robert Bedeski tabled an interesting methodology at the 4th International Symposium on *Sun Tzu's Art of War* in Beijing in 1998. It was titled "Human Security and Sun Tzu's Thought: An Alternative Approach to Peace-Building."[147] There is clear resonance between engagement management and Professor Bedeski's "Peacefare" that he calls "a process of building peace through understanding and implementing Human Security."

Consider Chinese Premier Zhu Rongji's stance concerning the spring 1999 Yugoslavian events. He offered a global caution against establishing a precedent that could have unpleasant implications. He said, "The world community is casting aside a vital principle when it interferes in the internal affairs of countries." They should not "imagine they can interfere in the China-Taiwan situation in the same way."[148]

Here the premier is speaking with the understated strength of *Ping-fa* and the Moral Law. Perhaps not unintentionally, he also speaks with the authority of a very long Western ethical tradition. Immanuel Kant's 1795 *Perpetual Peace* spoke of war as an unnecessary

---

145   *Saturday Night*, December 1999/January 2000, p. 42

146   See the Cohen and Tichy overview of Schoomaker's practices in *Fast Company* (September 1999).

147   Department of Political Science, University of Victoria. See: http://www.iir.ubc.ca/cancaps/bedeski.html.

148   *Toronto Globe and Mail*, April 3, 1999

evil, preventable by, among other things, treaties that disallow interference with the internal constitution of another state (Gallie 1979, 10).

Less strategic approaches without the inclusion of *qi* are not hard to find. Manwaring and Fishel say,

> Lacking an architecture for when, how, where and why to use the instruments of national and international power, the United States and the rest of the international community are forced to consider security problems on a case by case basis. We are left with vague entreaties that foreign policy and military management must serve the amorphous 'national well-being' and 'democracy' in a piecemeal and ad hoc crises management manner. (Fishel 1998, 197)

Practice Deception

All warfare is based on deception (I.18).

Deception in engagement management is next in importance after intelligence. There are twenty-one references to it in *Ping-fa*. Building and launching a strategy, deploying teams, and achieving victory with minimal disturbance in the organizational environment can't be done without deception. When you wish to remain unseen and of little concern to others, you must maintain a continuous program of deception. When you want to be open to others, your strength at such times must appear to be awesome, or of no significance. What is seen, and how it is interpreted, needs to be guided by you.

Deception is an important aid to cloaking activity and preventing discovery when gathering intelligence. We need intelligence to discover when another party needs to be nudged so that conflict, or perhaps even contact, does not occur. Awareness that interests are converging, or could converge, needs to be a closely guarded secret.

In managing the organization, and the organization in engagement all others must remain completely unaware of your plans. Visible activities should convey nothing of value to observers. Activity may be used strategically as a means of causing confusion or to intentionally mislead the other concerning your intentions. Deception is a key vehicle for achieving desired results without cost or loss, to anyone.

Ping-fa provides many techniques for disguise and the penetration of disguise. Indeed, we are even shown how we can, unobtrusively and painlessly, cause other players to give up key engagement intelligence, including their strength levels. Engagement managers do not allow other players to discover that they have been penetrated and evaluated.

That deception can cloak awareness, intent, and activity seems a hard lesson for civilians and the military in engagement. "Direct solutions and head-on attack are engrained in military psychology and will be difficult to eradicate" (Alexander 1993, 25). The commentary seems worried about what they see as unethical practices. But engagement activity, in war or in peace, can only be "unethical" where action is taken, and means are used that cause damage to another. *Ping-fa* is adamant that this must not happen: "A kingdom that has once been destroyed can never come again into being; nor can the dead ever be brought back to life" (XII.21).

Benevolence, which is benefit to all, is essential in *Ping-fa's* engagement management where self-interest is antithetical. An organization conducting sensitive intervention through the vehicle of strength management is acting in the interests of the greater good.

Deception remains an underdeveloped engagement art. This may be because it is considered "tainted" in the otherwise antiseptically clean field of engagement management. Others imagine it overrated, while some feel the risks from its use are just too great. Also, there may be some who feel the use of deception implies weakness, or the use of intellectual means when practical, physical devices would be more appropriate.

There is another important obstacle to overcome. It has to do with understanding what deception means in the *Ping-fa* engagement model. Consider the following observations concerning the Japanese attack on Pearl Harbor:

> *Sun Tzu's* works were known to influence Japanese military strategies and their conduct of war. During the Second World War the Japanese told the Americans that Pearl Harbor would never be attacked, when in reality it was making preparations and advances for the bombing. The Americans were caught totally off guard when the attack came. Many people still find it difficult to believe that the Japanese were capable of <u>lying</u> so blatantly. The act was an application of Sun Tzu's principle of deception. (We et al. 1996)

Spyclopedia, like (We *et al* 1996), asserts that Japanese tactics were based on (what we presume is a militarist) *Ping-fa,* but that has not been fully verified (Deacon 1988, 146). We can't know if the Japanese military understood *Ping-fa's* engagement management, but if they did they would have known that attacking Pearl Harbor represented a loss of control. *Ping-fa* says that such an attack could only bring greater cost than benefit, and indeed it did.

Ping-fa states the "worst policy of all is to attack walled cities." No *Ping-fa* adept would have recommended or condoned such an attack. The predictably huge losses for everyone involved made this an inefficient and ineffective engagement. Indeed, from a *Ping-fa* perspective, the Japanese and Americans were already engaged before the attack on Pearl Harbor came, and the engagement was failing. Pearl Harbor was nothing more than an escalation—a blunt representation of a conflict that had long been under way. If there was deception in the Japanese plan of attack it has not been made evident to this day.

Plain common sense would suggest that, whether one is playing poker or marshaling troops at the border, there would be an advantage in cloaking one's situation and intent. It would also seem eminently logical and fortuitous if the "enemy" thought you were heading in a different direction altogether from what you really intended. But most commentators think using deception is "not playing fair" (Aron 1976, 327; Tung 1994).

Sawyer allows that deception is all right in sports but is not acceptable in matters of real importance (1996, 43). Handel finds *Ping-fa* naive on the practice of deception, which he deems an insignificant military factor. *Ping-fa*

> relies heavily on deception as a 'cheap' solution, if not a panacea for many of the problems encountered in warfare. [*Ping-fa*] seems to ignore the fact one side does not have a monopoly on the art of deception, which, like the proverbial two-edged sword, can cut both ways. Therefore deception may not be as decisive as he assumes.

Handel says deception might well be dangerous and is really of no real practical value. Commanders could become too cautious by misreading the enemy, or by practicing deception they could get "ensnared by the enemy's carefully devised stratagems" (1992, 7–8, 103–104). O'Connell says we must continue with being "up front and honest" as we go head to head with competitors and enemies. There's no place for unethical practices in conflict.

Sun-tzu's belief in 'subjugating the enemy's army without fighting is the true pinnacle of excellence.' Yet this martial diffidence is strongly contrasted by a uniform tactical ruthlessness that supports surprise, deception, sudden attack, and feigned retreat in order to prey on enemies when they are least able to defend themselves—a style of fighting utterly at odds with the blunt confrontational ethic of Western combat. (O'Connell 1995, 171)

In a view that is beyond bizarre, R. K. Newland's *Tactical Deception* says, "If at all possible, the enemy *should be enticed to attack on our terms* so that we can control what he accesses and lead him to believe he has succeeded."[149] (The italics are his.) *Ping-fa* chapter IX—which illustrates how real intent may be discerned from signs, and conversely, how signs may be used to mislead—causes J. H. Huang to say, "Careless readers have twisted [smoke and dust] into deceptive warfare" (Huang 1993, 213). But this is precisely the message.

Dunnigan and Nofi, who evaluated deception in war, say that "the most potent weapon in any soldier's arsenal is deception" (1995). Some credit deception with saving Britain and significantly hastening the end of World War II. *The Transformation of War* says,

The essential principles of strategy will continue to be determined by its mutual, interactive character; that is, the fact that war is a violent contest between two opponents. The need to concentrate the greatest possible force and deliver a smashing blow at the decisive point will continue to clash with the need to outwit, mislead, deceive and surprise the enemy. (van Creveld 1991, 226)

---

149   http://www.jedefense.com/jed/html/new/dec98/feature.
html

Rosalie Tung (1994) feels the Western commentator distaste for the "unethical" practice of deception emanates from their overabundance of "Judeo-Christian influences." In her view, Asians without this moralistic framework find deception "a neutral term—amoral and acceptable if it results in a greater good." Cleary too references this "long tradition of deception in ancient China," with his half-hearted defense of the merits of deception.

Deception holds great promise for interorganizational management. With benevolence, it can reduce friction and allow harmonious relations. As a tool for beneficial engagement management, deception allows one to guide events sensitively, as strength is used as a powerful force for good.

Might we be missing a powerful opportunity to reduce, and possibly eliminate, tectonic plate clashes between people and organizations? Can we really afford to maintain myths around management and engagement practices because we are ignorant of them or find them offensive?

Be Adaptive

Adaptiveness is *Ping-fa's* third most frequent instruction. We first see it in chapter I: "According as circumstances are favorable, one should modify one's plans" (I.15). The *shuai-jan* mountain snake (see XI.29–30) is the *Ping-fa* metaphor for adaptive behavior. Doug Miller gives the metaphor new life with his "chameleon organization of the future [that] builds itself on a premise of flexibility" (Hesselbeing *et al.* 1997,120).

Organizations use intelligence gathering to set their engagement strategies but, more importantly, to modify their strategies according to what they are learning. Only a fool follows instructions blindly, when it is becoming evident that the instructions are inadequate or wrong. Chapter VIII.3 is the famous *Ping-fa* admonition that, where conditions warrant, the engagement leader should even disregard specific instructions of the chief.

Despite repeated instructions that leaders should adapt to circumstances, commentators consistently see and argue for the contrary. Tang Zi-Chang (1969, 37) imagines *Ping-fa* instructs that leaders should "adhere to the predetermined plan." Giles says line I.15 tells us not to "pin our faith to abstract principles." Then, he relates a story about Lord Uxbridge and Bonaparte, whose message is that one should be guided by the enemy (that is, respond to the enemy's initiatives). Such is, of course, completely at odds with *Ping-fa* instructions, where in the practice of engagement management, we must cause the other to move when it is favorable to us.

Another key *Ping-fa* line on adaptivity is the elegant and precise: "Let your rapidity be that of the wind, your compactness that of the forest" (VII.17). The commentary reads this the same way: as an instruction to remain both fast and compact. "Thus, they act as swiftly as the wind; they march as steadily as forests" (Huang 1993, 191). Ames says, "Thus, advancing at a pace, such an army is like the wind; slow and majestic; it is like the forest; invading and plundering" (1993, 130). Calthrop says, "Swift as the wind, calm like the forest." Cleary quotes himself incorrectly in *Mastering the Art of War*: "The rule is 'Move slowly as a forest'" (1989a, 120). Suggesting that one should be as fast as the wind and as tight as a forest would be to act predictably. How can you succeed when your every next move is evident to all?

The meaning of the line is self-evident, but if there was ever any doubt, it is immediately cleared up by looking at the context. Just before this line, we see "In war, practice dissimulation, and you will succeed." By using the infinitely variable wind and forest as illustrations, *Ping-fa* instructs those in engagements to be adaptive and unpredictable.

Sawyer makes the same mistake as his commentary colleagues when he says *Ping-fa's* adaptability instructions are all about "orthodox" and "unorthodox" tactics. Competency, in his view, means shifting from one to the other.

> 'Orthodox' tactics include employing troops in the normal, conventional, 'by-the-book,' expected ways—such as massive frontal assaults—while stressing order and deliberate movement. 'Unorthodox' tactics are realized primarily through employing forces—especially flexible ones—in imaginative, unconventional, unexpected ways. (1993, 428)

Nowhere does *Ping-fa* suggest that an activity is appropriate when it could give up valuable intelligence to the other party. The commentator practice of inserting their own views and expectations in defiance of *Ping-fa's* clear and adamant instructions has caused a great deal of misunderstanding. As these misinterpretations have been taught in military academies, one shudders at what the consequences may have been in some engagements.

Ping-fa uses ambiguity quite infrequently, actually only in two or three places where there is a need for contemplation and reflection. It uses no ambiguity when conveying the principles and practices of engagement management. Consider the admonition to move quickly. *Ping-fa* says, "Emulate the rapidity of a running hare" (XI.68).[150]

Ping-fa Views on Organizational Roles and Responsibilities

---

150   This is, of course a supporting admonition for adaptivity. No hare has ever run in a straight line.

Ping-fa says, "A ruler can bring misfortune ... by attempting to govern an army in the same way as he administers a kingdom" (III.12–15).

In an economical package, *Ping-fa* delivers principles, a mission statement, and information about the players, the processes, and the measures that guide, shape, and enable effective organizational and engagement management. We are thoroughly briefed on roles and responsibilities. There are statements concerning the ideals to which organizations and project leaders ought to aspire. These notions and instructions are as applicable today as they were over two thousand years ago.

Ping-fa used a military vocabulary and context for two reasons. First, because the subjects dealt with were new and difficult, the military metaphor made the subject "real" to its students, who could learn much more readily. Secondly, there simply were no words available then that could properly articulate the form and function of engagement management. Students could understand "army" and "war," when they might struggle with "team" and "engagement." Here we have replaced the military terms with generic, organizational labels. We will speak of "chiefs" (sovereigns), "leaders" (generals), "teams" (armies) and "observers" (spies) who have roles to play in "engagements" (wars).

These brief "biographical sketches" are intended for discussion. They are extracted and extrapolated from *Ping-fa* and the *Tao Te Ching*, combined with contemporary notions and ideas. Though liberties have been taken, there is nothing here inconsistent with the *Ping-fa* or *Tao Te Ching*.

The Chief ("Sovereign")

Chiefs are the personification of the organization. They are CEOs, mayors, chairs of boards, and presidents of public and private bodies. They may head countries or companies. Competent chiefs are powerful, visionary, and in complete touch with their organizations and its constituencies.

Chiefs are very important to organizations and in engagement management. *Ping-fa* opens and closes with admonitions directed at chiefs.[151] Little is said to and about them, but their role is clearly important. They are the authors of enterprise strategies that are built from what *Ping-fa* calls the "view from the heavens." They are the architect of the vision and builder of the solution.

Chiefs have high energy and are committed to success. They are awesome. The *Tao Te Ching* says, "The sage is guided by what he feels and not by what he sees. The truly great man dwells on what is real and not what is on the surface. (12)" Lawrence Fouraker, former dean of the Harvard Business School, said the most important contribution of chief executives was "intellectual capital" (Horton 1992, 30).

Good chiefs are always conscious of the impact of their behavior on the organization. While chiefs are visibly subdued, they are full of power. Their values are known to their people. Their limited encounters are strategic, forward-looking, and results-oriented.

Chiefs need to be "big picture" people, because their work is high level and strategic. They have sensitive feelers operating at many levels and in many different ways. They observe. They build and maintain value-based relationships within the organization. They appoint and empower leaders with whom they have a strong trust relationship. This trust flows throughout the organization. Machiavelli said, "The first opinion which one forms of a Prince is by observing the men he has around him" (McAlpine 1998, 103-104). And if one

---

151 *Ping-fa* refers specifically to chiefs in: I.1*, 5, 13*, III.12–15, VII.1*, VIII.1*, X.24*, XII.16*, 18–19*, 22*, XIII.4*, and 26*. (* means the line applies to both chiefs and leaders). I.1 is included because it is the principal admonition, applying to all.

does not see "good people" in the organization, one needs to look very carefully at the competence of the chief.

The best chiefs are nearly invisible outside their organizations. They are the perfect men (and women) that Fung Yu-Lan speaks of, where "tranquility and activity unite" (Fung Yu-Lan 1995, 16). They are the "hidden champions" of Hermann Simon:

> The chief of the world market leader in [a certain piece of equipment] remarked, 'We want neither our competitors not our customers to know our true market share'. The young chief of a service company commented, 'We have cherished our anonymity for years and feel very comfortable about it. Nobody has noticed our niche'. After substantial research, Philip Glouchevitch (1992) resignedly stated that these 'companies remain in many ways Inscrutable—a deliberate characteristic.' (1996, 4)

Chiefs eschew public profile, not because they do not care to be known, but because being known does not always help them achieve their objectives. Truly competent chiefs betray neither joy nor angst, unless there is a good reason for doing so. They are like "the best physician whose name does not get out of the house." They do not welcome accolades. Tom Watson Jr., IBM's former CEO, "frequently expressed irritation over the deference shown him. 'I think a sense of humility is vital, and the more humility the better'" (Horton 1992, 4).

Chiefs may be humble, but they are in recognized positions of authority and all understand their connection to the organizational mission. *Ping-fa* says organizations can't be successful if they are not benevolent, and they can't be benevolent if they don't have a values-based mission. Stephen Covey, who is completely in sync with *Ping-fa* on the importance of corporate missions, does not find wide support in the work world for missions or the necessity for getting them right. One executive told Covey that rather than take six months and involve all his people in a mission exercise, he would "whip this baby out this weekend."

Covey says that good chiefs take six months (or whatever it takes) and involve all their people (1991, 16). McNeil says he's worked with companies "where the process took a full year" (McNeil 1987, 87). W. Edwards Deming says, "Create and publish to all employees a statement of purpose of the aims and purposes of the company. Management must constantly demonstrate their commitment to this statement" (Covey 1991, 270). In his *Winning the Future*, Robert Russell (1986, 256) says, "Once we've established our values and direction and are comfortable with the means, we are ready to put all this to use: to develop strategies for action; making what we believe in happen."

Entrepreneur Portia Isaacson said, "I never deal with details, yet I never fail to give direction" (Horton, 1992). William Blackie, CEO of Caterpillar Tractor, said, "I deride the idea that an executive's function is problem solving. Bad executives are up to their necks in problems" (Heller 1985, 373).

Father T. M. Hesburgh, president of the University of Notre Dame for three decades, said, "Only an idiot would think they could run a place this size and this complicated alone." *The CEO Paradox* says, "If there is one skill that distinguishes leaders, it is their ability to delegate right."

Business psychologist Abraham Zaleznick says, "Managers prefer working with people; leaders stir emotion." Transforming leaders, says Warren Bennis, are "social architects" (Peters and Waterman 1982, 84–85). Chiefs are the "sages" of *Thunder in the Sky* (Cleary, 1993). They are "guardian spirits of heaven and earth ... who work against tremendous odds." They give the outside world "strategies for nipping problems in the bud" by "stopping gaps," which they do by "application of the arts of the Way" (i.e., *wu-wei*, or sensitive intervention). Good chiefs bring helpful changes that add to organization stability, sustainability, and excellence.

"Chuang Tzu" said,

> The mind of the perfect man is like a mirror. It does not move with things, nor does it anticipate them. It responds to things, but does not retain them. Therefore he is able to deal successfully with things, but is not affected.

When they act, they are decisive and move swiftly. They exercise flexibility, coolness, and judgment skills under trying conditions. Few, however, will ever know exactly what she or he has achieved, nor how they went about it.

> The best work often seems idiotically simple to group members who are unaccustomed to this sort of leadership. Yet a great deal happens. Sometimes just the lack of needless intervention permits the group to grow and be fertile. (Heider 1988, 89)

A colleague of Arthur Sulzberger, then CEO of the *New York Times*, said,

> I've seen him absorbing advice almost the way a sponge sucks up water. What I don't see ... is where does the squeezing process begin, and what is the factor. That starts to force some of the water that's been absorbed out. (Horton 1992, 31)

Chiefs engineer organizational consensus. The people are motivated by the chief's vision, values, and enthusiasm. He accomplishes his goals through the work of others. Some chiefs might imagine that— having achieved consensus where before there was only competition and confusion, having crafted strategies that articulate the consensus and the new goals for the organization, having wisely selected the best leaders available to achieve the strategy—they may now rest. But they cannot. Their vigilance must be constant. Chiefs remain observant and continually improve their understanding.

Proactive diplomats, competent chiefs see situations before anyone else sees them. They are cautious, not prone to either hasty decisions or actions. They are experts at knowing when intervention is necessary and when to avoid them at all costs. And when they must intervene, competent chiefs know exactly what minimal tweak will be effective in bringing things to right.

They are the gatherers and evaluators of intelligence. Their influence may be as subtle as the sweeping before a curling stone, and as invisible as a wedding gift that never arrives. They do not make these decisions lightly. Cleary speaks of "the importance of discerning observation in managing people."

> Sages govern not by trying to impose their own personal wills upon the national polity and the masses of the people, but by determining what is already there and skillfully arranging existing facts and forces such as they are in working relations designed to bring out the optimum efficiency and advantage possible under any circumstances. Thus in order to govern people, sages need to guide and direct them; to guide and direct people, sages need to know their aims and hopes; to know their aims and aspirations, sages need to watch what people undertake of their own accord. (Cleary 1993, 81, 86)

When the chief intervenes, he moves others in ways that will prevent or minimize the effects of encounters. The chief's subtle interventions, and noninterventions, achieve slight adjustments. These actions and nonactions keep the organization path clear. An impending connection that might have been unhelpful is averted.

Sometimes tweaking will not achieve the desired result. Perhaps conditions are too complex, events have moved too far forward, or the other is at too great a distance. At that point, the chief may decide to commence a formal engagement. It is a major point of departure when an engagement is decided upon.

Here the organization becomes an "instigator" in relation to one or more defined "others." A strategy is drafted and conveyed to a leader. *Ping-fa* says, "In war, the general receives his commands from the sovereign" (VII.1 and VIII.1).

Chiefs maintain a strategic role in engagement. Good chiefs (a) hire the best for engagements and (b) trust them. Good chiefs make sure their leaders are ready, and then (c) they are turned loose to do their jobs. They make sure that teams are adequately resourced.[152] Chiefs may monitor engagements when they are concerned about both details and the "big picture." But they do not interfere.

In the best engagements, the other is unaware that they have been so designated. They may never know it. Some commentators have seen this. Cleary spoke of "using creative interaction to achieve organizational objectives." Lau and Ames (1996, 79) speak of commanders with insight, who recognize critical moments and are able to capitalize on them. "The capacity of the small, incipient, and seemingly incidental to control the large by virtue of its pivotal position underlies the notion of getting the most from a situation while minimizing loss."

Chiefs engage for reasons other than meeting the direct "selfish" needs of an organization. In other words, engagements are not necessarily conducted for organizational gain. They could be undertaken to avoid loss—of the organization or of the other! Sometimes

---

152   Here *Ping-fa* and Machiavelli were in complete accord.

the chief will cause benefit to another, if that adds to environmental stability.

In 1999 *Fortune* magazine studied two "CEO factories"—General Electric and McKinsey. *Fortune* found that, though they were very different cultures, both produced excellent chief executives and had an "absolute insistence, blunt and uncompromising, on the best people—finding them, developing them, evaluating them, and getting rid of them if they don't measure up."[153] *The Book of Leadership and Strategy* says, "Rulers have to be careful about whom they appoint to office." As Cleary (1992a, 37) noted, they are the key to order, harmony, and loyalty.

The Leader ("General")

Chiefs determine when engagements are needed and how they shall be handled. The chief builds a strategy that draws on the organizational mission and the intelligence he has gathered. The engagement is unavoidable, is essential to the well-being of his and the other's organization, and will be minimal.

Leaders are hired by chiefs and carefully instructed in the principles and practices of engagement management. They are infused with virtue. Like their chiefs, they answer to higher values beyond that of the organization. Leaders are bound by the standards of their profession. They are discreet, yet forthright. Leaders avoid intrigue and confusion. Leaders cultivate relationships that will help their organizations, but in relationships they give up only what intelligence they must.

Leaders are able to combine observation and assessment skills with exceptional talent in leading and managing. They do all that while remaining in harmony with their organization, the strategy, and the Moral Law. Highly proficient planners, they have a proven capacity

---

153 *Fortune* (August 2, 1999). *CEO Super Bowl* by Geoffrey Colvin.

for learning and adaptability. They know intuitively when they need guidance, approvals, and refusals. They are at complete ease with decision-making. Leaders are found in all competent organizations, working in management and administrative capacities, or as negotiators and diplomats.

Engagement leaders know and believe in the mission. They are sagacious but not given to intemperance. Leaders know what bait will tempt them. They are both cautious and astute, and born risk-takers. They may appear outwardly calm, but inwardly they are a seething cauldron. Because they must balance foresight, wisdom, and action, they occupy the positions of greatest stress in organizations. Because they are fully informed, they are not surprised, and their timing is impeccable.

Competent leaders know they are utterly dependent on—and will be judged by—how well they develop their teams. They know the dynamics of teams and the techniques of control. They recruit them, teach them, and make them one.[154] Leaders train their teams so well that one member can perform any task as effectively as any other member. Leaders empower their team members, infusing them with strength. The team is not as strong as its weakest link, but as strong as the strongest link. When they are filled with energy and power, they are ready to move. They win when they engage. But they engage only when they must.

The *Tao Te Ching* and *Ping-fa* say that maintaining control is critical, despite how well equipped the team is, how attractive the prizes, or how great the opportunity for glory. If control is lost, there is failure, and then only weeds will grow where there were once fine gardens. Teams exist only to complete engagements. When the mission is accomplished, the team is disbanded.

---

154   According to Thomas Horton, Disney CEO Michael Eisner was an expert at building teams and getting the most out of them.

When leaders are most successful, few will know. When they are unsuccessful, all will know because losses have occurred, and perhaps conflict has broken out.

When leaders are trained they can be empowered to lead an engagement, governed by the strategy and new intelligence, gathered as the engagement advances. They carry out their instructions, shaped by what they learn in the field. They are fully authorized to modify the strategy if conditions dictate it, to the point of acting counter to specific instructions in that strategy. When they make adjustments, they do so without fear. They have absolute certainty that the chief will support every change. This "delegation" is far more than task assignment. "There are ... commands of the sovereign which must not be obeyed" (VIII.3). This is the *Ping-fa* principal directive on delegation and field authority.

Giles had a lot of trouble with this whole notion. He didn't like either the admonition or his translation of it. He then goes much too far in his interpretation of the admonition, not limiting the instruction to making a strategic field adjustment based on new intelligence. He says this all has to do with situations where "even Imperial wishes must be subordinated to military necessity" (1994, VIII.3). General Tao Hanzhang correctly identified the hazard of Giles's understanding when he noted that such field authority had the potential of causing "unremedial damage," if decisions made by commanders replaced or conflicted with state interests.

When *Ping-fa* tells the leader he is on his own and tells the chief to leave him alone, this does not mean the leader is "independent" or "adrift." But that is how much of the commentary reads it, thinking empowered leaders can do whatever they want. Sawyer says "generals" should be "empowered with absolute authority" and guide themselves, "irrespective of the ruler's directives." They should, he says, "conduct military affairs solely as his judgment might dictate" (1996, 21, 100).

Organizations need to be very careful in the recruitment and training of leaders. And they need to make sure that their chiefs do not imagine they are at the same time engagement leaders. Sound organizations have chiefs who are in the heavens and who appoint competent leaders who are on the earth. The business of chiefs is wisdom and strategic management. Their work is carried out by leaders. They translate strategies into action. They deliver results. *Ping-fa* spells out twenty-four leader directives. Mark well where he said chiefs should pay attention![155]

> World class team leaders facilitate the establishment and accomplishment of the team's goals. He or she is responsible for ensuring that the team fulfills the team's Charter and operates within its stated Boundaries. The team leader is the team's point of contact with the Sponsor. (McDermott 1998, 37)

Hermann Simons's *Hidden Champions* tells us that leadership is the most significant organizational success factor (Simon 1996, 221). But not everyone agrees. The literature is rife with lassitude. J. R. Hackman, who writes on "groups that work," observed the view that "leadership" should be informal—and that designating team leaders was really contrary to the team concept (Hackman 1990, 343).

---

155 *Ping-fa's* leader references are in I.1*; I.9, 11, 13*; I.15, 26; II.15; III.3, 5, 11; IV.7, 16; VI.8; VII.1, VIII.1*; VII.29; VIII.4, 5, 12, 13; IX.45; X.13, 14, 18, 19, 24; XI.34, 35, 40; XII.16*, 18–19*, 22*; XIII.4*, 26*. (I.1 is the general "mission statement" of *Ping-fa*: it states for *all* concerned that engagement management is of dire importance to the organization and its officers.) Line addresses both leaders and chiefs.

The hospital experimented to remedy the problem of inexperienced leaders. In one ward, the administrator removed a person from the team leader role and appointed a more experienced member as leader. Unfortunately the new leader (a psychologist) proceeded to dominate the group to the extent of intimidating the interns, so the ward administrator then eliminated the role of team leader entirely. (Hackman 1990, 343)

The Team ("Army")

Groups of all sorts are common in civilian and "uniform" workplaces, and in social and recreational settings. They handle projects and delegated tasks and often involve the coordination of multidisciplinary talents.

Sometimes groups are integrated to the point where we can say they are "teams" or "task forces." What they are doing is "teamwork." Peters and Waterman (*In Search of Excellence*) say they are "the basic organizational building blocks of excellent companies." But though the level of preparation, direction, control, and activity of these teams may at times be quite high, they rarely reach the heights of the "team" that *Ping-fa* requires for organizational engagements.

The culture and philosophy of *Ping-fa* teams may have originated with the *Tao Te Ching*. See, for example, "Yield and overcome; bend and be straight; empty and be full; wear out and be new; have little and gain; have much and be confused" (22). And as we see in the *Tao of Teams*, "Water! The image of moving water suggests an effortless flow that is yielding while supporting all things. Unlike water, values can clash, creating resentment and mistrust—the ebb and the flow" (Torres 1994, 29). Here is a remarkable resemblance to the ancient Chinese Triad that is a "motionless mover—in other words— of the center that governs the movement of all things without participating in it":

deriving from the Taoist hierarchy, which gave rise to them and which invisibly guides them for the purposes of a more or less outward activity in which it cannot itself intervene directly owing to the principle of 'non-action' (*wu-wei*). (Guenon 1991, 5)

Competent, integrated, and powerful, these are the teams that helped forge the first empire of China. They were not teams of soldiers, but civilians. *Ping-fa* teams are created by organizations and under the direction of leaders. There is a powerful trust relationship between team leaders and members where values, methods, rules, and objectives are fully internalized and adhered to. Teams are small, lithe, and mobile. With a short life expectancy, they are not "part" of organizations. They have no ongoing function, exactly as Donald Krause noted: "Armies came into existence to serve defined purposes ... in response to specific, definite threats or opportunities. [Such] armies were disbanded after the threat or opportunity had passed" (Krause, 1995).

The Qin academies provided instructions for the formation and development of teams. In *Ping-fa* XI.29–30, we are introduced to the *shuai-jan* mountain snake. It is *Ping-fa's* representation of a team in action. Giles says it has tenacity and unity of purpose and a spirit of sympathetic cooperation. It is also highly competent, immediately responsive, and extremely flexible.

Ping-fa teams know how engagements, when they are needed, are won. They are themselves invincible, achieving their victories often on nothing more than their evident strength. They fully understand that complete control is essential and that when in engagement, nothing is left to chance—not the choice of leader, not the members, and not the training of any of them. And these teams know that engagements respect the principles of benevolence.

They know and accept that the only *real* win is when everyone wins.[156]

Stephen Covey says success comes when you

unleash the energy and talent of people, [but if I am using] ... manipulative strategies and tactics to get other people to do what I want— while my *character* is flawed or my *competency* is questionable—I can't be successful over time. Rhetoric and good intentions aside, if there is little or no trust, there is no foundation for permanent success. (Covey 1991, 17)

Properly constituted and trained *Ping-fa* teams are conditioned to work in engagements inside and outside the organizational walls. They can be found where interdependence and focus are life and death factors—in health establishments, mountain climbing, and deep-sea diving expeditions, and in uniformed organizations. When you hear a team member say, "He has my back," you know you are hearing from a team member who understands and stands by the *Ping-fa* model.

Sergeant majors have known for centuries that discipline forges groups into high-performance teams that will not break when joint talents are needed most. Soldiers do not learn to march in order to give military bands something to do. They learn to march so they will move as a unit when they must. "Armies should create 'brain trusts.' Staff officers [should be] thinkers. They should not be used as copy clerks or orderlies. This is the only way in which a commander can pool the wisdom of his staff" (Tao Hanzhang 1987, 60).

In war, the most intelligible action units are relatively small groups of men, in close physical contact and operationally interdependent, who

---

156 Sawyer says "fostering welfare" is not on *Ping-fa's* agenda. (1993, 157 note 5).

share, as if by animal magnetism, the same reactions and feelings, whether in the form of resolution or faint-heartedness, of renewed dedication to, or of blind faith from, the demands of their terrible trade. (Gallie 1979, 104)

But in more pacific endeavors you must search hard to find *Ping-fa* teams. In the management theory genre, "team" and "group" are used interchangeably. In an analysis of "teamwork" in a medical setting, a psychologist said,

I don't see the [treatment] team as a group. I see the entire ward as a group. We don't have a strong sense of identity; we are more members of a ward than we are members of a team. Our team task is very narrow: we get together once a week to develop treatment plans. (R.B. Shaw on *Mental Health Treatment Teams*, in Hackman 1990, 341)

This psychologist is speaking neither of teams or teamwork, as envisioned in *Ping-fa*. In the business world, we rarely see teams operating at a high synergistic level. We find it difficult to imagine a group of civilians charged up and engaged with the same energy and commitment as soldiers at war or firemen battling a conflagration. A few see this as a serious organizational deficiency. Somerville and Mroz have said,

Organizations in the twenty-first century must find a way to make the spontaneous forming and re-forming of high-performing multidisciplinary teams a natural way of working. (Hesselbeing *et al* 1997, 71)

Organizations need competent teams, but management only infrequently understands how they can and should operate. In the civilian world, only minimum effort goes into team leadership, membership, and training. Little thought is given to conveying the mission, the strategy, or team roles when a team is established. Usually, a loosely formed group is told to "sort out the issues the first time you get together." About team membership, Doug Miller said, "Depending on the situation, people will find themselves as the leader on one team, a peer on another, and a subordinate on a third, the roles being defined by the nature of the work."[157]

Lipnack and Stamps say,

> *Empowered teams* are, [in their simplest form, where] people come together with a very clear common business *purpose.* *Members* are peers who interact laterally. *Leaders* emerge from within the group based on expertise and fit with group needs, rather than by superior appointment. (1993, 310)

Today, in the corporate world, the organizational and engagement value of real teams is generally unknown. And where it is, chiefs seem reluctant to spend the time and money needed to find the perfect leader and get the team into "combat" shape. Perhaps organizations have not seen the results they need to justify effort and cost.

> While a great many American firms have adopted 'team approaches' in recent years, success has been mixed. The reason could be that American managers don't quite realize what they are creating requires a lot of energy and attention from them to sustain. (Pascale and Athos 1981, 126)

This is a chicken-and-egg situation. Organizations are not seeing the benefits they expect, but those same organizations are not prepared to resource teams as

---

157 Doug Miller, *The Future Organization,* in Hesselbein *et al.* (1997, 123)

they should. Moreover, these organizations may have real difficulty approving the policy changes needed to ensure team effectiveness.

World Class Teams says when "real teams" are needed, "senior executives need to participate in a systematic process to set teams up for success."[158]

- They must provide visible support and commitment to the team.
- Teams need communications processes and technologies.
- Team leaders must be selected for their diversity and competency.
- Teams need a clear charter and boundaries.

Ping-fa and some of the contemporary management theory state that teams work best when they have freedom within a well-defined framework of principles. High performance happens when members know the limits and know how to work within (and sometimes outside) them. Stephen Covey says, "I teach [people] correct principles, and they govern themselves."

A team is different from a group: a team adds value. A group associates people by anything, whether deeply like a family, or superficially like a group of mostly random passengers on Flight 108. A team is more than individuals; it has synergy. It has an organizational advantage. (Lipnack and Stamps 1993, 85)

Rosabeth Moss Kanter agrees that structure is important:

Clear limits and guidelines and leadership are important in making an empowering, freedom-

---

158 (McDermott 1998, 21). These are lessons 1–3 and 8 of 15 listed.

generating process work. True 'freedom' is not the absence of structure—but rather a clear structure which enables people to work within established boundaries in an autonomous and creative way. (Foreword to L. J. Spencer's *Winning Through Participation*)

Groups That Work—and Those That Don't says the focus at the beginning should be on

task structure (clear task, consistent with the group's purpose, high on motivational potential); group composition (the right people, the right size) and core norms that regulate member behavior. (Hackman 1990, 10)

Focus is also important.

Teams are committed to achieving a specific *Performance and Business Challenge*. The Challenge must be aligned with and supporting the business's mission/vision. (McDermott *et al.* 1998, 32)

Pat Riley, who knows sports, teamwork, and a lot about winning, says teamwork means everyone's efforts are flowing in one direction. There is a value component. "Every team that wants to move toward significance and greatness has to decide what truths it will hold to be self-evident" (1993, 24). *World Class Teams* says, "Teams are the answer whenever there is an issue to be resolved" (McDermott *et al.* 1998, 7). *Winning Through Innovation* suggests teams are a key to competitive advantage.

But what makes a team both competent and effective? Authors Tushman and O'Reilly III (1997, 117) say it is efficient decision-making, flexibility, adaptability, and autonomy. Bob White (1987, 104) of the Canadian Autoworkers says when teams are engaged in collective bargaining, they must be full of strength and integrity. One *Ping-fa*-aware analyst says,

> It is important for the executive team to discuss strategic issues together frequently. By doing so you will become like any good team ... you learn to 'read each other's minds.' This becomes essential when it's necessary for the company to react quickly to marketplace changes or execute a strategy with vigor.[159]

World Class Teams says,

> World-class teams face turbulent waters on their journey. They are not for the unskilled, unprepared, or fainthearted. For most organizations [they] represent a different and complex way of working, thinking and behaving. They are complex. They require work. They *force change*. (Mcdermott *et al.* 1998, 8)

The Observer ("Spies")

Observers are supremely important to organizational success and endurance. Until the spies report, says *Ping-fa*, the army does not move.

> Hence it is only the enlightened ruler and the wise general who will use the highest intelligence of the army for purposes of spying and thereby they achieve great results. Spies are a most important element in water, because on them depends an army's ability to move. (XIII.26)

Whether there will be an engagement or not, what form it will take, and when it begins will be based on

159   *The Sun Tzu Strategy Newsletter*, second quarter issue (online) See: http://www.indiapolicy.org/lists/india_policy/1998/Jun/msg00157.html.

the data the observers deliver. Chiefs, leaders, and teams stand pat until the observers have reported. Only then can decisions be made, and if an engagement is indicated, a strategy crafted. When the engagement is under way, leaders need continuing intelligence to ensure their strategies remain appropriate.

As the eyes and ears of the organization, observers are carefully selected, trained, compensated, and utilized. They record everything, and they report everything exactly as seen and discovered. They do not know what is of value, because they do not know what is in the chief's head, nor do they have the chief's talents in strategic assessment.

Observers know they are important and valued and that they occupy positions of supreme trust. They know their livelihood and that of their organization heavily depends on their competence and their discretion.

Part V: *Ping-fa* Chapters

My contemporaries have failed to grasp the full meaning of [Master Sun's] instructions, and while putting into practice the smaller details in which his work abounds, they have overlooked its essential purport. (Ts'ao Ts'ao of the Han period)

Once, military adventures were often designed to obtain more resources to fight more wars. Once, business development depended on the favors of already rich men. This was the world in which Sun Tzu lived. It is why his teachings are more relevant to modern business than we might expect. Most of all, Sun Tzu understood that the most successful battles are those you do not have to fight. Modern business people obsessed by military analogies would do well to remember that. (*Financial Times*, August 4, 1999)

Structure and Content[160]

Ping-fa is in the form of a dissertation. It starts with a profound proposition and sets out the issues and actions related to it. Then, we have principles and practicalities that provide, in general and in specific detail, how the purpose is to be achieved. Terms, titles, structures, and processes are defined. We are told how to recognize competence and incompetence and how each should be dealt with. We are told, for example, that organizational leaders must be quiet, thoughtful, and benevolent. They must not be rash. They should cultivate their resources and carry out their orders. Finally, *Ping-fa* makes it abundantly clear what the consequences are of not conducting affairs appropriately.

This is a thesis on achieving beneficial results through the use of intelligence, patience, and strategic intervention.

160 Here we provide Giles's translation followed, line by line, with my interpretation. The Giles translation is available at http://ftp.sunet.se/pub/etext/wiretap-classic-library/suntzu.txt.

Ping-fa is an elegant and complete methodology, solidly grounded by a coherent philosophical framework. These methods are in harmony with the *Tao Te Ching*, which instructs us to "solve the difficult while it is still easy, make something big by starting with it when small. (63)"

The Sun Tzu School understood the malaise of complex organizations—with their slavish obedience to rules and structures and their fatalistic beliefs. Wishing for control of events but never achieving it, these organizations spend energy uselessly on activities that do not serve the organization. They either don't know or don't bother themselves about managing the organizational environment, where one needs to use trained and trusted observers and field agents in intelligence gathering that enables strategic analysis and planning.

Ping-fa has bookends. Chapter I defines the purpose of engagement management. Chapter XIII defines the single most important factor in achieving that purpose.

Each chapter has a general theme. Chapter I provides the high-level definition of the organization, the context, and the seriousness of engagement. Chapter II defines engagement failure. Chapters III through VI define what organizations are, how they are led, and the ways in which they articulate their objectives. Knowledge, planning, preparation, and strength are defined. We are given the rules to follow when an organization makes a decision to engage. There are instructions on timing, communication, control, and roles.

Chapters VII through X cover team movement and engagement conditions. We are told that when movement is necessary and appropriate, move carefully. Study the environment, including the others' behavior. Manage your team. Adjust the strategy as dictated by what you learn.

Chapters XI and XII are concerned with strength management, the operative factor in engagement management. Engagements are won through the management of strength, and the intelligence we learn about in Chapter XIII tells us where we are to find strength and weakness.

We are told how to specifically manage engagements in IV.17, V.3–11,and XII.1. The engagement environment is described in XI.1. The leader is instructed in organization and management in I.10. Physical and philosophical context is in I.5–8. What leadership is, and is not, is found in IV.8–9 and IV.11–16. Leadership faults are covered in X.14. The failure of a chief is in III.12. The very critical issue of knowledge gathering and use is seen in XIII.7 XI.53 and IX.10.

While we do not know why there are thirteen chapters, the number may have had spiritual or literary significance. There are thirteen chapters in *The Secret of the Golden Flower*. Paul Carus says there is great meaning in the thirteen "avenues of life" that are comprised of five senses and eight apertures (1964, 175).

What of the frequency of appearance of the number five? We see war governed by five constant factors, five situations, and there are five essentials for victory. There are five advantages, dangerous faults of a general, ways of attacking with fire, possible developments, and classes of spies. There are also five elements or energies (*wu hsing*).

Five is considered a powerful number in Chinese belief, being "the number of Heaven." Interestingly, it was the province where the emperor Chung Kuo lived (Guenon 1991, 59, 111).

There has been some debate around the order of the text, as we see it today, as well as whether the contemporary, widely distributed version is "original." The commentary often asks whether it has been added to or had sections removed over the last 2,200 years. Zi-Chang's *Principles of Conflict* completely reorders *Ping-fa*, because "all existing editions of Sun Zi in China and abroad are in disorder" (1969, 179). My research suggests only one apparent sequential disorder. It is the placement of chapter XII, which would more logically follow V.

Though there may be reasonable debate on the issue of the order of the chapters, it *is* clear that the methodology is all there. It reads as an integrated work, content flowing from subject to subject in a continuous stream. Should we seek significance in the fact that chapter VIII, which defines "leadership competence," is the shortest? Or that chapter XI, which illustrates "leadership in action," is the longest? I think not. Function in *Ping-fa* far outweighs form.

The framework of titled chapters may have been an aid to instruction or memorization, but the custom adds little value. In fact, that practice may have caused—over the millennia—more confusion than clarity. As there is no evident break between the chapters, the division seems arbitrary and a later modification.

There are many areas of potentially beneficial research here. If conducted from the perspective of engagement management, who can say what might be discovered? To date, the unbroken obsession with the military metaphor has not appreciably advanced either understanding or application.

The messages in *Ping-fa* reveal some extraordinary facts. First, though they are few in number, they are repeated again and again to a remarkable degree. The entire methodology, as it turns out, can be summarized in a short 31-word directive, but it is buttressed by 168 separate supporting references. Why should this be?

Ping-fa messages are repeated for two reasons. Primarily, the Sun Tzu School wanted no mistakes in meaning. Therefore, the admonitions and instructions are articulated again and again. They are expressed in different ways to ensure that there were no ambiguities.

There was also a pedagogical reason, as the school intended that shades of meaning and perspective would provide an aid to discussion and learning. Students had to learn a new and complex methodology.

Thunder in the Sky's "Master of Demon Valley" explains the use of redundancy and imagery:

> Always hold that net and motivate people. Use imagery to move them, in a manner responsive to their mentalities; seeing their feelings and states of mind, you can govern them accordingly. If you yourself turn around and go to them, they will turn around and come to you. When speech contains images and analogies, by their means you can establish a foundation. Repeat them over and over, reflect on them over and over, and the appropriate rhetoric and expressions for all affairs will not be lost. (Cleary 1993, 10)

The succinct nature of *Ping-fa*, the metaphorical elegance, and the meticulous way the methodology is designed and articulated make one wonder how so much of the commentary could be so wrong. One translator, encountering lines in the text that he deemed "obscure and redundant" material, simply deleted them. What he cut were prime admonitions on management, roles, delegation, strength, and values (Machell-Cox 1943, x).

There are similar examples of such treatment in all the major commentaries.

The Sun Tzu School *Ping-fa* Directive

Be strong and continually aware. Manage your strength and that of others. When essential, engage on your terms. Be observant, adaptive, and subtle. Do not lose control. Act decisively. Conclude quickly.[161]

The Principle Messages (occurrence frequency in brackets)

1. Manage engagements. (40)[162]
2. Manage strength (38)[163]
3. Gain knowledge. Modify plans. (37)[164]
4. Use deception. (21)[165]
5. Move decisively and with speed. (14)[166]
6. Manage commencement of engagement. (12)[167]
7. Get orders from the chief, and be guided by strategy. (6)[168]

The Sun Tzu School likely never imagined that their antiwar, pro-empire treatise would become known and accepted after the fall of the first empire as a text on

---

161   Robin Yates's "Sun Tzu Principles" come very close to this. They are found in his introduction to *Sunzi Speaks: The Art of War.*

162   II.1–15, 19; III.1–7; IV.11, 15; VI.26–27; VIII.12; XII.15–22; XIII.1–3

163   II.18; IV.1–2, 6–7; V.4, 15, 21–23; VI.7, 14, 21–24; VII.21, 28–34; VIII.1; IX.1–2, 17–40; X.19, 21, 27, 31; XI.33, 52; XIII.4

164   I.16–17; III.18; IV.13; VI.8, 13, 28–39; VII.12–14, 16–17, 22; VIII.3–4, 6–8; XI.52– XIII.9, 27; X 23; XI 37, 68; XIII.8

165   I.18–25; V.16–20; VI.9; VII.3–4, 12, 15, 26–27; XI.36

166   IV.12–15; V.13–15; VII.6, 17, 19; XI.19, 38–39, 65

167   VI.1–5, 11–12, 16, 19–20; IX.6; XI.66

168   I.15–16; VI.27; VII.1; VIII.1

military tactics. Likewise, they would have been surprised to see the *Ping-fa* military metaphor—an inspired teaching device—come to be seen as the message and not the medium.

That *Ping-fa* has been used to rationalize and justify military combat would have appalled the academicians of Qin. It is no less unsettling today.

Engagement Management: Strategy and Operational Models

A comprehensive and complete methodology, *Ping-fa* is grounded in well-defined and articulated principles. But it gives us as well the details of engagement management. Objectives are defined, as are the means by which the objectives are to be realized. Roles, responsibilities, and relationships are specified. Pitfalls to avoid are enumerated, and diverse success measures are identified.

Following are several transpositions of *Ping-fa's* methodology into operational models. That the methodology can be so easily modeled is proof to its intellectual creation and general application. Yes, *Ping-fa* can have a military application. But that application must focus more on *qi* than weaponry, more on intelligence gathering and sensitive intervention than on winning, more on achieving common goals than on defeating "competitors."

Ch'üan or Situation Weighing

(I.5–I.12)

Factor	Definition	Quality	Assessment
Moral Law	*The Moral Law causes the people to be in complete accord with their ruler so that they will follow him regardless of their lives, undismayed by any danger.*	Commitment, mission and leadership	*Which of the two chiefs is more imbued with the Moral Law?* *Which of the two leaders has the most ability?*
Heaven	*Night and day, cold and heat, times and seasons.*	Hard factors: demographics, conditions, issues	*With whom lie the advantages?*
Earth	*Distances, great and small; danger and security; open ground and narrow passes; the chances of life and death.*	Soft factors: Knowledge, benefits, risks and opportunities	*With whom lie the advantages?*
Commander	*The virtues of wisdom, sincerity, benevolence, courage, and strictness.*	Capability, values, strength, and control.	*On which side is leadership more effectively established? Which team is stronger?*

| Method and discipline | *The marshaling of the army in its proper subdivisions, the graduations of rank among the officers, the maintenance of roads by which supplies may reach the army, and the control of military expenditure.* | Training, order, delegation, empowerment, discipline, and capabilities. | *On which side are people and plans more ordered and prepared?*

On which side are resources best managed?

Which side better understands the management of qi? |
| Master Sun says: | *"These five heads should be familiar to every general: he who knows them will be victorious; he who knows them not will fail."* | | *By means of these considerations I can forecast victory or defeat.* |

Engagement Conditions ("Terrain")

(X.1–X.12)

Engagement Type	Instruction	Meaning
(1) Collaborative.	*Be before the enemy in occupying the raised and sunny spots, and carefully guard your line of supplies. Then you will be able to fight with advantage.*	Be strong, stay strong, and take the lead.
(2) Where the rules and objectives are not fixed and your knowledge is incomplete.	*If the enemy is unprepared, you may sally forth and defeat him. But if the enemy is prepared for your coming, and you fail to defeat him, then return being impossible, disaster will ensue.*	You may win if you move with greater strength and speed. If you have misjudged and lose the encounter, you may have lost the engagement.
(3) Where nobody benefits from initiation.	*Even though the enemy should offer us an attractive bait, it will be advisable not to stir forth, but rather to retreat, thus enticing the enemy in his turn; then, when part of his army has come out, we may deliver our attack with advantage.*	Cause the other to initiate. Then, engage before the other is fully prepared.

(4) In which only the initiator knows the real trophies. Move quickly, gain, and defend.

Should the army forestall you in occupying a pass, do not go after him if the pass is fully garrisoned, but only if it is weakly garrisoned.

If the other gains the trophy, challenge only if you are sure to gain it.

(5) Involving obvious trophies. Move and acquire. Await challenge.

If the enemy has occupied them before you, do not follow him, but retreat and try to entice him away.

If the other acquires such trophies before you, feign disinterest. Lure him away.

(6) Disadvantage. Control is not easily gained. There is a wide gap between the parties. A lack of good will and strengths are equal.

Why are there no instructions for engagement type six? We find the answer in Ping-fa's prime admonition: engage only when you must. Engage only when you know achieving success with mutual benefit is inevitable. In engagement type six, control will prove elusive, and conflict may be unavoidable. Avoid engaging.

The Conduct of Engagement

(VIII.1–VIII.5)

Condition	Meaning	Instruction	Meaning
In war	When an engagement is warranted	The general receives his commands from the sovereign, collects his army, and concentrates his forces.	An engagement begins only when a strategy is issued by the chief. Then a team may be deployed.
In a difficult country	You are distressed.	Do not encamp.	Radiate strength.
In a country where high roads intersect	There are many players.	Join hands with your allies.	Form alliances.
In dangerously isolated positions	You are vulnerable.	Do not linger.	Keep moving.
In hemmed-in situations	You see no way out.	You must resort to stratagem.	Use deception.
In a desperate position	There is no alternative.	You must fight.	Engage.

There are roads that must be followed, armies that must be not attacked, towns that must be besieged, positions that must not be contested, and commands of the sovereign that must not be obeyed.

Do not be bound by the strategy or driven by superiors who are not close to the action.

The general who thoroughly understands the advantages that accompany variation of tactics knows how to handle his troops.

Ensure your tactics and your management relate to the situation and need.

The general who does not understand these may be well acquainted with the configuration of the country, yet he will not be able to turn his knowledge to practical account.

Knowing the environment of the engagement is not enough to win.

So, the student of war who is unversed in the art of war of varying his plans, even though he be acquainted with the Five Advantages, will fail to make the best use of his men.

Only the adaptive succeed.

Hence in the wise leader's plans, considerations of advantage and of disadvantage will be blended together.

Continually assess whether decisions should be based on the strategy or emerging intelligence.

Ground

(XI.1–XI.10; XI.44–XI.50)

Ground Type	Description	Definition	Action	Meaning
Dispersive	*When a chieftain is fighting in his own territory*	Ground already held	*I would inspire my men with unity of purpose.*	Keep the team focused on the objective.
Facile	*When he has penetrated into hostile territory, but to no great distance; when you penetrate but a little way (XI.44)*	Ground you would like to possess	*I would see that there is close connection between all parts of my army.*	Consolidate the team. Engagement is likely.
Contentious	*Ground, the possession of which imports great advantage to either side*	Ground that benefits whomever possesses it	*I would hurry up my rear.*	Feign disinterest. Commence a feint.
Open	*Ground on which each side has liberty of movement*	Ground where possession is not an issue	*I would keep a vigilant eye on my defenses.*	Defend your rights.

Intersecting highways	*Ground that forms the key to three contiguous states so that he who occupies it first has most of the empire at his command*	Ground that, if possessed, enhances one's power over other ground	*I would consolidate my alliances.*	Join others to build strength.
Serious	*When an army has penetrated into the heart of a hostile country, leaving a number of fortified cities in its rear; when you penetrate deeply into a country (XI.44)*	Ground that has been won but is still attached to other ground	*I would try to ensure a continuous stream of supplies.*	Maintain strength.
Difficult	*Mountain forests, rugged steeps, marshes, and fens--all country that is hard to traverse*	Ground difficult to win, hold, and navigate	*I would keep pushing on along the road.*	Radiate strength.

Hemmed-in	*Ground that is reached through narrow gorges, and from which we can only retire by tortuous paths, so that a small number of the enemy would suffice to crush a large body of our men; when you have the enemy's strongholds on your rear and narrow passes in front (XI.45)*	Ground very hard to hold	*I would block any way of retreat.*	Consolidate your position.
Desperate	*Ground on which we can only be saved from destruction by fighting without delay; when there is no place of refuge at all (XI.24)*	There is no choice but immediate engagement.	*I would proclaim to my soldiers the hopelessness of saving their lives.*	Maximize the team's energy. Engage.

Six Ways of Courting Defeat
(X.20–X.30)

Ping-fa says, "The natural formation of the country is the soldier's best ally," but it is not enough to succeed in engagement. Those destined to fail will ignore the following admonitions:

Requirement	Skill	Cautions/Implications
A power of estimating the adversary, of controlling the forces of victory, and of shrewdly calculating difficulties, dangers, and distances	Strength management	He who knows these things, and in fighting puts his knowledge into practice, will win his battles. He who knows them not, nor practices them, will surely be defeated.
If fighting is sure to result in victory, then you must fight, even though the ruler forbids it.	Confidence and authority	
If fighting will not result in victory, then you must not fight even at the ruler's bidding.	Empowerment	
The general who advances without coveting fame and retreats without fearing disgrace, whose only thought is to protect his country and do good service for his sovereign, is the jewel of the kingdom.	Knowledge of the Moral Law and the practice of humility and humanity	

If, however, you are indulgent, but unable to make your authority felt; kindhearted, but unable to enforce your commands; and incapable, moreover, of quelling disorder, then your soldiers must be likened to spoiled children; they are useless for any practical purpose.

Hence the experienced soldier, once in motion, is never bewildered; once he has broken camp, he is never at a loss.

Hence the saying: If you know the enemy and know yourself, your victory will not stand in doubt; if you know heaven and know earth, you may make your victory complete.

Able to be one with, and support, your people

Knowledge of respective strengths

Regard your soldiers as your children, and they will follow you into the deepest valleys; look upon them as your own beloved sons, and they will stand by you even unto death.

If we know that our own men are in a condition to attack, but are unaware that the enemy is not open to attack, we have gone only halfway toward victory. If we know that the enemy is open to attack, but are unaware that our own men are not in a condition to attack, we have gone only halfway towards victory. If we know that the enemy is open to attack, and also know that our men are in a condition to attack, but are unaware that the nature of the ground makes fighting impracticable, we have still gone only halfway towards victory.

The Chapters

I. The Organization and Engagement

I. 1. Sun Tzu said: The art of war is of vital importance to the State.

Engagements are critical for organizational sustainability and growth. When they are not properly managed, the organization loses.[169]

I. 2. It is a matter of life and death, a road either to safety or to ruin. Hence it is a subject of inquiry which can on no account be neglected.

---

[169] "Vital political concerns" in the Chinese text reads *dashi*. It means "vital importance." *Dashi* was another way of saying "political concerns" in pre-Qin times. However, it concerned not everyday political affairs, but the extremely important activities directly under a lord's authority, which involved the entire country (Huang 1993, 122). R. L. Wing translates this as "Strategy is the Great Work of the organization" (1988, 21).

What is important to the state? The Master of the Hidden Storehouse speaks of the crown prince of Ch'I, who was approached by the lord of Yen. The lord of Yen asked, "Does the state of Ch'i have a treasure?" The crown prince said, "The ruler is trustworthy, the ministers are loyal, and the farmers support the government. This is the treasure of Ch'i." Hearing this, the lord of Yen took off his sword and left (Cleary 1993, 146).

Roger Ames on I.1: "The first priority is the avoidance of warfare if at all possible. Once, however, a commitment has been made to a military course of action, the project becomes to achieve victory at the minimum cost" (1993, 85). Tang Zi-Chang argues that military activity should be minimized to ensure troops remain fresh and thus able to achieve "Perfect Victory" (1969, 29).

Engagements can be peaceful and productive or typified by chaos and calamity. Study the nature of engagements and how to manage them.

I. 3, 4. The art of war, then, is governed by five constant factors, to be taken into account in one's deliberations, when seeking to determine the conditions obtaining in the field. These are: (1) The Moral Law;[170] (2) Heaven;[171] (3) Earth;[172] (4) The Commander; (5) Method and discipline.

Organizational values, ethics and the law are important in engagement. So too are various situations and conditions, including the capability and strength of the people involved.

I. 5. The Moral Law causes the people to be in complete accord with their ruler, so that they will follow him regardless of their lives, undismayed by any danger.

---

170   "Chinese philosophers hold that morality and law are not to be separated and that law-enforcement is only the last resort" (Bishop 1985, 49).

171   Cleary translates: "measure in terms of five things," of which the second is "the weather." Other commentators say this means "environmental conditions." Was *Ping-fa* so taken with "weather" it was built into first principles? I think not. The commentators take the literal road. See, for example, Teck and Grinyer (1994, 10, 15). "Weather" refers to people, their characteristics, and their conditions—old and young, trained and untrained, capable and not so capable. A person may be in the "spring of life." Being in "winter" may mean being too old to compete, not too cold to compete, as some of the commentary would have it. Huang says that "some have translated '*tian*' as 'the climatic condition' or 'weather' ... but 'the heavens', though still obscure, would have been a safer interpretation" (1993, 125). *Ping-fa* is an essay on strength and its management, so this is a reference to strength capability.

172   Tangible factors in the organization, the team, and the environment relevant to the engagement.

Moral Law binds people together. It is their identity. It is personified in the chief. As the Moral Law and the chief give meaning to people's lives, they serve willingly.[173]

I. 6. Heaven signifies night and day, cold and heat, times and seasons.

The condition of people will have a critical effect on their attitude, general behavior, and engagement performance. These are social considerations.[174]

I. 7. Earth comprises distances, great and small; danger and security; open ground and narrow passes; the chances of life and death.

There are also technical considerations, including placement, logistics, avenues, obstacles, and the assessment of both condition and chance of winning.

I. 8. The Commander stands for the virtues of wisdom, sincerity, benevolence, courage and strictness.

The chief must be of high integrity, intelligent, strong in the face of adversity, and able to guide and control.[175]

---

173 "Ruler" is an uncertain translation. Wing says the Chinese term *chun* is equally "monarch" or "king," meaning essentially "the highest authority, such as government and its laws and charters" (XI.3).

174 There are things known and unknown, visible and invisible. Some events happen with regularity and in a predictable way; still others come without notice. The degree of variation in people, situations, and events is immense.

175 The *Tao Te Ching* says, "The sage follows the light. He takes care of all men and abandons no one.... It is a serious mistake to engage in needless battles. Damage must result for all. But when battles must be fought, take care that kindness should survive" (Herman 1994, 113).

I. 9. By method and discipline are to be understood the marshaling of the army in its proper subdivisions, the graduations of rank among the officers, the maintenance of roads by which supplies may reach the army, and the control of military expenditure.

In engagement planning, ensure that plans include team task assignment, roles and responsibilities, intelligence gathering, and how strength is to be managed.[176]

I. 10. These five heads should be familiar to every general: he who knows them will be victorious; he who knows them not will fail.

Leaders who intend to win need to know these principles, conditions, and requirements.[177]

I. 11. Therefore, in your deliberations, when seeking to determine the military conditions, let them be made the basis of a comparison, in this wise: (1) Which of the two sovereigns is imbued with the Moral law? (2) Which of the two generals has most ability? (3) With whom lie the advantages derived from Heaven and Earth? (4) On which side is discipline most rigorously enforced? (5) Which army is stronger? (6) On which side are officers and men more highly trained? (7) In which army is there the greater constancy both in reward and punishment?

To determine which organization is better prepared for engagement, the chief needs to carry out a thorough comparison of his and the other's engagement conditions,

---

176   See R. L. Wing (1988, I.1) for a helpful "winning engagement" interpretation.
177   Huang says these are clearly peacetime, not wartime, activities. The issue here is building strength—or "raising forces," in Huang's words. He says Ts'ao Ts'ao was wrong to interpret this as a military matter (1993, 128–130).

strength and integrity, leadership capabilities, quality of situation analysis, and level of discipline balance.[178]

I. 12. By means of these seven considerations I can forecast victory or defeat.

When all this is known, the engagement result can be predicted.

I. 13. The general that hearkens to my counsel and acts upon it, will conquer: let such a one be retained in command! The general that hearkens not to my counsel nor acts upon it, will suffer defeat—let such a one be dismissed!

Leaders who adhere to these instructions will succeed. Get rid of the rest.

I. 14. While heeding the profit of my counsel, avail yourself also of any helpful circumstances over and beyond the ordinary rules.

Good leaders follow the rules of engagement, but they also harvest advice and assistance from all available sources.[179]

I. 15. According as circumstances are favorable, one should modify one's plans.

Strategies and plans need to be shaped by what is encountered in engagement.

---

178   Sawyer says the army is bound mainly by "the strict implementation of systems of rewards and punishments" (1996, 22).

179   Read with I.14. There is no conflict or contradiction here. The message is: "You know the rules [the Moral Law and the strategy]. Adhere to them. But don't be so foolish as to think I have seen and can anticipate everything."

I. 16. All warfare is based on deception.[180]

All strategies, plans, and initiatives need to be cloaked or disguised.

I. 17–23. Hence, when able to attack, we must seem unable; when using our forces, we must seem
inactive; when we are near, we must make the enemy believe we are far away; when far away,
we must make him believe we are near. Hold out baits to entice the enemy. Feign disorder, and crush him.[181]
If he is secure at all points, be prepared for him. If he is in superior strength, evade him. If your opponent is of choleric temper, seek to irritate him. Pretend to be weak, that he may grow arrogant. If he is taking his ease, give him no rest. If his forces are united, separate them. Attack him where he is unprepared, appear where you are not expected. These military devices, leading to victory, must not be divulged beforehand.

The engagement issue is strength—of all participants. Your strength is unknown to others. It is essential that you know, before engagements commence, that your strength is superior. There are many ways that a leader can raise the balance of strength in his favor. Combined with clever, undetectable planning, a rout can be predicted. If superior strength and favorable engagement conditions cannot be assured, then engagement must be avoided.

---

180   Tang Zi Chan, a former lieutenant general of the Army of the Republic of China, says this line means "war is an aberration of Dao" (Zi-Chang 1969, 187). I am eager to agree, for such supports my thesis. But lines 17–23 following are all on deception tactics.
181   Calthrop says "capture" rather than "crush."

I. 24. Now the general who wins a battle makes many calculations in his temple[182] ere the battle is fought. The general who loses a battle makes but few calculations beforehand. Thus do many calculations lead to victory, and few calculations to defeat: how much more no calculation at all! It is by attention to this point that I can foresee who is likely to win or lose.

Study situations well before entering into engagement. Inadequate study ensures defeat.

II. Maintain Control[183]

II. 1. Sun Tzu said: In the operations of war, where there are in the field a thousand swift chariots, as many heavy chariots, and a hundred thousand mail-clad soldiers, with provisions enough to carry them a thousand li, the expenditure at home and at the front, including entertainment of guests, small items such as glue and paint, and sums spent on chariots and armor, will reach the total of a thousand ounces of silver per day. Such is the cost of raising an army of 100,000 men.[184]

---

182   Sawyer's use of "ancestral temple" instead of "headquarters" conflicts with the *Ping-fa* admonition against omens and superstitions (1996, 42).
183   No fight: no blame. Achieve results, but not through violence (*Tao Te Ching* 8, 30).
184   Seeing numerical strength in this line when it is only illustrative, Calthrop says it should read, "A force of 100,000 men can be raised [therefore] you have the instruments of victory" (1908, 21).

Engagements are expensive.[185]

II. 2. When you engage in actual fighting, if victory is long in coming, then men's weapons will grow dull and their ardor will be damped. If you lay siege to a town, you will exhaust your strength.

Teams lose their edge in long engagements.

II. 3. Again, if the campaign is protracted, the resources of the State will not be equal to the strain.

There is also the risk that the team will lose its backing.

II. 4. Now, when your weapons are dulled, your ardor damped, your strength exhausted and your treasure spent, other chieftains will spring up to take advantage of your extremity. Then no man, however wise, will be able to avert the consequences that must ensue.

The longer the engagement, the greater your vulnerability.

---

185 Numbers of chariots and soldiers simply indicate scope and cost. Chapter II is the key admonishment that engagement is costly and to be avoided unless essential. Giles says the title is wrong, as it is really about "ways and means." Likewise, General Tao Hanzhang says don't engage until you have the necessary campaign resources (1987, 28, 83, 84, 97). "A very long distance" may mean many things. It could be distance from one's home or how deeply one has traveled into "unknown" territory. But less tactically it could also mean how far one has to go to solve the engagement or how far one has to "move" another to ensure his strength is less than your own. Griffith supports the view that distances were illustrative (1963, 144).

II. 5. Thus, though we have heard of stupid haste in war, cleverness has never been seen associated with long delays.[186]

It is not wise to move quickly into an engagement or to stay engaged any length of time.[187]

II. 6. There is no instance of a country having benefited from prolonged warfare.

Only short engagements make sense.

II. 7. It is only one who is thoroughly acquainted with the evils of war that can thoroughly understand the profitable way of carrying it on.[188]

---

186 Clavell imagines that, "once war is declared, [the skillful general] will not waste precious time in waiting for reinforcements, nor will he turn his army back for fresh supplies; but crosses the enemy's frontier without delay." If the situation was really one of combat, such behavior would be the "stupid haste" *Ping-fa* speaks of.

187 (Read with V.13, V.14, VII.17.) The commentators incorrectly interpret this to mean speed (as in blitzkrieg) in spite of *Ping-fa's* "haste is stupid." It is dumb to move too fast and dumb to hang around when you could finish the job. Move when you have the intelligence, and conclude just as quickly as you can. The "swoop of the falcon" does not suggest speed, but calculation.

Thunder in the Sky says, "Listen before speaking, coil before springing, start at the beginning, sow before reaping." The *Tao Te Ching* (36) calls this kind of strategy "subtle illumination" and explains its effectiveness by saying that "flexibility and yielding overcome adamant coerciveness." Strategic thinking involves "unexpected strategies [that] are unobstructed, by reason of their very unexpectedness. This is the value of inscrutability" (Cleary 1993, 81, 92).

188 Giles assumes this is a continuation of II.5–6 and reads it as an instruction to move rapidly.

Competent leaders who know what can go wrong in engagement make sure their planning prevents these mistakes.

II. 8. The skillful soldier does not raise a second levy, neither are his supply-wagons loaded more than twice.

Use no more resources or strength to conclude the engagement than you must.

II. 9. Bring war material with you from home, but forage on the enemy. Thus the army will have food enough for its needs.

Build your strength from the other while reducing his.

II. 10. Poverty of the State exchequer causes an army to be maintained by contributions from a distance.

Team strength needs are great. They must draw on many sources.

II. 11. On the other hand, the proximity of an army causes prices to go up; and high prices cause the people's substance to be drained away.

Be careful that another is not draining you at the same time.[189]

II. 12. When their substance is drained away, the peasantry will be afflicted by heavy exactions.

The consequences could be serious.

II. 13–14. With this loss of substance and exhaustion of strength, the homes of the people will be stripped bare,

---

189   Some of the commentary has this as an admonition against standing armies.

and three-tenths of their income will be dissipated; while government expenses for broken chariots, worn-out horses, breast-plates and helmets, bows and arrows, spears and shields, protective mantles, draught-oxen and heavy wagons, will amount to four-tenths of its total revenue.

There could be serious costs without benefit.

II. 15. Hence a wise general makes a point of foraging on the enemy. One cartload of the enemy's provisions is equivalent to twenty of one's own, and likewise a single picul of his provender is equivalent to twenty from one's own store.

The strength harvested from others is more powerful than the strength you develop yourself.

II. 16. Now in order to kill the enemy, our men must be roused to anger; that there may be advantage from defeating the enemy, they must have their rewards.

Teams need to be highly motivated and focused on achieving victory. They need to know what the engagement means for them and their organization.[190]

II. 17. Therefore in chariot fighting, when ten or more chariots have been taken, those should be rewarded who took the first. Our own flags should be substituted for those of the enemy, and the chariots mingled and used in conjunction with ours. The captured soldiers should be kindly treated and kept.

---

190   This means simply that fired-up teams perform well. Griffith says the line is out of place and gives it an odd translation that has R. L. Wing's support: "The reason troops slay the enemy is because they are enraged" (Griffith 1963, 75). Huang says "kill" is an incorrect translation of *shadi*. It should read as "trounce" (1993, 153).

Gained strength needs to be integrated into the strength of the team. Those of the other, who have been won over, need to be sheltered and nurtured.

II. 18. This is called, using the conquered foe to augment one's own strength.

Make what you gain part of your own.

II. 19. In war, then, let your great object be victory, not lengthy campaigns.

The objective is winning, not continuing the engagement.

II. 20. Thus it may be known that the leader of armies is the arbiter of the people's fate, the man on
whom it depends whether the nation shall be in peace or in peril. [191]

When engagements must be entered into, the organization must ensure they are appropriately managed.

III. Positioning for Engagement

III. 1. Sun Tzu said: In the practical Art of War, the best thing of all is to take the enemy's country whole and intact; to shatter and destroy it is not so good. So, too, it is better to recapture an army entire than to destroy it,

---

191   Only Huang interprets this line as "a commander who knows forces is the Guardian of the people's lives" (1993, 155).

to capture a regiment, a detachment or a company entire than to destroy them.[192]

The engagement objective is to achieve mutual benefit. Sometimes that benefit means absorption of the other into your organization.[193]

III. 2. Hence to fight and conquer in all your battles is not supreme excellence; supreme excellence consists in breaking the enemy's resistance without fighting.

You serve the organization best when you achieve your objectives with skill in sensitive intervention and nonintervention.

III. 3. Thus the highest form of generalship is to balk the enemy's plans; the next best is to prevent the junction of the enemy's forces; the next in order is to attack the enemy's army in the field; and the worst policy of all is to besiege walled cities.

The best strategies achieve results before the other's position has coalesced. The next best are able to derail the other's initiative before it gets under way. If these strategies are unsuccessful, you may have to engage.

---

192   In yet another bizarre intrepretation from the military community, R. L. Cantrell thinks "whole and intact" means "winning the whole battle" (http://www.centerforadvantage. com).

193   Simone Weil wrote, "There are peoples who have never recovered after having been conquered" (Walzer 1977, 228). Sawyer (1996, 53) wonders why one would want to gain another in an intact condition. Greene (1998, 112) says the wisdom of "crushing the enemy" goes right back to Moses. Air Marshal Evans, who advocates selective bombing, like many commentators just can't seem to understand that when *Ping-fa* says "whole and intact," it does not mean "somewhat whole and somewhat intact" (1997, 84).

But you do that only when you are able to overcome the other without conflict.[194]

III. 4. The rule is, not to besiege walled cities if it can possibly be avoided. The preparation of mantlets, movable shelters, and various implements of war, will take up three whole months; and the piling up of mounds over against the walls will take three months more.

Conflict expends vast time and resources.[195]

III. 5. The general, unable to control his irritation, will launch his men to the assault like swarming ants, with the result that one-third of his men are slain, while the town still remains untaken. Such are the disastrous effects of a siege.[196]

Conflict results from loss of control. Heavy cost without gain may result.

---

194   Debate rages on these lines. First, there is little agreement about the words "balk" and "plans." Some show these words as "attack" and "strategies." General Tao Hanzhang's translation is "upsetting the enemy's strategic plans" (1987, 17). No commentator explains how you can attack a strategy or upset a plan. Griffith uses an anecdote in an unsuccessful attempt to explain it (1963, 78). Sawyer comes closest with his thoughts about "diplomatic coercion" (1996, 19). There is a greater problem with "worst policy of all." Cleary says it means "last resort." Griffith says, "No alternative." The real meaning is "unacceptable."
195   Cleary (and many others) sees this as instruction: "Take three months to prepare your machines and three months to complete your siege engineering" (1988, 71).
196   Alexander says, "One of the factors that make a general great [and rare] is that he can withstand the urge of most men to rush headlong into direct engagements" (1993, 24).

III. 6. Therefore the skillful leader subdues the enemy's troops without any fighting; he captures their cities without laying siege to them; he overthrows their kingdom without lengthy operations in the field. [197]

Actual engagement is not always needed to achieve victory. The best leaders know how to win without encountering the other.

III. 7. With his forces intact he will dispute the mastery of the empire, and thus, without losing a man, his triumph will be complete. This is the method of attacking by stratagem.

Strategic engagement and competent leaders gain all while losing nothing.

III. 8. It is the rule in war, if our forces are ten to the enemy's one, to surround him; if five to one, to attack him; if twice as numerous, to divide our army into two.

Team strength—capacity and capability—dictate how engagements are to be managed. If far superior, quietly absorb the other. If superior, a simple engagement may

---

197   Cleary never fully appreciates this meaning of fire and water (1988, 72). Lau and Ames (1996, 55) are very unclear on the subject. Giles thinks this line is an admonition against striking prematurely. Commentator Jia Lin provides a correct military interpretation: "Just ingratiate yourself with the people while causing inward rifts among the military, and the city will conquer itself."

be necessitated. If in a position of only slight advantage, a complex engagement is indicated.[198]

III. 9. If equally matched, we can offer battle; if slightly inferior in numbers, we can avoid the enemy; if quite unequal in every way, we can flee from him.

Engagement can be undertaken if strengths are relatively equal but the results cannot be predicted. If at a disadvantage, engagement is not recommended. If overwhelmed, avoid engagement at all costs.[199]

III. 10. Hence, though an obstinate fight may be made by a small force, in the end it must be captured by the larger force.

Though they may try hard, teams of lower strength will fail.

---

198 Commentators say "surround" really means "surround and conquer." Cleary and General Tao Hanzhang go further. The general says "surround and annihilate" (1987, 92). "Surround" has a more subtle meaning. It means "to encompass"—that is, to achieve success by absorption. *The Tao of Leadership* says, "The feminine surrenders, then encompasses and wins." *Thunder in the Sky* gives us another possible meaning: "Prove them by surrounding," meaning see how people handle pressures, like being hemmed in on all sides (Cleary 1993, 93). If one's forces are "ten to the enemy's one," why would you test the enemy? Just go ahead and do it!

199 Read with X.7, X.11. "Fleeing" is the proper behavior of a leader who knows the other has far greater strength. This is not "retreat" in engagement, a behavior condemned in *Ping-fa*. Even the difficult XI.50 underscores the *Ping-fa* insistence on maintaining the offense. This line says engagement is out of the question. We agree with Cleary that "withdrawal does not mean regression, but a special kind of relaxation and removal, somewhat like the adjustment of a cooking soup from a preliminary boil to a maturing simmer" (1993, 93).

III. 11. Now the general is the bulwark of the State; if the bulwark is complete at all points; the State will be strong; if the bulwark is defective, the State will be weak.

Organizations prosper when their leaders are fully competent in all aspects of engagement management.

III. 12–15. There are three ways in which a ruler can bring misfortune upon his army: (1) By commanding the army to advance or to retreat, being ignorant of the fact that it cannot obey. This is called hobbling the army. (2) By attempting to govern an army in the same way as he administers a kingdom, being ignorant of the conditions which obtain in an army. This causes restlessness in the soldier's minds. (3) By employing the officers of his army without discrimination, through ignorance of the military principle of adaptation to circumstances. This shakes the confidence of the soldiers.

Chiefs can render teams ineffective. They can: (1) subvert the leaders in ignorance of conditions, (2) fail to recognize that engagements are different from normal management, and (3) fail to deploy the right leader.[200]

III. 16. But when the army is restless and distrustful, trouble is sure to come from the other feudal princes. This is simply bringing anarchy into the army, and flinging victory away.

An organization that does not clearly define, and respect, competency and relative roles and responsibilities will be unsuccessful.

---

200   Giles, confusing the functions of chiefs and leaders, says, "The general should not be in the thick of his own troops."

III. 17. Thus we may know that there are five essentials for victory: (1) He will win who knows when to fight and when not to fight. (2) He will win who knows how to handle both superior and inferior forces.[201] (3) He will win whose army is animated by the same spirit throughout all its ranks. (4) He will win who, prepared himself, waits to take the enemy unprepared. (5) He will win who has military capacity and is not interfered with by the sovereign.

Victory involves knowing when an engagement is proper and when it is not, knowing how to measure and manage strength,[202] knowing the dynamics of team management, knowing how to achieve greater strength and how and when to engage, and knowing that you have the authority to complete your mission.

III. 18. Hence the saying: If you know the enemy and know yourself,[203] you need not fear the result of a hundred battles. If you know yourself but not the enemy, for every victory gained you will also suffer a defeat. If you know neither the enemy nor yourself, you will succumb in every battle.

You have no need to fear engagement if you are knowledgeable and prepared. If you are prepared except

---

201   Giles thinks this concerns awareness of the time and place for engagement, when (1) and (2) are strength instructions (1994, III.17.2).

202   To commentators, "strength" means "numbers." Roger Ames says the issue is about "how to deal with numerical superiority and inferiority" (1993, 113).

203   "If a man lacks knowledge of what is harbored in his own person, how is he going to be able to win over those at a distance" (Lau and Ames 1998). "Effective negotiation at any level ... begins with an understanding of yourself" (Steinberg and D'Orso 1998).

for knowledge of others, your results will be average. Without preparation of any kind, you will fail.[204]

IV. The Use of Strength

IV. 1. Sun Tzu said: The good fighters of old first put themselves beyond the possibility of defeat, and then waited for an opportunity of defeating the enemy.

Experience proves: when you are too strong to be beaten, you need then only to define the details of engagement.

IV. 2. To secure ourselves against defeat lies in our own hands, but the opportunity of defeating the enemy is provided by the enemy himself. [205]

We are invincible, but the other provides the means to victory.[206]

IV. 3. Thus the good fighter is able to secure himself against defeat, but cannot make certain of defeating the enemy.

Some leaders are good at defense but are weak at offense.

IV. 4. Hence the saying: One may know how to conquer without being able to do it.

---

204   This is not an endorsement of wanton engagement. *Ping-fa* does not say, "You can engage in a hundred battles and never be defeated." It says, "You need not fear the result." Intelligent and strong organizations engage only when they must. When they engage, they win.
205   Some commentators think this, and IV.2 mean wait for the other to make a mistake.
206   Giles says wrongly, "That is, of course, by a mistake on the enemy's part." (1994, IV.2)

Leadership in engagement takes competence in both theory and practice.[207]

IV. 5. Security against defeat implies defensive tactics; ability to defeat the enemy means taking the offensive.

Defense and offense require very different engagement rules.

IV. 6. Standing on the defensive indicates insufficient strength; attacking, a superabundance of strength.

Those who are focused on defense are unprepared for engagement, while those who focus on offense are fully prepared. These conditions are evident to others.[208]

IV. 7. The general who is skilled in defense hides in the most secret recesses of the earth; he who is skilled in attack flashes forth from the topmost heights of heaven. Thus on the one hand we have ability to protect ourselves; on the other, a victory that is complete.

True leaders lead from a position of strength and do not burn energy in defensive tactics. True leaders engage and win.[209]

IV. 8. To see victory only when it is within the ken of the common herd is not the acme of excellence.

207   "Although the principles of war are simple and can be learned by anyone, application requires much care, skill, and caution" (Alexander 1993, 299).
208   Commentator Liu Yin says, incorrectly, that one defends because his strength is inadequate and attacks because his force is more than abundant (Sawyer 1993, 163 note 45). Engagements are won through fire and water, not fire alone.
209   *Ping-fa* makes it very clear that defense and offense are not equal tactics, decided upon by the exigencies of the moment. You do not win with defensive tactics.

The skills of engagement management are not commonly known.

IV. 9. Neither is it the acme of excellence if you fight and conquer and the whole empire says, "Well done!"

If everyone knows how victory was achieved, you have not performed as well as you should have.[210]

IV. 10. To lift an autumn hair is no sign of great strength; to see the sun and moon is no sign of sharp sight; to hear the noise of thunder is no sign of a quick ear.

Engagement management is about skills, activities, and processes that are beyond common experience and understanding.[211]

IV. 11. What the ancients called a clever fighter is one who not only wins, but excels in winning with ease.

It is not enough to win. You must win with minimal effort and cost.

IV. 12. Hence his victories bring him neither reputation for wisdom nor credit for courage.

It is best that your status as a winner goes unheralded.

IV. 13. He wins his battles by making no mistakes. Making no mistakes is what establishes the certainty of

---

210   Griffith translates this as "it is not the acme of skill [to] triumph in battle and be universally acclaimed 'Expert'."
211   If there is any truth at all to the "Burning of the Books" tale, it might have been caused by an inadvertent leak of this (engagement) knowledge outside the Qin academies.

victory, for it means conquering an enemy that is already defeated.

A brilliant strategy carried out by competent leadership means that strength has been properly managed and no mistakes made.[212]

IV. 14. Hence the skillful fighter puts himself into a position which makes defeat impossible, and does not miss the moment for defeating the enemy.

Secure against the other and fully aware, the leader knows when and how the engagement is to be won. Strength is one key factor. Timing is another.

IV. 15. Thus it is that in war the victorious strategist only seeks battle after the victory has been won, whereas he who is destined to defeat first fights and afterwards looks for victory.

Successful leaders engage when control is complete and the outcome is known. Incompetents strive to salvage a victory from the jaws of defeat.[213]

IV. 16. The consummate leader cultivates the moral law, and strictly adheres to method and discipline; thus it is in his power to control success.

---

212   Huang says the issues of "battle" and "victory" are completely distinct in the Linyi text. It is, therefore, not "achieving victory through battle" (1993, 167–168).
213   Giles sees paradox here, but *Ping-fa* says do not engage until you are certain of the outcome. Huang says the verb "seeks" was added after the Linyi text (1993, 168). This would suggest that competent strategists achieve victory before engagement. Incompetents try to wrest victory after the calamity of failure. Teck and Grinyer and Sawyer have unhelpful observations on this point (Teck and Grinyer 1994, 232; Sawyer 1996, 59, 25).

Effective leaders achieve success because they manage strength, ensure control, and behave in an ethical, benevolent manner.[214]

IV. 17. In respect of military method, we have, firstly, Measurement; secondly, Estimation of quantity; thirdly, Calculation; fourthly, Balancing of chances; fifthly, Victory.

Winning engagements entail assessment and management of the strength of all parties, examination of the potential for winning, and strategic and tactical adjustments.[215]

IV. 18–20. Measurement owes its existence to Earth; Estimation of quantity to Measurement; Calculation to Estimation of quantity; Balancing of chances to Calculation; and Victory to Balancing of chances. A victorious army opposed to a routed one, is as a pound's weight placed in the scale against a single grain. The onrush of a conquering force is like the bursting of pent-up waters into a chasm a thousand fathoms deep.

Success is assured when the calculation and management of all factors of engagement are done with care, and the engagement proceeds from a position of superior strength.

V. Building Strength

V. 1. Sun Tzu said: The control of a large force is the same principle as the control of a few men: it is merely a question of dividing up their numbers.

214 A common commentator interpretation: "Hold fast to military regulations" (Ames 1993, 116).
215 Opposing the literal, numerical approach of commentators, Huang says it is unsound to read "measurement" here as "size." Giles does recognize that only a small part of this is about "numbers" (1994, IV.17–18).

The principles of engagement management are constant. Practices may vary according to the situation.[216]

V. 2. Fighting with a large army under your command is nowise different from fighting with a small one: it is merely a question of instituting signs and signals.

When many are involved, effective communications will ensure integration and control are maintained.[217]

V. 3. To ensure that your whole host may withstand the brunt of the enemy's attack and remain unshaken—this is effected by maneuvers direct and indirect.

Protect your strength with diverse maneuvers.

V. 4. That the impact of your army may be like a grindstone dashed against an egg—this is effected by the science of weak points and strong.[218]

Achieve victory by avoiding strong points and attacking weak points.[219]

V. 5. In all fighting, the direct method may be used for joining battle, but indirect methods will be needed in order to secure victory.

---

216   Giles is very close. He says this has to do with bureaucratic organization.
217   Art McNeil's first leadership building block is "signaling skills" (1987, 35).
218   Here Calthrop's translation is way off the mark. He says engage the enemy with normal force and defeat with abnormal force (1908, 32).
219   "The true test of the great general is to decide where the 'Achilles heel' can be located" (Alexander 1993, 23).

Your strength and intent to win are clear when you commence an engagement, but that will be all that is evident about you.

V. 6. Indirect tactics, efficiently applied, are inexhaustible as Heaven and Earth, unending as the flow of rivers and streams; like the sun and moon, they end but to begin anew; like the four seasons, they pass away to return once more.

Your methods are many and diverse and ceaselessly varied.

V. 7–9. There are not more than five musical notes, yet the combinations of these five give rise to more melodies than can ever be heard. There are not more than five primary colors (blue, yellow, red, white, and black), yet in combination they produce more hues than can ever be seen. There are not more than five cardinal tastes (sour, acrid, salt, sweet, bitter), yet combinations of them yield more flavors than can ever be tasted. [220]

There are only so many things that can be done, but there are infinite ways they can be combined and applied.

V. 10. In battle, there are not more than two methods of attack—the direct and the indirect; yet these

---

220   Here the message is to manipulate what you know in different ways. "Do not repeat the tactics that won you a victory, but vary them according to the circumstances. This non repetitiveness of tactics implies a constant search for new and innovative ways of meeting the challenges offered by the ever-changing circumstances" (Wee *et al.* 1996, 226). Alan Watts says here the *Tao Te Ching* "is of course referring to the formal rules and classifications for these arts. [So] if you think there are only five colors, you must be blind, and deaf if you think that all music has to be in the pentatonic scale" (1957, 120).

two in combination give rise to an endless series of maneuvers.[221]

Complex arrays of tactics and techniques are drawn on for the engagement strategy.

V. 11. The direct and the indirect lead on to each other in turn. It is like moving in a circle—you never come to an end. Who can exhaust the possibilities of their combination?

Tools and techniques are applied in a planned sequence.

V. 12. The onset of troops is like the rush of a torrent which will even roll stones along in its course.

Deployed strategies eliminate resistance.

V.13. The quality of decision is like the well-timed swoop of a falcon which enables it to strike and destroy its victim. Methods must be variable and unpredictable to ensure that the opponent is unprepared and unbalanced by your initiative.

You are strong and decisive. When your activity is visible, it is obscure and misunderstood. The other's strength is reduced by his confusion.

V. 14. Therefore the good fighter will be terrible in his onset, and prompt in his decision.

There is no room for wobbling once the engagement begins.

---

221 Militarist commentators, including Wei Liao Tzu and Ts'ao Ts'ao, seem to think this line speaks of frontal, flank, and rear attacks (Machell-Cox 1943, 31).

*V. 15. Energy may be likened to the bending of a crossbow;
decision, to the releasing of a trigger.*[222]

Strength grows and reduces slowly. But it is applied
abruptly.

*V. 16. Amid the turmoil and tumult of battle, there may
be seeming disorder and yet no real disorder at all; amid
confusion and chaos, your array may be without head or
tail, yet it will be proof against defeat.*[223]

Your activity and the situation appear chaotic to the
other. But that apparent chaos is proof of your impending
success.[224]

*V. 17. Simulated disorder postulates perfect discipline,
simulated fear postulates courage; simulated weakness
postulates strength.*

Highly competent teams convey conditions opposite to
reality. Competent others understand this.

*V. 18. Hiding order beneath the cloak of disorder is simply
a question of subdivision; concealing courage under a
show of timidity presupposes a fund of latent energy;
masking strength with weakness is to be effected by
tactical dispositions.*

---

222   "The sage nurtures his spirit, harmonizes and retains
the fluency of his *qi*, calms his body, and sinks and floats,
rises and falls with *tao*. In using it, it is like touching off a
trigger" (Lau and Ames 1998, 41).
223   Your shape and intent are not discernible. Sawyer,
in grave error, imagines these lines describe a team losing
control (notes on text 71).
224   Which is exactly how Mao appeared to observers,
including Otto Braun (Stalin's "advisor" to the Central
Committee), during the Long March. "Mao's tactics drove the
KMT commanders dizzy. But Mao was acting on the hardest
kind of realism" (Salisbury 1985, 169).

It is not overly difficult to send out misleading messages.

V. 19. Thus one who is skillful at keeping the enemy on the move maintains deceitful appearances, according to which the enemy will act. He sacrifices something, that the enemy may snatch at it.

The other will move according to what he believes to be true. Sometimes the leader will sacrifice a point to reassure the other that his impressions are valid.

V. 20. By holding out baits, he keeps him on the march; then with a body of picked men he lies in wait for him.

The team causes the other to move until he is where you want him.

V. 21. The clever combatant looks to the effect of combined energy, and does not require too much from individuals. Hence his ability to pick out the right men and utilize combined energy.

Good leaders know that team development and its strength are far more important than the skills individuals bring to the team and what individuals contribute to the engagement.[225]

V. 22. When he utilizes combined energy, his fighting men become as it were like unto rolling logs or stones. For it is the nature of a log or stone to remain motionless on level

---

225   Read with V.22. Why does *Ping-fa* not "require too much from individuals"? This is pure group dynamics. The team is the viable unit in the engagement. It is truly effective only when it exudes "combined energy" and is able to maneuver as one. *Ping-fa* says "individualism" can get in the way.

ground, and to move when on a slope; if four-cornered, to come to a standstill, but if round-shaped, to go rolling down.

When the team is fully developed it moves as one.

V. 23. Thus the energy developed by good fighting men is as the momentum of a round stone rolled down a mountain thousands of feet in height. So much on the subject of energy.

Strong teams are unstoppable.

VI. Strategies and Field Changes

VI. 1. Sun Tzu said: Whoever is first in the field and awaits the coming of the enemy, will be fresh for the fight; whoever is second in the field and has to hasten to battle will arrive exhausted.[226]

Start an engagement when you are ready. Be ready before the other.

VI. 2. Therefore the clever combatant imposes his will on the enemy, but does not allow the enemy's will to be imposed on him.

Control the engagement.

VI. 3. By holding out advantages to him, he can cause the enemy to approach of his own accord; or, by inflicting damage, he can make it impossible for the enemy to draw near.

---

226   This is the measure of control. Sawyer got VI.1 mostly right by observing that one of *Ping-fa's* "fundamental principles is controlling others, rather than being controlled by others—and many of his tactical measures are devoted to appropriately manipulating the enemy" (1993, 166 note 75).

Cause the other to move when and where you want him.

VI.4. If the enemy is taking his ease, he can harass him; if well supplied with food, he can starve him out; if quietly encamped, he can force him to move.

You can cause the other to move regardless of his situation or intent.

VI. 5. Appear at points which the enemy must hasten to defend; march swiftly to places where you are not expected.

Use your own movements to cause the other to move and weaken.

VI. 6. An army may march great distances without distress, if it marches through country where the enemy is not.

As the other defends what is of no interest to you, you may advance unopposed.

VI. 7. You can be sure of succeeding in your attacks if you only attack places which are undefended. You can ensure the safety of your defense if you only hold positions that cannot be attacked.

Seize what is undefended. Occupy what cannot be taken.

VI. 8. Hence that general is skillful in attack whose opponent does not know what to defend; and he is skillful in defense whose opponent does not know what to attack.

Ensure the other knows what is neither valuable nor worthless.[227]

VI. 9. O divine art of subtlety and secrecy! Through you we learn to be invisible, through you inaudible; and hence we can hold the enemy's fate in our hands.

Unknown, you will succeed.

VI. 10. You may advance and be absolutely irresistible, if you make for the enemy's weak points; you may retire and be safe from pursuit if your movements are more rapid than those of the enemy.

Knowing where the other is weak and where he is not, you advance in confidence. Being faster than the other you can withdraw without concern.

VI. 11–12. If we wish to fight, the enemy can be forced to an engagement even though he be sheltered behind a high rampart and a deep ditch. All we need do is attack some other place that he will be obliged to relieve. If we do not wish to fight, we can prevent the enemy from engaging us even though the lines of our encampment be merely traced out on the ground. All we need do is to throw something odd and unaccountable in his way.

Knowing what the other must defend, we can force him into engaging us. Undefended and vulnerable, we can prevent engagement through the use of deception.[228]

---

227 With great insight, Giles said this is "the *Art of War* in a nutshell" (1994, VI.8 notes).
228 Consider the Zen koan tutorial practice: the master shakes the student out of his mental mind-set by doing something completely unexpected, causing confusion and disarray.

VI. 13. By discovering the enemy's dispositions and remaining invisible ourselves, we can keep our forces concentrated, while the enemy's must be divided.

Unobtrusive and cloaked, our observers gather intelligence. We are able to focus on what is important while the other has his resources scattered.

VI. 14. We can form a single united body, while the enemy must split up into fractions. Hence there will be a whole pitted against separate parts of a whole, which means that we shall be many to the enemy's few.[229]

We become more integrated and full of strength while the other becomes less and less.

VI. 15. And if we are able thus to attack an inferior force with a superior one, our opponents will be in dire straits.

We will prevail if we have effectively managed participant strength.

VI. 16. The spot where we intend to fight must not be made known; for then the enemy will have to prepare against a possible attack at several different points; and his forces being thus distributed in many directions, the numbers we shall have to face at any given point will be proportionately few.

Our plans remain secret. The other's strength is reduced and vulnerability increased, because he must prepare for several scenarios.

---

229 Lau and Ames say with a note of regret that "deploying in battle formation" is mentioned "only in passing" in *Ping-fa* (1996, 50).

VI. 17. For should the enemy strengthen his van, he will weaken his rear; should he strengthen his rear, he will weaken his van; should he strengthen his left, he will weaken his right; should he strengthen his right, he will weaken his left. If he sends reinforcements everywhere, he will everywhere be weak.

As there is no plan to counter yours, all his movements are ineffective.

VI. 18. Numerical weakness comes from having to prepare against possible attacks; numerical strength, from compelling our adversary to make these preparations against us.

Strength expended in defense is energy unavailable for offense. Strength lost by the other is strength gained by you.

VI. 19. Knowing the place and the time of the coming battle, we may concentrate from the greatest distances in order to fight.

Because we control the time and place of engagement commencement, we are able to concentrate on strength thoroughly, without interference.

VI. 20. But if neither time nor place be known, then the left wing will be impotent to succor the right, the right equally impotent to succor the left, the van unable to relieve the rear, or the rear to support the van. How much more so if the furthest portions of the army are anything under a hundred LI apart, and even the nearest are separated by several LI![230]

If you are not in control of your own team and the other, then you are unfocused and you will not succeed in strengthening yourself.

VI. 21. Though according to my estimate the soldiers of Yueh exceed our own in number, that shall advantage them nothing in the matter of victory. I say then that victory can be achieved.

Strength and control assure success even when you may be deficient in some areas.

VI. 22. Though the enemy be stronger in numbers, we may prevent him from fighting. Scheme so as to discover his plans and the likelihood of their success.

The other may exceed your strength in some aspects. You must prevent engagement until you assess likely outcomes.

VI. 23. Rouse him, and learn the principle of his activity or inactivity. Force him to reveal himself, so as to find out his vulnerable spots.

Use tactics to cause him to reveal his purposes, plans, and weaknesses.

VI. 24. Carefully compare the opposing army with your own, so that you may know where strength is superabundant and where it is deficient.

---

230   From more recent history: Sherman, "the greatest Union general in the American Civil War," said you have to put the enemy "on the horns of a dilemma, unable to defend two or more points and thus forced to cede at least one in order to save another" (Alexander 1993, 23).

Complete a thorough assessment of relative strengths and weaknesses.

VI. 25. In making tactical dispositions, the highest pitch you can attain is to conceal them; conceal your dispositions, and you will be safe from the prying of the subtlest spies, from the machinations of the wisest brains.

While you study, plan, and deploy, make absolutely sure you give nothing away. Frustrate and confuse the other.

VI. 26. How victory may be produced for them out of the enemy's own tactics—that is what the multitude cannot comprehend.

Engagements are won by what is gained from the other. Those trained in engagement management understand this.

VI. 27. All men can see the tactics whereby I conquer, but what none can see is the strategy out of which victory is evolved.

Team movements may be evident, but the way victory is achieved through the management of strength is not.[231]

VI. 28. Do not repeat the tactics which have gained you one victory, but let your methods be regulated by the infinite variety of circumstances.

---

231   A key line on "engagement management." Teck and Grinyer, seeing only military tactics, say this line means "the purpose of both strategy and tactics is to ensure the positioning, direction, movement, motivation and behavior of the troops will bring victory when they physically engage" (1994, 290).

Never repeat successful tactics. Be guided by conditions.

VI. 29. Military tactics are like unto water; for water in its natural course runs away from high places and hastens downwards.

When something works, claim victory and move on. Don't hang onto it.

VI. 30. So in war, the way is to avoid what is strong and to strike at what is weak.[232]

In engagement, avoid situations where you are less strong, and focus where strength is less than yours.

VI. 31. Water shapes its course according to the nature of the ground over which it flows; the soldier works out his victory in relation to the foe whom he is facing.

Tailor your plans to the problem at hand.

VI. 32. Therefore, just as water retains no constant shape, so in warfare there are no constant conditions.

Engagement conditions are always unique, and management within those conditions must also be unique.

VI. 33. He who can modify his tactics in relation to his opponent and thereby succeed in winning, may be called a heaven-born captain.

You are supremely competent if you are able to adapt to conditions.

---

232 Alexander quotes this line as "the way to avoid what is strong is to strike at what is weak." This is not a typographical error, as he repeats it later (1993, 29, 34).

VI. 34. The five elements (water, fire, wood, metal, earth) are not always equally predominant; the four seasons make way for each other in turn. There are short days and long; the moon has its periods of waning and waxing.

Be guided by the fact that variety and change are constants. But events are also known to follow a pattern.

VII. Engagement Management

VII. 1. Sun Tzu said: In war, the general receives his commands from the sovereign.

Engagements begin when the chief empowers the leader.

VII. 2. Having collected an army and concentrated his forces, he must blend and harmonize the different elements thereof before pitching his camp.

The team members have been assembled, and their strength is building. But before they can move they must be integrated into a coherent whole.

VII. 3. After that, comes tactical maneuvering, than which there is nothing more difficult. The difficulty of tactical maneuvering consists in turning the devious into the direct, and misfortune into gain.

Integrated, the team now learns how to move.

VII. 4. Thus, to take a long and circuitous route, after enticing the enemy out of the way, and though starting after him, to contrive to reach the goal before him, shows knowledge of the artifice of deviation.

Moving with competence means that the team is able to move itself with aplomb but is also able to move the other to a more helpful position.

VII. 5. Maneuvering with an army is advantageous; with an undisciplined multitude, most dangerous.

The strong, trained, and integrated team is able to engage effectively.[233]

VII. 6. If you set a fully equipped army in march in order to snatch an advantage, the chances are that you will be too late. On the other hand, to detach a flying column for the purpose involves the sacrifice of its baggage and stores.

Sometimes the team may have to move before it is fully prepared. In such cases, there could be considerable loss of strength.[234]

VII. 7. Thus, if you order your men to roll up their buff-coats[235] and make forced marches without halting day or night, covering double the usual distance at a stretch, doing a hundred LI in order to wrest an advantage, the leaders of all your three divisions will fall into the hands of the enemy.

If you move before you are ready, make very sure that you do not require more of the team than they are able to give. There could be issues around loyalty.

233　Giles says the commentators think this means "good generalship means good maneuvers." Sawyer incorrecrly reads "undisciplined multitude" as "masses" and misses the point of training and discipline (1993, 169, notes on text 98).

234　Giles says this line is unintelligible and very likely corrupted.

235　Another military take: Griffith and Ames say "armor" instead of "buff-coats" (Griffith 1963, 103; Ames 1993, 129).

VII. 8. The stronger men will be in front, the jaded ones will fall behind, and on this plan only one-tenth of your army will reach its destination.

You can't depend on everyone being in place and operating at full capability.

VII. 9–10. If you march fifty LI in order to outmaneuver the enemy, you will lose the leader of your first division, and only half your force will reach the goal. If you march thirty LI with the same object, two-thirds of your army will arrive.

You need to assess very carefully how much you are prepared to give up to gain the trophy that you seek.

VII. 11. We may take it then that an army without its baggage-train is lost; without provisions it is lost; without bases of supply it is lost.

If you give up too much you jeopardize the enterprise.

VII. 12. We cannot enter into alliances until we are acquainted with the designs of our neighbors.[236]

Collaborative effort is appropriate when methods and goals are harmonious.

VII. 13. We are not fit to lead an army on the march unless we are familiar with the face of the country—its mountains and forests, its pitfalls and precipices, its marshes and swamps.

---

236 Militarist commentator Machell-Cox says this means you can never really trust a neighbor. He quotes Field Marshal Count Schlieffen, who said, in 1909, that you can never be sure that your ally is going to be there when you need him.

Leaders must be full of knowledge about the situation and environment.

VII. 14. We shall be unable to turn natural advantage to account unless we make use of local guides.

Seek out and use the advice of experts.[237]

VII. 15. In war, practice dissimulation, and you will succeed.

You are fully competent, but success depends on the other's ignorance.

VII. 16. Whether to concentrate or to divide your troops, must be decided by circumstances.

Test what you know against what you are seeing.
VII. 17. Let your rapidity be that of the wind, your compactness that of the forest.[238]

The team is adaptive, reacting to conditions as appropriate. It moves as slowly or as quickly as warranted. Its concentration is highly variable.

VII. 18. In raiding and plundering be like fire, is immovability like a mountain.

---

237   Lassere and Probert on "Asia competition" say
that their research data "confirms the critical role that a regional headquarters can play in collecting, analyzing and consolidating competitive information as well as fostering [local visibility]."
238   Sawyer gets it wrong with his "speed like the wind, slowness like the forest, invasion and plundering like a fire, unmoving like the muntains" (1993, 169). He fails to see the contradiction between this rendering and his comments in chapter 6: "Predictability means having form; therefore [repetition] would contradict Ping-fau's principle of being formless" (1993, 168).

Be fluid yet firm.

VII. 19. Let your plans be dark and impenetrable as night, and when you move, fall like a thunderbolt.

Reveal nothing. Move decisively. Move as one and without hesitation.

VII. 20. When you plunder a countryside, let the spoil be divided amongst your men; when you capture new territory, cut it up into allotments for the benefit of the soldiery.

Share success among the team members.

VII. 21. Ponder and deliberate before you make a move.

Never move rashly.

VII. 22. He will conquer who has learnt the artifice of deviation. Such is the art of maneuvering.

Innovation, surprise, and unorthodox tactics work. Acting predictably does not.

VII. 23. The Book of Army Management says: On the field of battle,[239] the spoken word does not carry far enough: hence the institution of gongs and drums. Nor can ordinary objects be seen clearly enough: hence the institution of banners and flags.

In the midst of engagement, use all available methods of communication.

---

239   Giles says in his notes that "on the field of battle" is "implied, but not actually in the Chinese."

VII. 24. Gongs and drums, banners and flags, are means whereby the ears and eyes of the host may be focused on one particular point.

Clear directions demand clear communications.[240]

VII. 25. The host thus forming a single united body, is it impossible either for the brave to advance alone, or for the cowardly to retreat alone. This is the art of handling large masses of men.

With clear direction the team advances in unison.

VII. 26. In night-fighting, then, make much use of signal-fires and drums, and in fighting by day, of flags and banners, as a means of influencing the ears and eyes of your army.

Circumstances dictate what communication forms and devices should be used.

VII. 27. A whole army may be robbed of its spirit; a commander-in-chief may be robbed of his presence of mind.[241]

---

240   Read with VII.25–26. Communications are important. Chuang-tzu said, "Nothing compares to using clarity." *Thunder in the Sky* says, "To work effectively with others, particularly in a supervisor or leadership capacity understand their mentalities so as to be able to predict their patterns of response. Skillful use of language to establish a basis of communication also demands perceptive attention to the effects of specific words and images on each individual and each team in order to evolve a workable attunement of minds and ideas" (Cleary 1993, 80).
There is another important, yet implicit, message. Communications can be used to inform, but they can also be used to confuse.
241   It is not wise to rush about. If too much energy is used, exhaustion follows (*Tao Te Ching*, 55).

Highly effective communications can cement your team and crumble the other.[242]

VII. 28. Now a soldier's spirit is keenest in the morning; by noonday it has begun to flag; and in the evening, his mind is bent only on returning to camp.

Communications must always relate to audience condition.

VII. 29. A clever general, therefore, avoids an army when its spirit is keen, but attacks it when it is sluggish and inclined to return. This is the art of studying moods.

The leader's communications take advantage of audience receptivity.

VII. 30. Disciplined and calm, to await the appearance of disorder and hubbub amongst the enemy—this is the art of retaining self-possession.

Be patient. Watch for evidence of conflict that can be exploited.

VII. 31. To be near the goal while the enemy is still far from it, to wait at ease while the enemy is toiling and struggling, to be well-fed while the enemy is famished— this is the art of husbanding one's strength.

---

242   Chang Yu says you rob the enemy of his "keen spirit" by simply waiting "until their ardor and enthusiasm have worn off." Sawyer comes close to understanding that signs and symbols have a communication and strength-reduction role (1993, 170 note 101). General Li Ching understood these issues very well: "attacking must include the art of assailing the enemy's mental equilibrium" (Giles 1994).

Good teams, good plans, and good execution mean that you remain strong and have a far better chance of realizing your goals.

VII. 32. To refrain from intercepting an enemy whose banners are in perfect order, to refrain from attacking an army drawn up in calm and confident array—this is the art of studying circumstances.

The other team will betray its capability if you pay attention. Govern yourself accordingly.

VII. 33. It is a military axiom not to advance uphill against the enemy, nor to oppose him when he comes downhill.

Do not engage another whose strength is greater than yours. Do not forestall an other in decline.

VII. 34–35. Do not pursue an enemy who simulates flight; do not attack soldiers whose temper is keen. Do not swallow bait offered by the enemy.[243] Do not interfere with an army that is returning home.[244]

There are numerous situations where team movement is not advised.

VII. 36. When you surround an army, leave an outlet free. Do not press a desperate foe too hard.

---

243 "Li Ch'uan and Tu Mu, unable to see the metaphor, say these words refer to food and drink that have been poisoned by the enemy" (Giles 1994; see the footnote on IX.6).

244 Giles says this means " an army set on returning home will fight to the death." The more important message is that it is not only unnecessary but foolish to continue when the other is leaving the engagement.

Always leave the other with a way out. Assess whether the application of pressure is advisable.[245]

VII. 37. Such is the art of warfare.

These are the directions for management within engagement.

VIII. Leadership Competence[246]

VIII. 1. Sun Tzu said: In war, the general receives his commands from the sovereign, collects his army and concentrates his forces

When the leader receives the strategy from his chief, the engagement has begun. He assembles the team and commences strength building.

VIII. 2. When in difficult country, do not encamp. In country where high roads intersect, join hands with your allies. Do not linger in dangerously isolated positions. In hemmed-in situations, you must resort to stratagem. In desperate position, you must fight.

Your principal responsibility is ensure you remain strong and invulnerable. Confront the other if you must.

VIII. 3. There are roads which must not be followed, armies which must be not attacked, towns which must

---

245 Desperate people with nothing to lose may cause a great deal of damage. When another is in difficulty, wise leaders watch and wait. General Tao Hanzhang says this notion is "simply ludicrous" (1987, 92). Clavell misses again by noting that when one leaves an outlet, "this does not mean that the enemy is to be allowed to escape" (1983, 35).
246 Sawyer calls this chapter "Nine Changes" and then complains that there are actually ten (1993, notes on text 113).

not be besieged, positions which must not be contested, commands of the sovereign which must not be obeyed.

Conditions will dictate where you must adjust your operations and plans, and where the engagement strategy must be modified.

VIII. 4. The general who thoroughly understands the advantages that accompany variation of tactics knows how to handle his troops.

Competent leaders know that they must remain open, aware, and flexible.

VIII. 5. The general who does not understand these, may be well acquainted with the configuration of the country, yet he will not be able to turn his knowledge to practical account.

A less competent leader may understand conditions very well, but he must know how to relate action to condition.

VIII. 6. So, the student of war who is unversed in the art of war of varying his plans, even though he be acquainted with the Five Advantages, will fail to make the best use of his men.

Teams perform best when their leader is able to observe, learn, and modify.

VIII. 7. Hence in the wise leader's plans, considerations of advantage and of disadvantage will be blended together.

Changes are based on cost against benefit.

VIII. 8–9. If our expectation of advantage be tempered in this way, we may succeed in accomplishing the essential part of our schemes. If, on the other hand, in the midst of difficulties we are always ready to seize an advantage, we may extricate ourselves from misfortune.

Engagements are conducted in accordance with an approved strategy. Good leaders make changes as engagements proceed when assessment indicates a plan change is warranted. There are, in addition, circumstances where an immediate reaction to unforeseen or emerging events may be essential.

VIII. 10. Reduce the hostile chiefs by inflicting damage on them; and make trouble for them, and keep them constantly engaged; hold out specious allurements, and make them rush to any given point. [247]

Team activities have a defined outcome: to reduce the strength of the other.

VIII. 11. The art of war teaches us to rely not on the likelihood of the enemy's not coming, but on our own readiness to receive him; not on the chance of his not attacking, but rather on the fact that we have made our position unassailable.

Good planning is not based on what you wish for but on what needs to be done. [248]

---

247   Huang says "hostile chiefs" (in Giles's translation) and "enemy" (Ts'ao Ts'ao, Du Mu, and others) are a mistranslation. The term should, in his view, be "other lords," meaning both friends and competitors (1993, 203).
248   Military commentators say this line embraces arming for defense. But "readiness" and "unassailable" refer to strength (qi), not armament.

VIII. 12–13. There are five dangerous faults which may affect a general: (1) Recklessness, which leads to destruction; (2) cowardice, which leads to capture; (3) a hasty temper, which can be provoked by insults; (4) a delicacy of honor which is sensitive to shame[249] *(5) over-solicitude for his men, which exposes him to worry and trouble. These are the five besetting sins of a general, ruinous to the conduct of war.*[250]

Leaders can suffer five serious character deficiencies: (1) acting unwisely, [251] (2) unable or reluctant to act, (3) inability to resist manipulation, (4) narcissism,[252] and (5) unable to give direction. These traits can singly, or in combination, cause an engagement to be lost.

VIII. 14. When an army is overthrown and its leader slain, the cause will surely be found among these five dangerous faults. Let them be a subject of meditation.

When engagements fail, look to these failures of leadership.

IX. Situation Assessment

IX. 1. Sun Tzu said: We come now to the question of encamping the army, and observing signs of the enemy. Pass quickly over mountains, and keep in the neighborhood of valleys.

---

249   Avoidance of, or withdrawal from, engagement is not shameful, but a reasonable and honorable tactic. The admonition is repeated in X.24, "the general who retreats without fearing disgrace."

250   Wautzu says, "Rash encounter, which is ignorant of the consequences, cannot be called good" (Calthrop 1908, 101).

251   This is the danger of "losing it," when the leader recklessly plunges into engagement. See: Ordeal by Fire.

252   Pat Riley, speaking of self-interest (as against team interest), calls it the "Disease of Me" (1993, 41).

The team's first work is situation assessment. Remain invisible.

IX. 2. Camp in high places, facing the sun. Do not climb heights in order to fight. So much for mountain warfare.

Observe. Expend no energy. Do not be confused by the other's obscurity and deceptive tactics.

IX. 3. After crossing a river, you should get far away from it.[253]

If messages are unclear, sort them out. Move when you achieve understanding.

IX. 4. When an invading force crosses a river in its onward march, do not advance to meet it in mid-stream. It will be best to let half the army get across, and then deliver your attack.

Do not engage until you are sure that your own deception has been adequately effective and that the other can perceive your strength.[254]

IX. 5. If you are anxious to fight, you should not go to meet the invader near a river which he has to cross.

---

253   This may also suggest conditions are confused, or there is possible deception by the other. The *Ping-fa* message is: "Gain clarity. Act."
254   Roger Ames says, with profound illogic, "When the invading army crosses water in his advance, do not meet him in the water. It is to your advantage to let him get halfway across and then attack him" (1993, 139).

If there is an urgent need to start the engagement, don't move until you are clear on both the strength and deception factors.[255]

IX. 6. Moor your craft higher up than the enemy, and facing the sun. Do not move up-stream to meet the enemy.[256] So much for river warfare.

Allow a degree of visibility. Move when it is strategically beneficial.

IX. 7–8. In crossing salt-marshes, your sole concern should be to get over them quickly, without any delay. If forced to fight in a salt-marsh, you should have water and grass near you, and get your back to a clump of trees. So much for operations in salt-marches.

When you are denied invisibility, ensure that situation is of short duration. Seek opportunities for obscurity and deception.

IX. 9. In dry, level country, take up an easily accessible position with rising ground to your right and on your rear, so that the danger may be in front, and safety lie behind. So much for campaigning in flat country.

Where neither obscurity nor deception can be had, work to achieve favorable positioning and ease of movement. Make sure you have an escape route.

IX. 10. These are the four useful branches of military knowledge which enabled the Yellow Emperor to vanquish four sovereigns.

---

255 Giles thinks one shouldn't meet the invader, "for fear of preventing his crossing!"
256 Giles says several commentators warn against the enemy throwing poison in the river upstream. The same absurd notion was raised regarding VII.34.

Situation assessment means observing and analyzing in a condition of safety while carefully managing what the other may learn about you.

IX. 11. All armies prefer high ground to low and sunny places to dark.[257]

You need to be quite clear on this point: the other will also be assessing the situation.

IX. 12. If you are careful of your men, and camp on hard ground, the army will be free from disease of every kind, and this will spell victory.[258]

Don't be so involved with external events and analysis that you are blind to what could be happening to your team.[259]

---

257   "Some scholars have interpreted *di* here as 'terrain' which is problematic" (Huang 1993, 205, 125). General Tao Hanzhang says "ground" is "a concept which has the implications of the modern 'topography' and 'military geography'" (1987, 65).

258   This is the strength of *qi*. Huang, quite rightly, says these references concern yin and yang (that is, balancing forces).

259   Huang is uncomfortable with the reference to disease (1993, 208). *Thunder in the Sky* offers this: "Excellent indeed are the words of Confucius: 'Eat enough in winter, and the body is warm; eat enough in summer and the body is cool'. When warmth and coolness are appropriate to the season, then people have no sickness or fever. When people have no sickness or fever, then epidemics do not go around. When epidemics do not go around, all, can live out the years given by Heaven" (Cleary 1993, 156). To be "free from disease" then is more "to be healthy." "Disease of every kind" could refer to mental as well as physical health. *Ping-fa* may mean to ensure that discipline and focus are maintained to prevent the team "wasting away."

IX. 13. When you come to a hill or a bank, occupy the sunny side, with the slope on your right rear. Thus you will at once act for the benefit of your soldiers and utilize the natural advantages of the ground.

Occupy a position where you can watch everything simultaneously.

IX. 14. When, in consequence of heavy rains up-country, a river which you wish to ford is swollen and flecked with foam, you must wait until it subsides.[260]

Sometimes there is too much data and you can't fully assess the situation. Wait.[261]

IX. 15–16. Country in which there are precipitous cliffs with torrents running between, deep natural hollows, confined places, tangled thickets, quagmires and crevasses, should be left with all possible speed and not approached. While we keep away from such places, we should get the enemy to approach them; while we face them, we should let the enemy have them on his rear.[262]

Some situations defy understanding. Don't dwell on them, but cause the other to move so that intelligence is

---

260   Observers of the Tao wait quietly while the mud settles (Feng and English). Tang Zi-Chang (1969, 39) says, "Do not engage the enemy by moving against the current."

261   If there is just too much information to absorb, or if the information is conflicting or not conclusive, you must wait. Judgment is "difficult enough to apply when plans are drafted in an office, far from the sphere of action; the task becomes infinitely harder in the thick of fighting itself, with reports streaming in" (Howard and Paret 1976, 227). Not seeing this as an intelligence issue, Griffith says the line is out of place and is likely part of a commentary that has "worked its way into the text" (1963, 118).

262   Sawyer calls these conditions "Heaven's Well," "Jail," "Net," "Pit," and "Fissure"!

given up. As you know, these are important situations to understand; you must not betray that to the other.

IX. 17. If in the neighborhood of your camp there is any hilly country, ponds surrounded by aquatic grass, hollow basins filled with reeds, or woods with thick undergrowth, they must be carefully routed out and searched; for these are places where men in ambush or insidious spies are likely to be lurking.

Look carefully at ground close to you where the other's team and his observers could be secreted.

IX. 18. When the enemy is close at hand and remains quiet, he is relying on the natural strength of his position.

If the other is near and tranquil, he is both strong and active.

IX. 19–20. When he keeps aloof and tries to provoke a battle, he is anxious for the other side to advance. If his place of encampment is easy of access, he is tendering a bait.

The other will deploy tactics similar to you in order to cause you to move.

IX. 21. Movement amongst the trees of a forest shows that the enemy is advancing. The appearance of a number of screens in the midst of thick grass means that the enemy wants to make us suspicious.

Distinguish between real and feigned appearances.

IX. 22. The rising of birds in their flight is the sign of an ambuscade. Startled beasts indicate that a sudden attack is coming.

Look for evidence not subject to deception.

IX. 23. When there is dust rising in a high column, it is the sign of chariots advancing; when the dust is low, but spread over a wide area, it betokens the approach of infantry. When it branches out in different directions, it shows that parties have been sent to collect firewood. A few clouds of dust moving to and fro signify that the army is encamping.

Be skilled at reading signs.[263]

IX. 24. Humble words and increased preparations are signs that the enemy is about to advance. Violent language and driving forward as if to the attack are signs that he will retreat.

The other may inadvertently give away strategic information.

IX. 25. When the light chariots come out first and take up a position on the wings, it is a sign that the enemy is forming for battle.

Watch how the other positions his team.

IX. 26. Peace proposals unaccompanied by a sworn covenant indicate a plot.

Watch for lures and deceptions.

---

263 A series of illustrations is provided on gathering intelligence unobtrusively. Griffith thinks this line is about the manner of collecting firewood. He asks if "men whispering together" (IX.35) "means disaffection, or men considering desertion" (1963, 119, 122). *Ping-fa* says to see past the obvious, and learn to interpret signs. Seek evidence of possible discontent. If confirmed, exploit the opportunity (with fire).

IX. 27–28. When there is much running about and the soldiers fall into rank, it means that the critical moment has come. When some are seen advancing and some retreating, it is a lure.

Haste and ordered movement indicate the other is preparing to engage. If there is not full involvement, a deception is in progress.

IX. 29–31. When the soldiers stand leaning on their spears, they are faint from want of food. If those who are sent to draw water begin by drinking themselves, the army is suffering from thirst. If the enemy sees an advantage to be gained and makes no effort to secure it, the soldiers are exhausted.

Watch for signs that indicate the other's morale and strength.[264]

IX. 32–36. If birds gather on any spot, it is unoccupied. Clamor by night betokens nervousness. If there is disturbance in the camp, the general's authority is weak. If the banners and flags are shifted about, sedition is afoot. If the officers are angry, it means that the men are weary. When an army feeds its horses with grain and kills its cattle for food, and when the men do not hang their cooking-pots over the camp-fires, showing that

---

264   Read with IX.30–31. *Thunder in the Sky* says, "To establish power and control affairs, first it is imperative to discern sameness and difference: to distinguish right and wrong speech, see expressions of what is inside and what is outside, know the logic of what is and what is not, decide which plans are safe and which dangerous, and determine what is nearby and what is far off" (Cleary 1993, 23). Handel is not impressed: "Although more reliable than spies, such indicators are susceptible to deliberate manipulations by the enemy and should not be trusted without the benefit of extensive collaboration" (1992, 114).

they will not return to their tents, you may know that they are determined to fight to the death. The sight of men whispering together in small knots or speaking in subdued tones points to disaffection amongst the rank and file. Too frequent rewards signify that the enemy is at the end of his resources; too many punishments betray a condition of dire distress.

There are a great many ways that the other's situation and plans can be discerned from a distance.

IX. 37. To begin by bluster, but afterwards to take fright at the enemy's numbers, shows a supreme lack of intelligence.[265]

Only fools act without a thorough situation analysis.

IX. 38. When envoys are sent with compliments in their mouths, it is a sign that the enemy wishes for a truce.

Watch carefully for signs that the other wishes to avoid engagement or disengage.

IX. 39. If the enemy's troops march up angrily and remain facing ours for a long time without either joining battle or taking themselves off again, the situation is one that demands great vigilance and circumspection.[266]

Be equally careful in conditions of stalemate.

IX. 40. If our troops are no more in number than the enemy, that is amply sufficient; it only means that no direct attack can be made. What we can do is simply to concentrate all

---

265   Sawyer, for unknown reasons, thinks this is about commanders and their troops (1993, 175 note 137).
266   This is an expression of strength. Ts'ao (and Giles, I assume) think this means a ruse.

*our available strength, keep a close watch on the enemy,
and obtain reinforcements.*[267]

When strengths are equal, engagement is unlikely.
Remain vigilant. Build your strength.

*IX. 41. He who exercises no forethought but makes light
of his opponents is sure to be captured by them.*

Leaders who, without evidence, dismiss the capability of
others will be defeated.

*IX. 42. If soldiers are punished before they have grown
attached to you, they will not prove submissive; and, unless
submissive, then will be practically useless. If, when the
soldiers have become attached to you, punishments are
not enforced, they will still be useless.*

Team members must be compliant. Achieving compliance
requires careful nurturing and management.

*IX. 43. Therefore soldiers must be treated in the first
instance with humanity, but kept under control by means
of iron discipline. This is a certain road to victory.*[268]

267　Giles finds this obscure and says other commentators
do as well. He feels Li Ch'uan comes closest with: "Only
the side that gets more men will win." When in doubt,
commentators speak of numerical strength. This line means
only "stay put, build your strength!"
268　In serious oversimplification, and in a clear miss of
Moral Law, Min Chen says, "Qi Ji-guang, a general of the
Ming Dynasty, once said 'Although soldiers are not very
smart, they are most easily moved.' Because the majority of
soldiers were peasants, they could be easily motivated by a
little care from their generals" (*Business Horizons*, Mar/Apr
1994, Vol. 37, Issue 2).

Care and control ensure team effectiveness.[269]

IX. 44. If in training soldiers commands are habitually enforced, the army will be well-disciplined; if not, its discipline will be bad.

Discipline is maintained through consistent enforcement.

IX. 45. If a general shows confidence in his men but always insists on his orders being obeyed, the gain will be mutual.

When leaders empower and direct, everyone benefits.

X. Parties in Engagement

X .1 – X.12 Sun Tzu said: We may distinguish six kinds of terrain.[270]

There are six engagement conditions.

269　Read in the context of the other admonitions on benevolence (I.8; II.8; II.13, 14; II.17; XIII.16).
Not everyone agrees that good generals are also "old softies." Says *Sun Tzu: War and Management,* "Having a human orientation must not be equated with adopting a welfare-oriented approach to management—giving in to every request and demand by the employees" (162). And the Machiavelli perspective in managing people is that "clemency is a commodity that should be administered in small doses" (McAlpine 1998, 95). Cleary has a very different, troublesome translation: "Direct them through cultural arts, unify them through martial arts" (1988, 141).
270　Huang says, "No definition has been given (in this section) for *di* (zone; terrain). As this is contrary to Sun Wu's style of writing, his explanatory passage must have been mislaid somewhere" (1993, 201). "Terrain" is almost always read by commentators as "ground." But the issue here is form and function, not landscape.

(1) Accessible ground. Ground which can be freely traversed by both sides is called accessible. With regard to ground of this nature, be before the enemy in occupying the raised and sunny spots, and carefully guard your line of supplies. Then you will be able to fight with advantage.[271]

Conditions of profit.[272] Choose the most favorable position, and commence the engagement. Your chances of winning are good if you maintain your strength.

(2) Entangling ground. Ground which can be abandoned but is hard to reoccupy is called entangling. From a position of this sort, if the enemy is unprepared, you may sally forth and defeat him. But if the enemy is prepared for your coming, and you fail to defeat him, then, return being impossible, disaster will ensue.

Win–lose conditions. Winning may be straightforward if the other is unprepared for you. But if the other is prepared and you engage and fail, the consequences to the organization could be serious, as you may not be able to recover.

(3) Temporizing ground. When the position is such that neither side will gain by making the first move, it is called temporizing ground. In a position of this sort, even though the enemy should offer us an attractive bait, it will be advisable not to stir forth, but rather to retreat, thus enticing the enemy in his turn; then, when part of

---

271   Giles finds *Ping-fa* woefully deficient here for, unlike Napoleon, missing the critical importance of "communications." Giles failed to discover the instructions on communications in VII.24 and elsewhere.

272   There is no serious disagreement or retrenchment.

his army has come out, we may deliver our attack with advantage.[273]

Stall conditions. Cause the other to initiate before he is ready by withdrawal. Then engage.

(4) Narrow passes. With regard to narrow passes, if you can occupy them first, let them be strongly garrisoned and await the advent of the enemy. Should the army forestall you in occupying a pass, do not go after him if the pass is fully garrisoned, but only if it is weakly garrisoned.

Tactical advantage. Protect this key position well. If held by the other, seek to take it only if it is not well protected.

(5) Precipitous heights. With regard to precipitous heights, if you are beforehand with your adversary, you should occupy the raised and sunny spots, and there wait for him to come up. If the enemy has occupied them before you, do not follow him, but retreat and try to entice him away.

Strategic gain.[274] Broadcast your success and prepare for challenge. If the other acquires such trophies before you, feign disinterest. Lure him away.

---

273 Sawyer says this is a "stalemate." Other commentators consider it a lengthy standoff (1993, 176 note 143).

274 Commentators and translators disagree about the "sunny" and "dark" spots ("yin" and "yang" in the Chinese text). This could well be a Taoist injunction, but the tactile commentators see this as geography. Griffith is one of them: "in the context of Sun Tzu [yin and yang] have no cosmic connotations" (1963, 125).

(6) Positions at a great distance from the enemy. If you are situated at a great distance from the enemy,[275] and the strength of the two armies is equal, it is not easy to provoke a battle, and fighting will be to your disadvantage.

Engagements of disadvantage.[276] There is no evident room for compromise, strengths are equal, and the other cannot be lured into initiation. Do not engage.

X. 13. These six are the principles connected with Earth. The general who has attained a responsible post must be careful to study them.

These are the principal engagement conditions and how they are to be handled. Give this careful study.

X. 14. Now an army is exposed to six several calamities, not arising from natural causes, but from faults for which the general is responsible. These are: (1) Flight; (2) insubordination; (3) collapse; (4) ruin; (5) disorganization; (6) rout.

There are six failures of leaders.

X. 15. Other conditions being equal, if one force is hurled against another ten times its size, the result will be the flight of the former.

Confronting an evidently superior adversary.

X. 16. When the common soldiers are too strong and their officers too weak, the result is insubordination. When the

---

275   Why is there no seventh format: *positions near the enemy?* It is because 1 through 5 involve being "near the enemy"—that is, in engagement. Format 6 engagements are to be avoided.
276   Giles says this means you should not make a long march to meet the enemy.

officers are too strong and the common soldiers too weak, the result is collapse.

Failure to effectively manage team strength. [277]

X. 17. When the higher officers are angry and insubordinate, and on meeting the enemy give battle on their own account from a feeling of resentment, before the commander-in-chief can tell whether or no he is in a position to fight, the result is ruin.

Failure to maintain control.

X. 18. When the general is weak and without authority; when his orders are not clear and distinct; when there are no fixed duties assigned to officers and men, and the ranks are formed in a slovenly haphazard manner, the result is utter disorganization.

There is no leadership, communications are faulty, work is not properly assigned, and discipline is weak or nonexistent.

X. 19. When a general, unable to estimate the enemy's strength, allows an inferior force to engage a larger one, or hurls a weak detachment against a powerful one, and neglects to place picked soldiers in the front rank, the result must be rout.[278]

---

277   This line makes no sense if one assumes the discussion is about power and authority. The only reasonable explanation is to be found in the "strength" of "*qi.*"

278   An important line. To understand the *Ping-fa* instruction, recognize the subject and object in the sentence. The message is: if you don't use intelligence (picked soldiers), you fail.

Failure to use intelligence effectively to conduct assessments and modify strategies as needed. [279]

X. 20. These are six ways of courting defeat, which must be carefully noted by the general who has attained a responsible post.

Leaders, when appointed, need to pay attention to how one can lose.

X. 21–22. The natural formation of the country is the soldier's best ally; but a power of estimating the adversary, of controlling the forces of victory, and of shrewdly calculating difficulties, dangers and distances, constitutes the test of a great general. He who knows these things, and in fighting puts his knowledge into practice, will win his battles. He who knows them not, nor practices them, will surely be defeated.

Team members benefit from what they know of people and events; however, they need the leader's abilities in assessment and leadership to win.

X. 23. If fighting is sure to result in victory, then you must fight, even though the ruler forbid it; if fighting will

---

279 Commentators read this line (along with VII.8) as "put your best [strongest, best-armed] people out in front." Cleary likes to speak of "elite fighters" and "crack troops." Chang Yu speaks of "keenest spirits." Griffith calls these people "select shock troops." Ames and Wang Xuanming says they are a "vanguard of crack troops." If one is "unable to estimate" or with an "inferior force" or "weak detachment," *Ping-fa* says you are bound to be defeated. Why then would a leader put his "picked soldiers in the front rank"? The message here is about, inter alia, the failure to use intelligence gatherers. Giles recognizes the point in chapter XIII. There he references Cromwell's "scout masters," who were spies that contributed to his victories. See Cleary's dissertation on this issue (1989, 78–79).

not result in victory, then you must not fight even at the ruler's bidding.

Your decision to engage must be driven by assessing the chances of success, not by the instructions in the strategy.[280]

X. 24. The general who advances without coveting fame and retreats without fearing disgrace, whose only thought is to protect his country and do good service for his sovereign, is the jewel of the kingdom.

Leaders whose focus is on the organization and the engagement and not on themselves are to be treasured.

X. 25. Regard your soldiers as your children, and they will follow you into the deepest valleys; look upon them as your own beloved sons, and they will stand by you even unto death.

Leaders should be as benevolent with their team as they are with others in engagement.

X. 26. If, however, you are indulgent, but unable to make your authority felt; kindhearted, but unable to enforce your commands; and incapable, moreover, of quelling disorder: then your soldiers must be likened to spoilt children; they are useless for any practical purpose.

---

280   Here we must be very careful. "Victory" is not in the eyes of the beholder. It is in the context of *Ping-fa's* benevolence. This is not victory over another. It is victory with another.

That does not mean leaders should spoil members of their team to the point where control and effectiveness are lost.[281]

X. 27–28. If we know that our own men are in a condition to attack, but are unaware that the enemy is not open to attack, we have gone only halfway towards victory. If we know that the enemy is open to attack, but are unaware that our own men are not in a condition to attack, we have gone only halfway towards victory.

The leader knows the condition of all participants.

X. 29. If we know that the enemy is open to attack, and also know that our men are in a condition to attack, but are unaware that the nature of the ground makes fighting impracticable, we have still gone only halfway towards victory.

The leader also knows when an engagement is one of disadvantage.

X. 30. Hence the experienced soldier, once in motion, is never bewildered; once he has broken camp, he is never at a loss.

Competent leaders begin engagements fully aware and remain confident throughout.

X. 31. Hence the saying: If you know the enemy and know yourself, your victory will not stand in doubt; if you know Heaven and know Earth, you may make your victory complete.

---

281 Every soldier who has gone through basic training, and every member who has gone through effective team building, understands this distinction.

They know they are going to win because they have full knowledge of all the players and are fully competent in engagement management.

XI. Dynamics

XI. 1–14. Sun Tzu said: The art of war recognizes nine varieties of ground: [282]

Engagements are about gaining, holding, and losing "ground." There are nine types, and they demand specific actions:

(1) Dispersive ground. When a chieftain is fighting in his own territory. Fight not.

Do not engage another for whom concession is an impossibility. [283]

(2) Facile ground. When he has penetrated into hostile territory, but to no great distance. Halt not.

When an engagement is entered into, do not rest until significant gains have been made.

(3) Contentious ground. Ground, the possession of which imports great advantage to either side. Attack not.

---

282   The commentary insists that ground is "battleground" or "terrain." But this is not about land. Ground is whatever you wish to gain or retain in an engagement. This might be a good, power, or any other benefit. "Turf" approximates "ground." Huang speaks of *qing,* which has meaning both in "zone" and "power" (1993, 221). Griffith's trouble with this chapter is understandable, given his understanding of "terrain" and "ground" (1963, 130, 133).
283   Calthrop thought dispersive ground was a battleground too close to the soldier's homes (1908, 58).

Do not betray interest in areas of great importance to you.

(4) Open ground. Ground on which each side has liberty of movement. Do not try to block the enemy's way.

If an element is of minor importance, do not forestall its acquisition by the other.

(5) Ground of intersecting highways. Ground which forms the key to three contiguous states, so that he who occupies it first has most of the empire at his command. Join hands with your allies.

Deploy all available resources on those targets that are gateways to success.[284]

(6) Serious ground. When an army has penetrated into the heart of a hostile country, leaving a number of fortified cities in its rear. Gather in plunder.

If significant advances have been made but all opposition has not been eliminated as the campaign proceeded, strength enhancement is in order.

(7) Difficult ground. Mountain forests, rugged steeps, marshes and fens—all country that is hard to traverse. Keep steadily on the march.

Keep moving in areas of complexity and potential high vulnerability.

---

284   General Tao Hanzhang speaks of "focal ground" ("intersecting highways"). The sovereign of Wu asks Sun Tzu what he should do, as he cannot reach the focal ground first, "even if we drive our horses and chariots as fast as possible." The reply? "The distance is the same to us and to the enemy." This answer is completely illogical if discussing physical reality (1987, 67).

(8) Hemmed-in ground. Ground which is reached through narrow gorges, and from which we can only retire by tortuous paths, so that a small number of the enemy would suffice to crush a large body of our men. Resort to stratagem.

Use a variety of techniques to achieve objectives that are of very high risk. Keep your own exposure to the minimum.

(9) Desperate ground. Ground on which we can only be saved from destruction by fighting without delay. Fight.

If you have no option but to engage, engage immediately.[285]

XI. 15–17. Those who were called skillful leaders of old knew how to drive a wedge between the enemy's front and rear; to prevent cooperation between his large and small divisions; to hinder the good troops from rescuing the bad, the officers from rallying their men. When the enemy's men were united, they managed to keep them in disorder. When it was to their advantage, they made a forward move; when otherwise, they stopped still.

The competent leader manages his team and that of the other. He moves only when he has a reason to do so.

XI. 18. If asked how to cope with a great host of the enemy in orderly array and on the point of marching to the

---

285 Huang translates this line as "where fierce combat leads to survival, but lack of fierce combat leads to destruction is lethal." But then he tells us "combat" is not in the Linyi text, having been "erroneously dropped," and the expression should really be "fierceness" (1993, 224). This line then means "issues which can only be resolved through engagement are desperate ones."

attack, I should say: "Begin by seizing something which your opponent holds dear; then he will be amenable to your will."

If threat is imminent, seize ground of great importance to the other.

XI. 19. Rapidity is the essence of war: take advantage of the enemy's unreadiness, make your way by unexpected routes, and attack unguarded spots.

Your observers have briefed you completely. You know what you can achieve and how by a rapid advance.[286]

XI. 20. The following are the principles to be observed by an invading force: The further you penetrate into a country, the greater will be the solidarity of your troops, and thus the defenders will not prevail against you.

The more ground you gain, the stronger you get, the harder it is to defeat you.

XI. 21. Make forays in fertile country in order to supply your army with food.

Ensure the team has opportunities for strength building and maintenance.

XI. 22. Carefully study the well-being of your men, and do not overtax them. Concentrate your energy and hoard

---

286   Read with XI.65. Speed *is* essential when an opportunity presents itself. Chapter XI is on leadership. Though *Ping-fa* warns again and again that acting abruptly is hazardous, it commands that when you are fully aware, pounce!

your strength. Keep your army continually on the move, and devise unfathomable plans.[287]

Stay mobile and in complete control. Build strength. Do not waste it. Ensure your plans remain undetectable and meaningless to others.

XI. 23. Throw your soldiers into positions whence there is no escape, and they will prefer death to flight. If they will face death, there is nothing they may not achieve. Officers and men alike will put forth their uttermost strength.

When you need all that the team can give, dramatically reduce their options.[288]

XI. 24. Soldiers when in desperate straits lose the sense of fear. If there is no place of refuge, they will stand firm. If they are in hostile country, they will show a stubborn front. If there is no help for it, they will fight hard.

Reducing choices can cause strength to focus.

XI. 25. Thus, without waiting to be marshaled, the soldiers will be constantly on the qui vive; without waiting to be

---

287   Giles offers two equally incorrect interpretations here. He says you keep moving to avoid detection and/or link your army together.

288   Read with XI.40, XI.50, and XI.58–59. "According to Sun Tzu, a military leader skilled in the art of command must be able to create a situation in which he leaves his own troops no choice but to stand and fight, or die" (Handel 1992, 81). *Ping-fa* says sometimes the team must believe achieving the objective is of greater importance than their own well-being.

The seriousness which these lines convey can only reflect: (1) the great importance of engagements and (2) the fact that people perform better under pressure.

asked, they will do your will; without restrictions, they will be faithful; without giving orders, they can be trusted.[289]

The team will show initiative and be energetic, trustworthy, and obedient.

XI. 26. Prohibit the taking of omens, and do away with superstitious doubts. Then, until death itself comes, no calamity need be feared.

Successful engagements rely on facts and discourage supposition.[290]

XI. 27. If our soldiers are not overburdened with money, it is not because they have a distaste for riches; if their lives are not unduly long, it is not because they are disinclined to longevity.[291]

---

289 "The leader who controls others through fear will find that the control is reactive and temporary. It is gone when the leader is gone" (Covey 1991, 103). Effective teams work well even in the absence of the leader.

290 Teams should be governed by the facts and their training, rather than seeking guidance from spirits. "It is the pride of our natural culture that Sun Tzu was an atheist even more than two thousand years ago" (Hanzhang 1987, 77). Machiavelli says you will fare better with force than prayers. Huang is quite wrong here when he says, *"Xiang* is a belief in good or bad luck. Superstition and *yi* [apprehension] here are both manifestations of the soldier's emotional instability" (Huang 1993, 227).

291 Chang Yu and Giles think this line has to do with choice and temptation. Rather, this is as Peters and Waterman had it: "We desperately need meaning in our lives and will sacrifice a great deal to institutions that will provide meaning for us" (1982, 56). With a strictly militarist view, O'Connell says, "Going to war, because of the distinct possibility of personal annihilation, constitutes perhaps the most 'altruistic' of social gestures" (1995, 6).

Team motivation emerges from less evident factors.[292]

XI. 28. On the day they are ordered out to battle, your soldiers may weep, those sitting up bedewing their garments, and those lying down letting the tears run down their cheeks. But let them once be brought to bay, and they will display the courage of a Chu or a Kuei.[293]

All teams suffer from inertia and trepidation; however, once the engagement has begun, they are driven to succeed.

XI. 29. The skillful tactician may be likened to the shuai-jan. Now the shuai-jan is a snake that is found in the ChUng mountains. Strike at its head, and you will be attacked by its tail; strike at its tail, and you will be attacked by its head; strike at its middle, and you will be attacked by head and tail both.[294]

The leader builds his team so that it is fluid and mobile. Strength is infused throughout, and the team responds as circumstances require.[295]

---

292   *Thunder in the Sky* says, "People may be drawn to organizations by prospects of success and reward, or they may be drawn by a sense of affinity of aims and ideals, or they may be drawn by admiration and faith. It is essential to understand the nature of the attraction in order to understand the character of those attracted" (Cleary 1993, 80).
293   Here the commentators see only war and potential death. Giles says the men are expressing "genuine grief." Clavell says the tears do not mean the soldiers are afraid, but that "they have all embraced the firm resolution to do or die" (1983, 62).
294   "Therefore the stiff and unbending is the disciple of death. The gentle and yielding is the disciple of life" (*Tao Te Ching*, 76).
295   This direction is repeated in V.16: *your array may be without head or tail, yet it will be proof against defeat.*

XI. 30. Asked if an army can be made to imitate the shuai-jan, I should answer, Yes. For the men of Wu and the men of Yueh are enemies; yet if they are crossing a river in the same boat and are caught by a storm, they will come to each other's assistance just as the left hand helps the right.

These teams are adaptive and able to exercise judgment.[296]

XI. 31. Hence it is not enough to put one's trust in the tethering of horses, and the burying of chariot wheels in the ground

Effectiveness is not assured by adhering to what has been prov en and seen before.[297]

---

296   *In Search of Excellence* says, "The true power of the small group lies in its flexibility" (Peters and Waterman 1982, 127). There are other messages:

(a) Benevolence is important. *Thunder in the Sky* says, "The course from the center means helping those in distress and attending to emergencies. Intelligent and benevolent people are needed to carry this out. Those who are rescued and given support in distress never forget the favor" (Cleary 1993, 71). Wee *et al.* do not agree. War draining the national economy could be a problem if it "distracts" the general. "If he is distracted by human sufferings and becomes indecisive in taking military actions, the war may be prolonged and the sufferings will continue even longer."

(b) Circumstances change. Today's enemy is tomorrow's ally. But Sawyer thinks the story has to do with "casting people onto fatal terrain" (1996, 110). Giles says this means different parts of an army should work together.

(c) Taoists may see this as a demonstration of the Way in practice (Cleary 1992, 63).

297   Huang is very close here: "concentrating on steadfastly digging in is not as suitable as flexible techniques" (1993, 229).

XI. 32. The principle on which to manage an army is to set up one standard of courage which all must reach.

Nevertheless teams require firm values, objectives, and guidance.

XI. 33. How to make the best of both strong and weak— that is a question involving the proper use of ground.

Leaders must instinctively understand where people are flexible and where they are immobile, what they might be prepared to give up and what they will die to retain.

XI. 34. Thus the skillful general conducts his army just as though he were leading a single man, willy-nilly, by the hand.

One can transpose and apply what one knows of individuals to an entire group.

XI. 35. It is the business of a general to be quiet and thus ensure secrecy; upright and just, and thus maintain order.

Leaders should limit their communications to matters of order and value, and refrain from conveying details of engagement.

XI. 36. He must be able to mystify his officers and men by false reports and appearances, and thus keep them in total ignorance.

Only the leader has the complete picture. There is, then, less chance for internal conflict or inadvertent betrayal.[298]

---

298   Read with XI.57.

XI. 37. By altering his arrangements and changing his plans, he keeps the enemy without definite knowledge. By shifting his camp and taking circuitous routes, he prevents the enemy from anticipating his purpose.

His plans, evident to nobody, ensure he is able to move freely and without opposition.

XI. 38. At the critical moment, the leader of an army acts like one who has climbed up a height and then kicks away the ladder behind him. He carries his men deep into hostile territory before he shows his hand.

When he is ready, he has the team advance to its objective with strength and determination. Moving rapidly, he is well into the engagement before the other is clear that it is under way.

XI. 39. He burns his boats and breaks his cooking-pots; like a shepherd driving a flock of sheep, he drives his men this way and that, and nothing knows whither he is going.

Despite his powerful movements, the objective is not apparent.

XI. 40. To muster his host and bring it into danger—this may be termed the business of the general.[299]

The leader's task is ensuring rapid commencement and significant gain in engagement.

XI. 41. The different measures suited to the nine varieties of ground; the expediency of aggressive or defensive tactics; and the fundamental laws of human nature: these are things that must most certainly be studied.

---

299 Giles says this means when you mobilize you should not delay in "aiming a blow at the enemy's heart."

Leaders must know what individuals and groups believe and how they think. They need to know what motivates them and what restrains them. They need to know what people will do in certain circumstances and how those circumstances can be managed to ensure activity occurs in a certain way.

XI. 42. When invading hostile territory, the general principle is, that penetrating deeply brings cohesion; penetrating but a short way means dispersion.

Teams fully engaged are more integrated than those wobbling at the fringes.

XI. 43. When you leave your own country behind, and take your army across neighborhood territory, you find yourself on critical ground. When there are means of communication on all four sides, the ground is one of intersecting highways.[300]

The nature of events is far different when the team is in engagement than when it is not. Influences will multiply and reach their peak when the team is in areas of supreme importance.

XI. 44. When you penetrate deeply into a country, it is serious ground. When you penetrate but a little way, it is facile ground.

These influences grow as you move further into the engagement.

---

300   These instructions are clearly misplaced and should adjoin XI. 1–14, which sets out the types of ground. They are, however configured in a much different form. These variations suggest that editing occurred following Ping-fa's original publication.

XI. 45. When you have the enemy's strongholds on your rear, and narrow passes in front, it is hemmed-in ground. When there is no place of refuge at all, it is desperate ground.

Conditions and activity need to continuously relate.

XI. 46–50. Therefore, on dispersive ground, I would inspire my men with unity of purpose.[301] On facile ground, I would see that there is close connection between all parts of my army. On contentious ground, I would hurry up my rear. On open ground, I would keep a vigilant eye on my defenses. On ground of intersecting highways, I would consolidate my alliances. On serious ground, I would try to ensure a continuous stream of supplies. On difficult ground, I would keep pushing on along the road. On hemmed-in ground, I would block any way of retreat. On desperate ground, I would proclaim to my soldiers the hopelessness of saving their lives.

The leader's style and tactics must be appropriate to the situation at hand.

XI. 51. For it is the soldier's disposition to offer an obstinate resistance when surrounded, to fight hard when he cannot help himself, and to obey promptly when he has fallen into danger.

The leader who best knows his team and what moves them is best able to manage them in engagement.

XI. 52. We cannot enter into alliance with neighboring princes until we are acquainted with their designs. We are not fit to lead an army on the march unless we are familiar

---

301   When the team is subjected to strength reduction, the leader must build focus on values and objectives. Tu Mu says this line means go on the defensive and avoid battle (Giles).

with the face of the country—its mountains and forests, its pitfalls and precipices, its marshes and swamps. We shall be unable to turn natural advantages to account unless we make use of local guides.

A good leader knows his people, but he must also know the environment within which the team is functioning. He knows his people from what he has learned and experienced himself; knowledge of the environment he must gain from observers.

XI. 53. To be ignorant of any one of the following four or five principles does not befit a warlike prince.

Excellence in leadership is evident in the way certain contextual situations are handled.

XI. 54. When a warlike prince attacks a powerful state, his generalship shows itself in preventing the concentration of the enemy's forces. He overawes his opponents, and their allies are prevented from joining against him.

Team leadership and power are evident. They are able to influence the other's abilities and the other's capability to gather additional support.

XI. 55. Hence he does not strive to ally himself with all and sundry, nor does he foster the power of other states. He carries out his own secret designs, keeping his antagonists in awe. Thus he is able to capture their cities and overthrow their kingdoms.[302]

Such teams are selective in who they align with, empowering nobody. They move mysteriously and with ease. They are awesome.[303]

---

302 Ames says this means "you can take his walled cities and lay waste to his state" (1993, 161).
303 XI.54–55 is clearly the biography of Qin Shih Huangdi.

XI. 56. Bestow rewards without regard to rule, issue orders without regard to previous arrangements; and you will be able to handle a whole army as though you had to do with but a single man.[304]

Competent leaders, not bound by convention, are successful in people management.

XI. 57. Confront your soldiers with the deed itself; never let them know your design. When the outlook is bright, bring it before their eyes; but tell them nothing when the situation is gloomy.

There are things that the team needs to know and things they should not know.

XI. 58–59. Place your army in deadly peril, and it will survive; plunge it into desperate straits, and it will come off in safety. For it is precisely when a force has fallen into harm's way that is capable of striking a blow for victory.

Team management involves both direct and indirect factors.

XI. 60–62. Success in warfare is gained by carefully accommodating ourselves to the enemy's purpose. By persistently hanging on the enemy's flank, we shall succeed in the long run in killing the commander-in-chief. This is called ability to accomplish a thing by sheer cunning.

---

304   Here we have another misplaced section. XI.56–59 should follow XI.35, as it is concerned with the team itself, not the team in its environment.

Know the other and what motivates him. Establish a tight link with those characteristics. Eventually you will overcome resistance.[305]

XI. 63. On the day that you take up your command, block the frontier passes, destroy the official tallies, and stop the passage of all emissaries.[306]

Leaders ensure control of logistics, procedures, and communications.[307]

XI. 64. Be stern in the council-chamber, so that you may control the situation.

Leaders manage the decision-making process.

---

305   Read with XII.61. Sheer cunning is engagement management. It happens at a distance, both literally and figuratively. "Killing the commander-in-chief" is equivalent to "killing the king" in chess. Huang says "killing" should read "trouncing" (1993, 237, 238). Ts'ao Ts'ao defined *sha* as "even over a thousand miles one is able to qin [capture] their commanders."

306   This starts an interesting series of admonitions that speak more to governance than engagement management. Did *Ping-fa* provide then for instructions on how to consolidate victories while instituting good government?

307   Among other things, the leader must instill vision in the team without delay. McNeil says, "What great leaders have shared has been a carefully articulated set of core values that attracted followers and a clear sense of where they wanted to go. They signaled their vision and values with action and visibility. Visionary leaders do this sort of thing on Day One. And they keep it up. In winning organizations, values and vision do not change from day to day" (1987, 43, 54). Giles, in great error, says this line means cease communications with the enemy. Machell-Cox, making only a slightly less grievous error, says he favors the perspective of Ts'ao Ts'ao that the actions follow the plans having being "fixed."

XI. 65. If the enemy leaves a door open, you must rush in.

The environment must be continually scanned. When opportunities appear, they should be seized.

XI. 66. Forestall your opponent by seizing what he holds dear, and subtly contrive to time his arrival on the ground.

Use clever devices to manage the commencement of engagement.

XI. 67. Walk in the path defined by rule, and accommodate yourself to the enemy until you can fight a decisive battle.[308]

Be pliant and compliant until your strength and position can ensure victory.

XI. 68. At first, then, exhibit the coyness of a maiden, until the enemy gives you an opening; afterwards emulate the rapidity of a running hare, and it will be too late for the enemy to oppose you.

---

308   Giles and Chia Lin say this means you should act conventionally. Tu Mu is fine with his "conform to the enemy's tactics." But we get more help from the *Yuan Dao: Tracing Dao to its Source*, which speaks of "The Efficacy of Accommodation." Through "genuineness of purpose and acting through the heart-and-mind, [one] is able to shape the values and customs of the world to a degree that far exceeds the power of laws and punishments" (Lau and Ames 1998, 54). There is an admonition for ethical behavior here. "Walking the path defined by rule" is Stephen Covey discussing the importance of principles. "They are the laws of the universe that pertain to human relationships and human organizations. They are part of the human condition, consciousness and conscience" (1991, 18).

When your path is clear, pounce. The kingdom is yours.

XII. Reducing Strength[309]

XII. 1. Sun Tzu said: There are five ways of attacking with fire. The first is to burn soldiers in their camp; the second is to burn stores; the third is to burn baggage trains; the fourth is to burn arsenals and magazines; the fifth is to hurl dropping fire amongst the enemy.

Winning an engagement demands that the strength of the other be reduced. There are a number of direct and indirect ways this can be done.[310]

XII. 2. In order to carry out an attack, we must have means available. The material for raising fire should always be kept in readiness.

Always have a suite of tools and techniques at hand to instigate strength reduction.

XII. 3. There is a proper season for making attacks with fire, and special days for starting a conflagration.

Know when strength reduction can be initiated, and know when it will be highly successful.

XII. 4. The proper season is when the weather is very dry; the special days are those when the moon is in the

---

309   Military commentators are not sure what chapter XII means or what to do with it. *Sun Tzu: War and Management* ignores it altogether.
310   Ts'ao Ts'ao attempted, unsuccessfully, to add clarity to this line by saying it means "conform to fire in attacking the enemy" (Huang 1993, 241).

constellations of the Sieve, the Wall, the Wing or the Cross-bar; for these four are all days of rising wind.[311]

Strength reduction works when the subjects are receptive to it; it works best when it is able to regenerate and spread itself.

XII. 5–10. In attacking with fire, one should be prepared to meet five possible developments: (1) When fire breaks out inside the enemy's camp, respond at once with an attack from without. (2) If there is an outbreak of fire, but the enemy's soldiers remain quiet, bide your time and do not attack. (3) When the force of the flames has reached its height, follow it up with an attack, if that is practicable; if not, stay where you are. (4) If it is possible to make an assault with fire from without, do not wait for it to break out within, but deliver your attack at a favorable moment. (5) When you start a fire, be to windward of it. Do not attack from the leeward.

(1) If the other's strength is already reducing, fuel it at once externally. (2) Be wary of deception. (3) Commence the engagement if you are ready when reduction initiatives are at their most influential; otherwise, don't move. (4) If conditions are favorable for an external initiative, do not wait for strength reduction to begin spontaneously. (5) Make certain your initiatives do not adversely affect your own team.

---

311   XII.4–10 should have tested the credulity of those who refuse to see war as metaphor in *Ping-fa*. Giles and other commentators dwell on the seasons of rising wind. None have yet questioned the sheer inanity of an instruction to be sure you don't get burned in your own fire.

XII. 11. A wind that rises in the daytime lasts long, but a night breeze soon falls.[312]

Strength reduction initiatives should begin early in the day.

XII. 12. In every army, the five developments connected with fire must be known, the movements of the stars calculated, and a watch kept for the proper days.

Every team needs to be alert to the techniques of strength reduction and the conditions under which they will prove successful.

XII. 13. Hence those who use fire as an aid to the attack show intelligence; those who use water as an aid to the attack gain an accession of strength.[313]

Skilled leaders reduce the strength of the other and build their own.

XII. 14. By means of water, an enemy may be intercepted, but not robbed of all his belongings.

A strong team may challenge, but winning requires that the other be weak.[314]

XII. 15. Unhappy is the fate of one who tries to win his battles and succeed in his attacks without cultivating

---

312   The tactician Mei Yaochen, who lived five hundred years after *Ping-fa* emerged, explained, "A daytime wind will stop at night, a night wind will stop at daylight."
313   Might the Chinese character from antiquity for "show" also have suggested "use"?
314   Giles says, "Water can do useful service but it lacks the terrible destructive power of fire."

the spirit of enterprise; for the result is waste of time and general stagnation.[315]

Manage strength in the engagement. To do otherwise is ineffective.

XII. 16. Hence the saying: The enlightened ruler lays his plans well ahead; the good general cultivates his resources.[316]

Engagement management is about good strategies and effective strength management. The first is the role of the chief, the latter the task of the leader.

XII. 17. Move not unless you see an advantage; use not your troops unless there is something to be gained; fight not unless the position is critical.

Engage only when you must or when an opportunity is presented. Seek only objectives of value.[317]

---

315   Giles calls this "one of the most perplexing passages in Sun Tzu." He favors Mei Yao-ch'en's interpretation: strike while the iron is hot. Machell-Cox calls on Napoleon's tactics and condemns those of Japan and Russia, saying this instruction is to finish the job at once after an initial victory against an enemy. But here *Ping-fa* simply summarizes the admonitions on strength management.
316   "The only way we can reap the harvest in the fall is to plant in the spring and to water, weed, cultivate and fertilize during the long summer" (Covey 1991, 164).
317   Giles says, "Sun Tzu may at times appear to be over-cautious." Griffith and I see this line similarly. "If not in the interests of the state, do not act. If you cannot succeed, do not use troops. If you are not in danger, do not fight." Unfortunately, he was moved to add as a footnote, "The commentators make it clear that war is to be used only as a last resort" (1963, 142).

XII. 18–19. No ruler should put troops into the field merely to gratify his own spleen; no general should fight a battle simply out of pique. [318] *If it is to your advantage, make a forward move; if not, stay where you are.*

Unless you have a very good (common and beneficial) reason for entering into an engagement, don't.

XII. 20. Anger may in time change to gladness; vexation may be succeeded by content.

Engagements are not intended to address issues of the moment, but those of consequence and the long term.

XII. 21. But a kingdom that has once been destroyed can never come again into being; nor can the dead ever be brought back to life. [319]

Precipitous acts can have serious, irreversible consequences.

XII. 22. Hence the enlightened ruler is heedful, and the good general full of caution. This is the way to keep a country at peace and an army intact. [320]

---

318 "People who have a marked tendency to emotionalize or personalize every issue … will also have more trouble [using advanced negotiation techniques]" (Albrecht 1993, 53).

319 Could the *Ping-fa* have been more clear in its anticonflict admonition? Sawyer says in the same breath that "destroying is only second best" and "occupying a thoroughly devasted state was never espoused by any ancient Chinese military thinker" (1993, 160 note 33).

320 Ames translates "heedful" as "approaches battle with prudence" (1993, 166).

When chiefs are full of knowledge about their organization and its environment, and leaders engage only when they must, conditions are beneficial and losses are minimal.

XIII. Intelligence

XIII. 1. Sun Tzu said: Raising a host of a hundred thousand men and marching them great distances entails heavy loss on the people and a drain on the resources of the State. The daily expenditure will amount to a thousand ounces of silver. There will be commotion at home and abroad, and men will drop down exhausted on the highways. As many as seven hundred thousand families will be impeded in their labor.[321]

Engagements are expensive and disruptive.

XIII. 2. Hostile armies may face each other for years, striving for the victory which is decided in a single day. This being so, to remain in ignorance of the enemy's condition simply because one grudges the outlay of a hundred ounces of silver in honors and emoluments, is the height of inhumanity.[322]

To enter into and maintain a state of prolonged engagement, when intelligence could have prevented or minimized it, is foolish.[323]

XIII. 3. One who acts thus is no leader of men, no present help to his sovereign, no master of victory.

The competent know when something must be done and when doing nothing is appropriate.

---

321   Again and again, *Ping-fa* repeats the chapter II admonition: engage only when you must.
322   The *Tao Te Ching* says, "Ignoring knowledge is sickness" (69).
323   It is foolish to engage without knowing how the engagement will be resolved.

XIII. 4–6. Thus, what enables the wise sovereign and the good general to strike and conquer, and achieve things beyond the reach of ordinary men, is foreknowledge.[324] *Now this foreknowledge cannot be elicited from spirits; it cannot be obtained inductively from experience, nor by any deductive calculation. Knowledge of the enemy's dispositions can only be obtained from other men.*

Intelligence gathering is critical for organizational well-being. Experts who know how to harvest it are given this responsibility.

XIII. 7. Hence the use of spies, of whom there are five classes: (1) Local spies; (2) inward spies; (3) converted spies; (4) doomed spies; (5) surviving spies.[325]

This role is performed by observers. There are several types.

XIII. 8. When these five kinds of spy are all at work, none can discover the secret system. This is called "divine manipulation of the threads." It is the sovereign's most precious faculty.

The supreme chief is one who excels at observer management. His talents and activities are unknown and unrecognized.

XIII. 9–13. Having local spies means employing the services of the inhabitants of a district. Having inward

---

324   Warspeak for this is "those who dominate the electromagnetic spectrum and the information that flows from it will achieve direct success on the battlefield" (*Review Magazine* 1996).

325   Calthrop gratuitously noted that "as the sages dealt with war between members of the same race, the work of spies was greatly facilitated" (1908, 13).

spies, making use of officials of the enemy. Having converted spies, getting hold of the enemy's spies and using them for our own purposes. Having doomed spies, doing certain things openly for purposes of deception, and allowing our spies to know of them and report them to the enemy. Surviving spies, finally, are those who bring back news from the enemy's camp.[326]

Observers are stationed in strategic situations. They use diverse techniques for gathering intelligence.

XIII. 14. Hence it is that which none in the whole army are more intimate relations to be maintained than with spies. None should be more liberally rewarded. In no other business should greater secrecy be preserved.[327]

Observers are your most critical assets. Bind them closely to you. Reward and cloak them well.

---

326 Clavell says, "Your surviving spy must be a man of keen intellect, though in outward appearance a fool; of shabby exterior, but with a will of iron. He must be active, robust, endowed with physical strength and courage: thoroughly accustomed to all sorts of dirty work, able to endure hunger and cold, and to put up with shame and ignominy" (1983, 80). His source for this material is unknown. Nor is it known where Tang Zi-Chang got the impression Sun Tzu speaks of "Counter spies [who] are employed to spy on spies" (1969, 75).
327 The "picked troops" in the front ranks of Qin Shih Huangdi's terra-cotta "army"

XIII. 15. Spies cannot be usefully employed without a certain intuitive sagacity. [328]

The chief must have a natural talent for instruction and deployment.

XIII. 16. They cannot be properly managed without benevolence and straightforwardness. [329]

Observers need to know that the object of the exercise is effecting change for the benefit of the whole.

XIII. 17. Without subtle ingenuity of mind, one cannot make certain of the truth of their reports.

A report of people and events is one thing. What that report means could be something else altogether.

XIII. 18. Be subtle! be subtle! and use your spies for every kind of business.

That you use observers, how, and for what reasons must never be revealed.

---

328   Here is an ambiguity. Is it the "users" (leaders) or the "used" (observers) who need to have "intuitive sagacity"? I assume both. Giles says, "Tu Mu strangely refers these attributes to the spies themselves." Clavell adds his own thoughts: "A brazen face and a crafty disposition are more dangerous than mountains or rivers; it takes a man of genius to penetrate such."

329   Another ambiguity. Who precisely must be "benevolent and straightforward"? Here I assume *Ping-fa* speaks of a requirement of the leaders given the risk that an observer might serve more than one master.

XIII. 19. If a secret piece of news is divulged by a spy before the time is ripe, he must be put to death together with the man to whom the secret was told.[330]

Observers are critical to the engagement and the organization. Everything depends upon their discretion.

XIII. 20. Whether the object be to crush an army, to storm a city, or to assassinate an individual, it is always necessary to begin by finding out the names of the attendants, the aides-de-camp, and door-keepers and sentries of the general in command. Our spies must be commissioned to ascertain these.[331]

Charge your observers with discovering who is in charge and who the contacts and confidants of those in charge are. All these details are of importance.[332]

XIII. 21–25. The enemy's spies who have come to spy on us must be sought out, tempted with bribes, led away and comfortably housed. Thus they will become converted

---

330   This must be a later addition or an error in translation. It is is the sole endorsement of violence in *Ping-fa*. Further, for spies, the time for divulgement is never "ripe." Though much less likely, this admonition could be a device for benchmarking loss of trust as the most serious offense in engagement. Zhao Benxue says "both must die" is an incorrect translation (Huang 1993, 252). Calthrop may be responsible for the "both" translation (1908, 72).

331   Here *Ping-fa* is not advocating "crushing an enemy." Whatever you have to do, there is certain basic data you need to have. Recognized Taoist authority Alan Watts states that "obliterating" enemies is a destruction of balance and would therefore be wholly inappropriate.

332   "When highly successful warriors choose which relationships to cultivate, they woo the gatekeepers (even incompetent ones) and thereby gain access to the decision makers" (Roberts 1993, 42).

spies and available for our service. It is through the information brought by the converted spy that we are able to acquire and employ local and inward spies. It is owing to his information, again, that we can cause the doomed spy to carry false tidings to the enemy. Lastly, it is by his information that the surviving spy can be used on appointed occasions. The end and aim of spying in all its five varieties is knowledge of the enemy; and this knowledge can only be derived, in the first instance, from the converted spy. Hence it is essential that the converted spy be treated with the utmost liberality.

Your best observers are those who are in the employ of the other.

XIII. 26–27. Of old, the rise of the Yin dynasty was due to I Chih who had served under the Hsia. Likewise, the rise of the Chou dynasty was due to Lu Ya who had served under the Yin. Hence it is only the enlightened ruler and the wise general who will use the highest intelligence of the army for purposes of spying and thereby they achieve great results. Spies are a most important element in water, because on them depends an army's ability to move.[333]

Organizational management requires an effective intelligence system that provides the data that the chief may assess to determine when action, and inaction, is warranted.[334]

---

333   Though Giles said these lines created great controversy, as they alleged that important, honorable men were really nothing more than spies for their government, they say no such thing. *Ping-fa* says two dynasties had competent leadership. As they were competent, they must have used spies.

334   Chuang Tzu says, "Those who understand the conditions of life do not seek to do what life cannot accomplish. Those who understand the conditions of destiny do not seek for that which is beyond the reach of knowledge" (James Legge quoted in Creel 1953, 103).

Part VI: The Past, Present, and Future

Dissonance: The Commentators[335]

Ping-fa has been translated a number of times and published in many commentaries, the bulk of which have been militaristic in whole or in part. Calthrop (1908. 14) says that when *Sun Tzu: The Art of War* was introduced to Japan, it generated "an army of Japanese commentators."

The commentary makes much of the assumption that *Ping-fa* was written as an "experience of war that was often savage, cruel and deadly serious" in the "vastly different context" of "military operations in China during the period of the Warring States" (Teck and Grinyer 1994, 289). An element of this tale is that *Ping-fa* was a commissioned work, written by a general for one of the warring lords. There is no reliable evidence supporting these notions. Nevertheless, they continue to define the *Ping-fa* context.

Rudnicki says *Ping-fa* is simply "Thirteen Chapters about war." Lau and Ames (1996, 59) say *Ping-fa* is "an important classical text on the subject of warfare [which explains] why it has come down to us through an unbroken transmission." General Griffith, Captain Calthrop, and General Tao Hanzhang obviously speak from the perspective of their lifelong military professions. Ames (1993, 7) tells us he consulted exclusively with "China's leading scholars in military affairs" to write his "definitive Sun Tzu."

Marginal issues dominate the commentary, with unchallenged assumptions and interpretations repeated without question since the Han dynasty. Consequently, the commentary has to a very large degree molded and shaped today's understanding of *Ping-fa*. New

---

335   There have been many commentaries on *Ping-fa*, but not so many as the *Tao Te Ching*. Paul Lin, writing in 1977, believed there were then more than six hundred Chinese commentaries on the *Tao Te Ching*, and seventy or eighty translations, of which forty-four were English.

releases of *Sun Tzu: The Art of War* are for the most part commentators commenting on commentators. Today, in what is an utterly bizarre outcome, a brilliant treatise that played a key role in establishing the Chinese empire, now about 2300 years old and published in millions of copies, is thought by many to be instructions on how to start a fire and kill enemies crossing a river.

The commentary, with only rare exceptions, deems *Ping-fa* practical and tactical. James Clavell adds what he imagines is helpful content about river navigation when he reviews chapter IX. "Do not move upstream to meet the enemy. Our fleet must not be anchored below that of the enemy, for then they would be able to take advantage of the current and make short work of you." In another invention he says, "In crossing salt marshes ... get over them quickly because of the lack of fresh water, and poor quality of the herbage." And again, "dispersive ground" means that "soldiers, being near to their homes and anxious to see their wives and children, are likely to seize the opportunity afforded by a battle and scatter in every direction" (1983, 42–43, 56). He may have borrowed this fascinating idea from Calthrop, who describes "distracting ground" this way (1908, 58).

When commentators read in IX.14 about waiting until the river subsides before crossing it, they understand only that it is foolish to cross a swollen river. They take an equally literal meaning from IX.3–5, where *Ping-fa* discusses "getting away from rivers" and "meeting enemies at, or in rivers." Chapter IX illustrates how one can derive facts from appearances though careful observation and interpretation. Using woodlore metaphors, *Ping-fa* speaks of forests and dust clouds. Oblivious to the metaphor, commentators debate the details. This has been taken to an absurd level by Machell-Cox, who discusses the tactical uses of trees and shrubs. He suggests that in the upcoming (1940s) Japanese campaign, "the Services" would benefit if data were assembled on such matters (Machell-Cox 1943, 43).

Zi-Chang (1969, 54) says that when the army is in "disturbed country ... help the rulers to unite." Krause (1995, 2) says, "Sun Tzu's central idea is that battles or competitions are won by the organization or person who, first has the greatest competitive advantage and who, second, makes the fewest mistakes." Speaking of "the army on the march," *Ping-fa* says, "Camp in high places, facing the sun. Do not climb heights in order to fight. So much for mountain warfare." Moving from mountains to streams, *Ping-fa* says, "After crossing a river, you should get far away from it." Sawyer (1996, 26) says the *Ping-fa* lines on "terrain" were the first systematic study of the subject. But *Ping-fa*, when it suggested "camp[ing] in high places, facing the sun," was not suggesting where the army should pitch its tents.

Sawyer (1993, 172 note 118) says that armies shouldn't camp downstream from their enemies because of the possibility of "suddenly released flood waters." That might well be a threat if the army was encamped under the "enemy's" dam. The *Ping-fa* instructions on fighting with fire and water are, from a literal view, plainly absurd.

Ping-fa is not written in "very specific and operational terms," as one (better) commentator has it (Teck and Grinyer 1994, 289). But such an analysis is up against powerful forces. "Really sound knowledge of topography, movement and supply are the foundations of military knowledge, not tactics and strategy as most people think" (Machell-Cox 1943, 6).

Where *Ping-fa* says ensure you will be victorious before you engage, they see an admonition to pick on weaklings. Wee *et al.* (1996, 110) say it is essential that you "find the right victim [as] the chosen target must be an easy prey." This represents a serious misunderstanding of *Ping-fa's* strength management methodology. It also is in direct

320

conflict with the ethical standards set out in both *Ping-fa* and the *Tao Te Ching*.

General Griffith (1963, 87) shows some minor advance over Wee *et al.* when he tells us, "Anciently those called skilled in war conquered an enemy easily conquered." Nevertheless, it is still a long journey to achieve compliance (or even resonance) with the admonitions of the *Tao Te Ching*:

> If actions are approached,
> and carried out in the natural way,
> the power of evil is reduced,
> and so the ruler and the ruled
> are equally protected.
> They will not contrive to harm each other,
> for the virtue of one refreshes the other.
> (60)[336]

Bizarre interpretations have resulted from forcing *Ping-fa* into the military genre with Machiavelli, Clausewitz, and Antoine Henri, Baron de Jomini. Is it reasonable that a manual on military tactics has gained *Ping-fa* "a place in the world's literature," philosophical or not? Manuals do not as a rule make great literature, and as a war manual *Ping-fa* just doesn't cut it. It is in fact often discredited in the military canon.

Considerable pain has been taken at times to maintain the militaristic charade. The commentary achieves this by the insertion of new material or by an extravagant and convoluted interpretation of what *Ping-fa* must have meant. These machinations continually miss the mark. To date, no commentator has seen that *Ping-fa* is focused on peaceful engagement, engagement conducted with the express purpose of achieving objectives *without* conflict. When the practical matters of the conduct of war cannot

---

336 http://www.clas.ufl.edu/users/gthursby/taoism/ttcstan3.htm#38

be found, the commentators become apologists for *Ping-fa's* inadequacy, or they simply add in the missing bits.

Stefan Rudnicki's *Art of War* contains material from General Colin Powell, Marshal Turenne, and Stonewall Jackson. He even arranges to have "Sun Tzu the warrior" commenting on Sun Tzu. Like General Tao Hanzhang, Rudnicki does not favor us with references, but he does tell us unhelpfully that his "version is mostly derived" from the Giles translation.

In *Ping-fa* there is nothing on how to conduct a siege, how to treat sickness and wounds, and how to set up and maintain supply lines. We must look elsewhere for instructions on the care of horses and other beasts of burden. Lau and Ames say *Ping-fa* mentions crossbows only twice because they weren't popular at that time (1996, 43).[337] Griffith provides reams of information on weaponry gathered from other sources, because in his view there just isn't enough in *Ping-fa*. He adds to this misdemeanor with strange extrapolations that have no foundation in the text:

> The organization described by Sun Tzu permitted considerable flexibility in march formations, while articulation made possible rapid deployment into those suitable for battle. The five man squad or section could obviously march either in rank or file. (1963, 37)

The commentary, frustrated at its inability to see what *Ping-fa* is really all about, blames it and never themselves. Vaughan Yarwood reviewed Krause's work in July 1996 in *Management* and was favorably impressed. But *Ping-fa* did not fare so well. Yarwood noted that Krause "included nuggets of the original's sketchy and disordered text for flavor." But Handel (1992, 22, 54) disagrees with that take to a point. "Many strategists

---

337   The crossbow was likely introduced to China in 500 BC (Ames 1993, 24).

are more comfortable reading Sun Tzu rather than Clausewitz's *On War*, whose methodology and style are not as easy to follow. *On War* lends itself to facile, hence erroneous, comparisons because it is seldom read in its entirety." But, says Handel, one gets real value by taking the time to read all of Clausewitz. "The concepts for which Clausewitz is most renowned are all set forth by Sun Tzu in *The Art of War*, although Clausewitz analyzes them in more detail and may express them in more elegantly worded aphorisms."

General Tao Hanzhang (1987, 90) says, "The main shortcomings of *Sun Tzu's Art of War* are that it does not discuss the nature of war." Michael Handel is unsure what you can use *Ping-fa* for, unless you want to study how a prince sees things from a lofty perch.

> Unlike *On War, The Art of War* does not offer the reader a systematic explanation or step-by-step reconstruction of the logical process through which concepts are developed. From this point of view, *The Art of War* reads more like a manual written as a compact guide for the 'prince' or higher ranking military commander. Thus, while Clausewitz leads the reader through a tortuous - though educationally rewarding—reasoning process, Sun Tzu, for the most part presents the reader with his conclusions. (1992, 22)

In 1929, Tang Zi-Chang said that his military science mentor told him that while "Sun Zi wrote a very profound book, it is not well organized." In Zi-Chang's view, *Ping-fa* is in disorder because of the effects of time and deterioration of writing materials (1969, 13).

Equal to the war they see in *Ping-fa* has been the war that commentators have been practicing among themselves for almost two millennia. Tu Mu was isolated for his pacific views about *Ping-fa*.

Though Giles calls Ts'ao Ts'ao (155–220 CE) a military genius and a great writer, he also says his commentary was "scarcely intelligible" and as much in need of analysis as *Ping-fa* itself. Much of the argument has focused on the translation of passages. Griffith translates III.4 this way: "Thus what is of supreme importance in war is to attack the enemy's strategy." Giles, he says, not only translates the passage incorrectly, but (predictably) is being too soft, as usual, in imagining *Ping-fa* had in mind "to balk the enemy's plans." Griffith apparently missed Giles's definition of "balking." To him it meant "an active policy of counter-attack."

Ou-yang Hsiu, a thousand years after *Ping-fa* was created, praised Mei Sheng-yu and offered his reaction to those who imagined that *Ping-fa* was not an army manual:

Later scholars have misread Sun Tzu, distorting his words and trying to make them square with their own one-sided views. Thus, though commentators have not been lacking, only a few have proved equal to the task. My friend Sheng-yu has not fallen into this mistake. In attempting to provide a critical commentary for Sun Tzu's work, he does not lose sight of the fact that these sayings were intended for states engaged in internecine warfare; that the author is not concerned with the military conditions prevailing under the sovereigns of the three ancient dynasties, nor with the nine punitive measures prescribed to the Minister of War. Again, Sun Wu loved brevity of diction, but his meaning is always deep. Whether the subject be marching an army, or handling soldiers, or estimating the enemy, or controlling the forces of victory, it is always systematically treated; the sayings are bound together in strict logical sequence, though this has been obscured by commentators who have probably failed to grasp their meaning. In his own commentary, Mei Sheng-yu has brushed aside all the obstinate prejudices of these critics, and has tried to bring out the true meaning of Sun Tzu himself. In this way, the clouds of confusion have been dispersed and the sayings made clear. I am convinced that the present work deserves to be handed down side by side with the three great commentaries; and for a great deal that they find in the sayings, coming generations will have constant reason to thank my friend Sheng-yu. Making some allowance for the exuberance of friendship, I am inclined to endorse this favorable judgment, and would certainly place him above Ch'en Hao in order of merit.[338]

Cheng Hou dared suggest that *Ping-fa* might have been a work of philosophy that simply used military tactics for illustration. In reaction, Chu His expressed his astonishment and resentment to this,

audacious comparison with the venerated classical works of a document that encourages a ruler's bent towards unrelenting warfare and reckless militarism. (Giles 1910)

The first translation done in a European language was published in Paris in 1772, under the title *"L'art de la guerre."* Its author was a Jesuit missionary to China, Jean-Jacques Amiot. His translation was Tao-sensitive. He says he translated *Ping-fa* because of the inadequacy of the work done to that time. Following Amiot were Captain E. F. Calthrop and Lionel Giles. More recently,

---

338   http://www.online-literature.com/suntzu/artofwar/1/

the field has been dominated by General Samuel B. Griffith and Thomas Cleary.

Griffith dismissed Amiot's work because he saw it as overly focused on moral and humanitarian issues, which caused him to "misinterpret" *Ping-fa*. He didn't like what Lionel Giles achieved either. It was

> marred throughout by tasteless criticisms. Had this eminent orientalist devoted to his own effort the energy he wasted in denigration of Captain Calthrop's, one may surmise that his would have been somewhat better than it is. (Griffith 1963, 181)

D. C. Lau has little good to say about Griffith, while Ames agrees with Griffith. Ames (1993, 8) said Giles made a "vitriolic and undignified assault" with "unrelenting unkindnesses to poor pioneering Calthrop." Though Roger Ames commends the "invaluable insights" of Griffith, he can't find an equal reason to praise Giles and Cleary. Griffith's work "is superior to Giles's [*sic*] and to recent popular attempts such as the Thomas Cleary translation, informed as the latter is by neither practical military wisdom nor scholarship."

Says Handel (1992, 158),

> None of the currently available translations of *Sun Tzu* is entirely accurate. Each translator has employed some modern Western phrases or words that do not exist in the original and has inevitably, even if unintentionally, contributed some of his own ideas. This is particularly true of General Griffith's readable translation, and less so of the Giles translation.

Cleary got his turn with Wilhelm's translation of *The Secret of the Golden Flower*. He accuses Wilhelm of "reading weird and superstitious ideas into the text," and in a burst of indignation, refers to him in the space of three sentences as having published a work that was confused, misconstrued, unreliable, flawed, and dysfunctional (1991). Tang Zi-Chang (1969, 175) says Griffith's work has "chapter headings [that] do not correspond with the accurate Chinese meanings nor are they proper English military terminology." A good example of the never-ending debate can be seen in Wee *et al.* (1996, 296).

In the latter years of the twentieth century, *Ping-fa* became the darling of martial artists, militarists, and writers enamored with the wars and warriors of ancient Asia. James Clavell enthusiastically proposed that military officers should be required to write examinations on *Ping-fa*, which, if they fail, would lead to dismissal or demotion.

> I truly believe that if our military and political leaders had studied [Sun Tzu], Vietnam could not have happened, we would not have lost the war in Korea; the Bay of Pigs could not have occurred; the hostage fiasco in Iran could not have come to pass; the British Empire would not have been dismembered; and in all probability, World Wars I and II would have been avoided— certainly they would have not been waged as they were waged, and the millions of youths obliterated unnecessarily and stupidly by monsters calling themselves generals would have lived out their lives. (Clavell 1993, 1–2)

Clavell never does explain just how *Ping-fa* could influence or prevent all these events, but he tells us he "believe[s] The Art of War shows quite clearly *how to take the initiative* and combat the enemy—any enemy." This is not *Ping-fa* but Clausewitz, who said there is really only one key decisive element in war: "sheer overwhelming force." In the commentator's linear universe there is little or no room for alternate methods of interorganization management and dispute resolution. Some even dismiss the value of intelligence gathering in situations leading to, or in the midst of, conflict. They never challenge the notion of inherent value in competition and the inevitability of conflict.

Some imagine conflict to be beneficial. "Strategic management" to these folks is all about the economics of loss prevention. The competent general, in this view, achieves the objective, without completely destroying the objective or his own forces. But if subduing the enemy takes destruction, then so be it. Those who can blithely speak of "Mutually Assured Destruction" as a military strategy are patently unable to see *Ping-fa* in any way other than a reflection of their own views. That has not prevented their being able to articulate war as a beneficial activity—for its goals are right. James Clavell says, "Since ancient times, it has been known that the true object of war is *peace*" (1983, 7). R. L. Wing says the purpose of *Ping-fa* was "to outline specific strategies to overcome conflicts while viewing the world as a complete and interdependent system that must be preserved" (1988, 13).

Consider one of the most quoted *Ping-fa* admonitions: victory is achieved before war. Every commentator reads this as an admonition for war preparedness. But this statement does not say, "He who prepares appropriately wins the battle." It says victory is achieved before war. Why would war be needed if victory has already been achieved?

Now consider an example of missing information—in this case, what the militarist really needs to know about types of warfare. About "mountain warfare," *Ping-fa* says you should camp high up, but don't climb to fight. On the subject of "river warfare," it says to moor your craft higher up than the enemy's and not to move upstream to meet him. Instructions for campaigning in salt marshes and in dry level country total three lines.

The commentators agree that chapter X describes six types of "ground," but then imagine that chapter XI defines nine types of "situations" or "grounds." The evident redundancy escapes them. As we indicate elsewhere, chapter X is about engagement situations, and as Krause and Tang Zi-Chang have seen, chapter XI is about engagement dynamics. It is nonsensical to imagine that two chapters of the thirteen would focus on the same subject.

The commentary is not, however, all misguided. Lau and Ames (1996, 41) suggest *Ping-fa's* imagery "naturalizes the military culture, by bringing together military detail and philosophical ideas."

> Contemporary scholars who work on classical Chinese military thought [consider Sun Tzu to be] a philosophical text. In a highly conceptual and even philosophical way, Sun-tzu addresses the issues of warfare, the operations of the military, its strategy, tactics, and so on. It is, in their view, the fact that Sun Tzu is philosophical, that has assured it a place in the world's literature, while the *Sun Pin* has been 'lost to posterity.' (ibid., 57)

Roger Ames (1993, 35, 40-41, 73) shows insight when he tells us that "military strategy can be used as a source of metaphors to shape philosophical distinctions and categories." He says teaching practices at the time *Ping-fa* was created "grounded" theory and philosophy in experiences and "evocative metaphors."[339] These devices were intended to aid learning and the development of knowledge, not through rote but through cognitive processes. This is all very good. But he then says, "The place of [*Ping-fa*] as the fundamental work in classical military literature is unassailable."

Though hardly free of the militarist view, McNeilly is one of the modern commentators who has helped move *Ping-fa* from the battlefield to the boardroom. But he confesses that it has not been easy.

> Because business, like warfare, is dynamic, fast-paced, and requires an effective and efficient use of scarce resources, modern executives have found value in Sun Tzu's teachings.[340] But The Art of War is arranged for the military leader and not the CEO, so making connections between ancient warfare and today's corporate world is not always easy.[341]

Consider how much more fruitful his contribution would have been if he had shown that *Ping-fa's* messages and benefits were all about careful observation, evaluation, and settlement with the least possible inconvenience. This is the stuff of strategic planning and management, and business and social institutions are in woeful need of help along these lines.

But there are other problems with the commentary. Over the last 2300 years, it is possible that modifications may have been made to the text. It could well be that elements, including some of Sun Pin could have been

---

339   Similar conditions and motives could have led to the veiling of *The Masters of Huainan* and Zhang's *Understanding Reality* (Cleary 1989b, xxvii).
340   Author of *The Six Principles from Sun Tzu,* and the *Art of Business: Six Principles for Managers*
341   August 1996, on Amazon.com. Also see http://cazmedia.com/suntzu/sixprin.html.

blended into Ping-fa.[342] The 1972 discovery of the oldest known *Ping-fa* manuscript from an ancient tomb near Linyi in Shandong differs from all known versions of *Ping-fa*. The content on which the military commentary has focused is absent from this version. What this means is that not only is a good deal of the military commentary incorrect, it is based on text not part of the Ping-fa that helped found the Chinese empire.

J. H. Huang has made a very significant contribution to linking today's "Art of War" with Qin's Ping-fa. His first challenge was to the accepted meaning of the word "war" in "Art of War." "Art of War," he feels, may be no more than a later added mistranslation.[343] Huang's knowledge of the *Ping-fa* epoch, culture, language, philosophy, and writing style, and his focus on the Linyi text have enabled him to examine *Ping-fa* from a fresh perspective. He followed the same linguistic analysis process Paul Lin used with the *Tao Te Ching*, and achieved a high level of coherence as a result. His conclusion: the persistent war context and application of *Ping-fa* is highly suspect.

But it is more than "suspect"—it is utterly incorrect. The *Ping-fa* thesis is crystal clear: engagements are critically important. Enter into them only when you must. Ensure control. Ensure minimal loss and costs. Conclude them quickly. With great clarity and even stridency, *Ping-fa* says that if relations have dissolved into conflict, then the cause and consequence is failure. Organizations – and perhaps the wider community - will suffer.

End Game: Sun Tzu's "Art of War"

The Art of War has remained a very popular work for two hundred years in the West, occupying bookshelves in the military, business and recreational worlds. Though it

---

342   Just as it is alleged Wang Pi's work became part of the *Tao Te Ching* (Lin 1977, xii)
343   It is actually simply extracted from the text. It is not certain that *Ping-fa* ever had any title.

has gained a place in the civilian domain, it still carries the cachet of conflict. Whether used in soccer coaching or corporate information technology management, the messages—and we assume applications—are all about conflict.

Deemed a manual for defeating enemies or opponents and for "winning at any cost," some see it as a hallowed justification for ruthlessness: forget ethics—just do what you have to do to destroy your enemies. But some of the commentary has (to a degree) picked up on *Ping-fa's* admonition that destroying cities is not good practice. The militarist argument for a conservative application can be seen in these remarks from Air Marshal David Evans, who references *The Art of War*:

> Another factor pertinent to the use of precision guided munitions is that it has never been economical or preferable in war to destroy the enemy's civil infrastructure, beyond the extent to which it is supporting his military operations. (1997, 84)

These interpretations and applications miss the point. *Ping-fa* says conflict means failure and benefits are often elusive. Winston Churchill, very much later, had a similar message: "Of what use is decisive victory in battle if we bleed to death as a result of it?" Collaboration and cooperation deserve their day at court as vehicles for achieving mutually beneficial goals.

Those whose livelihoods depend on adversity will not be easily convinced that the authors of *Ping-fa* were appalled at the whole notion of conflict, and that *The Art of War* should be more accurately called *The Art of Peace*.

It is unfortunate that a work of great historical significance and potentially very wide application and benefit has been defined in this way. Not only are we seeing misapplication with possibly serious consequences, but research on the work has all but stopped. There have been no significant challenges to the *Ping-fa* as manual of war paradigm. Until now.

This is not to say that *Ping-fa* is irrelevant for military engagement. Quite the contrary, there are models and messages here for all domains. But it is far less valuable for conflict management than it is for conflict prevention. *Ping-fa* drives for success before, not during, conflict. It says if you let matters get out of hand and conflict emerges, the chances of recovery or of a satisfactory conclusion are low to negligible. Jane Jacobs has said that Machiavelli, Sun Tzu, and publications such as the *Wall Street Journal* are perpetuating misunderstanding – but we are not entirely sure what misunderstandings she is referring to, and what corrective actions she proposes. We assume she is advocating a less militarist approach to problem solving.

Such approaches and initiatives, however, pale in the face of the onslaught of videos, books, audio tapes, and even comic books that perpetuate the "Sun-Tzu-as-warrior" concept. The translator of one such comic book said he studied "Napoleon, Clausewitz, Jomini, Moltke and Fuller" to make sure he got "Sunzi's ideas in the most appropriate terminology."[344]

There is no end to the range and variety of Sun-Tzu-as-warrior "analysts." We can purchase *The Art of War for Lovers* by Dr. Cowan Connell.[345] And when love goes wrong, there is *The Tao of Divorce: A Woman's Guide to Winning (based on Sun Tzu's the Art of War)*, by Fuchs and Sooho.[346] Consider *Sun Tzu's Ancient Art of Golf* by Chapin and McDonald. Several years ago a Chapters Bookstore employee won a prize for an essay that applied Sun Tzu to the perilous world of bookselling.[347] A doctor

---

344   C. C. Tsai, which is the pen name of Tsai Chih Chung
345   http://www.amazon.com/exec/obidos/
ASIN/0671000632/002-1639198-8367219.
346   *http://www1.shore.net/~tao/*
347   *Canadian Bookseller*, October 1989

named Catlin has written *The Art of Soccer*. It was reviewed by Craig Hartley in *Soccer Shorts* of the Palo Alto Soccer Club, where he noted that he didn't see the relevance between soccer and quotes from the Chinese general Sun Tzu.

Khoo Kheng-Hor, a prolific Sun Tzu as warrior exponent, has authored *Sun Tzu and Management, Sun Tzu and the CEO's Conscience, War at Work,* and *The Art of War in Corporate Politics*. One of his works shows how to fight corporate wars with samurai techniques.[348] Martial artists can also buy Kaufman's *The Art of War: The Definitive Interpretation of Sun Tzu's Classic Book of Strategy for the Martial Artist*. There is even an instant Sun Tzu. New technologies allow books to be printed on demand. The second book produced by this new technology was "The Art of War, a 2000 year old Chinese treatise on competition and conflict."[349]

The prize for the most bizarre juxtaposition must go to John Hanson. He linked Sun Tzu with charitable giving in an essay titled, "Borrow a Corpse for the Soul's Return."[350] The survival-of-the-most-brutal Sun Tzu commentary is well demonstrated in Phil Porter's *Eat or Be Eaten* and Robert Slater's *Get Better or Get Beaten*. These "take-no-prisoners" management studies occupy bookstore shelves near serious works in business and militaria.

Oliver Stone's 1987 movie *Wall Street* features a financier corrupting a young broker by teaching him how to apply a warlike Sun Tzu in the game of corporate takeover. Said the financier, "It's a zero-sum game kid, somebody wins, somebody loses."

The CEO course in the University of Manitoba MBA program uses only two texts for its leadership seminars:

---

348 *New Straits Times*, Malaysia (May 15, 1999)
349 *Business Line,* India (July 8, 1999)
350 *Fund Raising Management* (May 1997, Vol. 28, Issue 3)

Machiavelli's *The Prince* and Sun Tzu.[351] If your interest is "takeover investing," Gulf Al Baraka Investment Company LLC in Dubai says you needn't study the "corporate strategy tomes published by B-school professors from Harvard and Wharton"—just read "Machiavelli's Prince and Sun Tzu's Art of War."[352] We are told Newt Gingrich reads Sun Tzu.[353] His fascination with the connection between war and politics has been mentioned in the *Congressional Record*.[354] Angolan rebel leader Dr. Jonas Savimbi is described as a "pure military strategist. Close associates say his favored text is Sun Tzu."[355] Lee Atwater, credited with electing George Bush in 1988, and selected as chairman of his party in 1989, was fond of both Sun Tzu and Machiavelli.[356]

Ian Harley, chief executive of Abbey National, uses Sun Tzu as his "management guru."[357] According to a 1996 *Christian Science Monitor* (CSM) article, "more than 1,600 [sic] years later, China's Communist leaders are trying to adhere to [Sun Tzu's] dictum in a mounting confrontation with Taiwan, by firing missiles near the

---

351   Despite the course leader's view that the genre is military. He is also chair of Manitoba Hydro. See: *Ivey Business Journal*, Spring 1998, Vol. 62, Issue 3, p. 63.
352   *Khaleej Times*, UAE (June 15, 1998)
353   According to *The Economist* (December 23, 1995); *Window of Opportunity* (226, 237). He also is very familiar with General Heinz Guderian's *Panzer Leader* and Isaac Asimov's *The Foundation Trilogy*. See: http://www.pbs.org/wgbh/pages/frontline/newt/newtlist.html.
354   Congressional Record (October 1996), Mrs. Schroeder (Colorado) speaking on the subject of "Concern Expressed Over Use Of Military Personnel For Political Purposes"
355   "Angolan Rebel; Leader Thrives on Media Ban" in *Irish Times* (August 16, 1999)
356   http://www.intellectualcapital.com/bibliotech/rev-031397.html
357   Interview in *The Guardian*, UK (March 20, 1999)

island and making other provocative gestures."[358] In another, CSM writer J. L. Tyson offers advice in the campaign against Saddam Hussein, using "Ancient Words of War: Wisdom from Beijing's most venerated military strategist." He says US generals should "at the beginning, when enticing the enemy into combat, appear as shy as a young maiden."[359]

A Sun Tzu quote adorns the wall of John Grieve, head of the Metropolitan Police Race and Violent Crimes Task Force.[360] Joseph Estrada, elected Philippine president in 1998, confesses to gaining inspiration from Sun Tzu.[361] Ronald Mendell has developed what he calls a "Sun Tzu classic wartime strategy" to deal with the problem of parking lot crime.[362]

The Institute for Advanced Interdisciplinary Research recommends Sun Tzu study for those who aspire to a leadership position in the "globally interlinked economy."[363] Another management consulting organization stated that Sun Tzu "provides the reader with the principles of strategy and teaches the importance of conflict resolution without battle." This was fine until they added, "The intent, however, is to be victorious."

The Indian Army runs a management school in Calcutta that uses Sun Tzu and other works to "bring the clockwork precision and efficiency of [the military] to the corporate workplace."[364] *Profit: The Magazine for Canadian Entrepreneurs* wrote in April/May 1998 of the importance of forging alliances with competitors. This is a clear Sun Tzu instruction, yet *Profit* said enterprises

---

358   CSM 1996-03-01. J.S. Landay, in article titled "China Military Thumps Chest At More Agile, Potent Taiwan"
359   CSM 1991-01-04
360   *The Observer*, UK (January 31, 1999)
361   *Agence France Presse Intl.* 29 May 1998
362   *Security Management* (December 1995, Vol. 39, Issue 12, p. 46)
363   http://www.systems.org/HTML/books/sun-tzu.htm
364   *Business Line* (February 9, 1998)

should follow the "science of peace [rather than] the art of war."

The beneficial analyses and applications of *Ping-fa* are few in number. But they do exist. Henry Mintzberg, who wrote *The Rise and Fall of Strategic Planning,* felt that "Sun Tzu" invented strategic planning.[365] Franco Bernabe, chief executive of Olivetti, told the *Harvard Business Review* that Sun Tzu is "the first comprehensive text on strategy that can still be applied to all kinds of human activity."[366]

We know with some assurance that business and military leaders are not reading Sun Tzu as *Ping-fa.* What we need to know is what interpretation these leaders and writers are taking from *The Art of War* and applying in their various domains. The popular press never questions *The Art of War* or its alleged ("beneficial") applications, but then the commentators— who are allegedly authorities on the subject—don't raise these questions either. The all too frequent message is militaristic, and it is all about winning, using whatever weapons you can pull out of your arsenal. There seems to be a real reluctance to challenge the notion that military practices are simply inappropriate in peacetime interpersonal and interorganizational relations. At the same time, the military shows some degree of adversity to drawing on the lessons, and lessons learned, from peace authors and architects in the civilian domain.

In the Work World

Is the theory and practice of gung-hoism[367] finding a niche in the corporate world? The *Toronto Sun* in August

---

365   Published by Doubleday of New York and Asiapac of Singapore.
366   *Financial Times* (February 27, 1999)
367   For yet another expression that has taken on quite a different meaning in the West, see Blanchard and Bowles's *Gung Ho!* where we are told it is a Chinese expression meaning "teamwork."

1995 reported that "hard-nosed superagent" Mike Ovitz, reportedly a dedicated student of Sun Tzu, had just been made president of Disney. Croda International chief executive Mike Humphrey "half jokingly, says there are only two management books worth reading, Sun Tzu and *The Prince* by Machiavelli."[368] From Min Chen we "learn" that "the Chinese expression *shang chang ru zhan chang* in English means 'The marketplace is a battlefield.' This is how Asians view success or failure in the business world."[369]

On April 2, 1997, the *Asia Times* complained bitterly about the proliferation (in Southeast Asia) of management texts based on the classics, which were "on the low end of the intelligence spectrum." Ong Hock Chuan asked, "How many times have you seen poor Sun Tzu exploited by a management hack, trying to cash in on the aspirations of would-be business warriors?" Author Douglas Fetherling reached his exasperation limit in 1999 with what he called the "nonsense publishing" of "trash" around Taoism and Sun Tzu (which he calls a "deeply spiritual work"). He begged his readers to "read the real goods, not the denatured, exploitative and false works by people seeking to capitalize on a fad."[370] Even Cleary got on the bandwagon with his *Mastering the Art of War.* Mark Kingwell, in an April 1996 story in the *Globe and Mail*, found Cleary "trying much too hard" to establish a Sun Tzu business link.

Stefan Rudnicki said Sun Tzu can be used for everything from sports to business to love, "provided you are willing to see the world in which you live and work as a network of actual and potential combat zones, where the stakes are high, and struggle is the primary mode of being; where no one is to be trusted, and survival depends on unconditional victory" (1996,

---

368 Interview in *Yorkshire Post*, UK (March 29, 1999)
369 Min Chen in *Business Horizons* (Mar/Apr 1994)
370 *Toronto Star* (April 18, 1999)

7).[371] The ferocity of business competition has gotten so bad, according to some, that "individual payoffs" are becoming so highly valued that "North Americans will quite often sacrifice [winning in negotiations] to beat the opponent, to embarrass him, or to reduce his outcomes" (Leung and Tzosvold, 1998, 317). The Albrechts (1993, 57) say the vocabulary used in the workplace is only reflecting the "warrior values" that exist there.

Evoking the images of Sun-Tzu-as-warrior, Jeffrey Arlen, editor of *Discount Store News*, says, "War is raging between the retailing superpowers" in a way that brings back memories of the "slam-bam, take no prisoners of the 1980's."[372] Executives of advertising agency MZD believe their success "in today's hyper-competitive business environment" comes from their focus on aggressive strategic planning. "Strategic planning is the art of war," says Montgomery, "because business is war, every day. War is opportunity." His *Become Strategic or Die* (written with Peter J. Plus) has been described as "a unique blend of Sun Tzu's *Art of War* and cutting-edge strategic business theory."[373]

Lucio Tan, allegedly the richest man in the Philippines, is described as a "latter day Sun Tzu" with a "Sun Tzu management style" by an April 1999 story in *Business World Philippines*. The article makes it clear that the Sun Tzu references illustrate his "aggressive management, dis-empowering subordinates, inscrutability and impulsiveness." One reviewer of *The Art of War for Executives* said, "If this is not the daftest [book on business], it may be the most alarming."[374] He had some difficulty relating incendiary attacks to everyday work

---

371   http://www.fortunecity.com/victorian/beardsley/288/praises1.html
372   Discount Store News, March 22, 1999, Vol. 38 Issue 6
373   Montgomery Zukerman Davis at http://www.mzd.com.
374   *The Economist* (June 24, 1995)

situations and studying how to "permanently defeat a competitor."

The April 1995 *Milwaukee Business Journal*, as uncomplimentary about this book as was *The Economist*, said that author Krause had "admitted to a certain amount of literary license." Krause sees *Ping-fa* chapter XII, for example, which is really about strength management, as "Destroying Reputation." Dehumanization and suboptimization are Machiavelli, not *Ping-fa*.[375]

Dangerous ideas are also to be found in *48 Laws of Power*, a book that misreads and misapplies *Ping-fa* in a remarkable way. Robert Greene says you can "forget about morality—that's strictly for losers. I maintain that believing that true, long-lasting power ultimately relies on honest and fair means is pure nonsense."[376]

> 'Crush the enemy' is a key strategic tenet of Sun-tzu. The idea is simple: Your enemies wish you ill. There is nothing they want more than eliminate you. The solution: Have no mercy. Crush your enemies as totally as they would crush you. The only peace and security you can hope for from your enemies is their disappearance. (1998, 112)

Competitive Strategy says that the practice by some companies to view competitive moves as "entirely a game of brute force" may not always be enough to ensure the right outcome, if "competitors will be tough (or worse, desperate or seemingly irrational) in their responses or if competitors are pursuing greatly different objectives. Even with clear strengths, a war of attrition is costly to the victor and vanquished alike and is best avoided." This would have been a perfect opportunity for author Michael Porter to suggest something akin to *Ping-fa's* "sensitive intervention." But Porter concludes with "Making competitive moves in oligopoly is best thought

---

375 See McAlpine 1998, 123.
376 *Financial Times* (January 16, 1999)

of as a combination of whatever brute force the firm can muster, applied with finesse" (1980, 92).

Donald Krause (1995, 109) says that in the business world, "conflict is inevitable [and] we cannot learn too much about how to compete." He says if conflict isn't happening, we should be making it happen. "Competition should occur when we have something important to gain or when we are in danger."

Here's a sampling of Sun-Tzu-as-warrior news clips:

- Sun Tzu has gone high-tech. And developers have taken the military metaphor right along with them. The makers of PalmPilot provide Sun Tzu as a downloadable text file that you can install and read at your leisure. *Palmpower* magazine announced this in September 1998 with the headline: "Meet Sun Tzu, avoid flogging and keelhauling."[377]

- *The Star* (Malaysia) announced in November 1998 a new interactive Sun Tzu CD that would use "text, animation, sound effects and interactive designs" to give managers the sort of stuff that "the King of Wu used to deadly effect." The publisher expected to sell 7,500 copies in six months in English, Bahasa Malaysian, Japanese, and Koren. This release was followed by *Sun Tzu on the Andromeda Interactive Classic Library CD.* An Indonesian reviewer wished his nation's military leaders, during the "nerve-wracking and tear-jerking riots which pounded out nation over the last year," had spoken more like Sun Tzu and less like "social scientists."[378]

- Henry Juszkiewicz, chairman and chief executive, wants to make Gibson Guitar the

377 http://www.palmpower.com/issues/issue199809/bookmonth998001.html
378 *The Jakarta Post* (March 29, 1999)

"largest instrument manufacturer in the world. The key is to be aggressive." Says the *Financial Post* in June 1998, "Perhaps that explains why his boardroom gives prominent space not to guitar manuals, but to copies of his required reading for new executives—*The Art of War.*"

- Dean Lundell says *The Art of War*, which is "not a methodology but a philosophy," teaches (1) "concepts, but mostly it teaches you how to exploit your opponent; (2) that people will blindly follow a leader without regard to danger; (3) not to fight in a river."[379]
- "Keep the CEO informed! When war begins one of the most critical aspects in ensuring the general is kept informed on the progress of the battle, the conditions of his army, and that of the enemy is the establishment of effective communications systems."[380]
- "'In order to <u>kill</u> the <u>enemy</u>, our men must be roused to <u>anger</u>,' reads *The Art of <u>War</u>*, and the corporate <u>battleground</u> of today's Internet is most evident when it comes to the Microsoft/Netscape <u>face-off</u>. Since December, the statements have been <u>raining like shells</u>. Netscape CEO Jim Clark said recently, 'I don't have anything against Microsoft, except that <u>they want to kill us.</u>'"[381] (The underlining is mine.)
- Steve Zelnak, president and CEO of Martin Marietta Materials Inc., hands out copies of *Sun Tzu* as he works to make his company the "nation's second-largest producer of rock and

---

379   *Futures*, February 1998, Vol. 27, Issue 2, p. 40

380   (Wee *et al* 1996, 168)

381   *Electronic Engineering Times* (May 13, 1996)

gravel. Business is really a military game, said the former Army bomb disposal expert."[382]

- Kenneth Kaye has written *Workplace Wars and How to End Them.* His work is targeted at "anybody who is affected by or involved in personal vendettas, animosities, or grudges that can make a workplace environment pure hell. For these situations ordinary conflict resolution isn't enough. Sometimes," he says, "it IS personal."

- James D. Laughlin and Graham Tort's article in *Commentary Magazine*[383] is titled "The New Art of War." Far from being concerned about using Sun Tzu war stories in the workplace, the July 1995 *Indianapolis Business Journal* story says the authors are not writing about "disemboweling or light brigade charges" but rather a "most civilized sort of war."

- Richard Marcinko has published *Leadership Secrets of the Rogue Warrior,* a "business-as-war" best seller. *Businessweek* reviewed it under the heading "Buzz Off, Sun Tzu!"

- James L. Wade III, writing in *Oncology Issues* (1997, 12[5]:5), noted that Sun Tzu's teachings are applicable to health care. He speaks of the "sheathed sword stratagem,"[384] which is apparently the "defeat of the target using intimidation, coercion, and gradual erosion of the target's will." These images support his argument against "managed health care."[385]

---

382 *Triangle Business Journal* (April 3, 1998)
383 US National Council for Urban Economic Development
384 This notion comes from Clavell. It apparently means "supreme excellence is breaking the enemy's resistance without fighting."
385 George Silver, writing about US health care, quotes both Sun Tzu and Clausewitz. *American Journal of Public Health*, March 1995, Vol. 85, Issue 3.

- Sal Marino has created "Sun Tzuisms." These are "what wins wars and markets," he says. For example, "In publishing, in manufacturing, as well as in war, firepower will beat manpower; expressions of personality and creativity will defeat intellect." He says, "Don't attack a tank with a peashooter. Protect your assets."[386]
- Professor John B. McKinnon says the benefit of Donald Krause's 1995 work (on *Ping-fa*) is that it has saved business executives all the bother of "having to mentally transfer Ping-fa's instructions on how to wage war to how to successfully conduct a business."[387]

This business-as-war, interpersonal-relations-as-martial-arts mentality is starting to raise concerns. And those concerns focus on scholarship and application. In August 1997, Bruce Rubenstein of the *Corporate Legal Times* reviewed the "manager as warrior" phenomenon and declared it an "insidious conceit." He described Dean Lundell's *Sun Tzu's Art of War For Traders and Investors* as "breathless and portentous. McGraw-Hill exhibits the brass balls of a Samurai warrior by charging $19.95 for this silly book." The *Philadelphia Inquirer* called applying war metaphors in the workplace dangerous because

it can all blow up in your face. Managers study dog-eared copies of *Sun Tzu's Art of War* or *The Black Belt Manager* or whatever is the latest business book based on combat strategies, [as they] find ways to translate warlike ideas to work.[388]

---

386   Editorials in *Industry Week* (October 1997 and December 1998)
387   He is dean of Babcock Graduate School of Management, Wake Forest University.
388   January 4, 1998 See: http://www.phillynews.com/inquirer/98/Jan/04/lifestyle/OFFIC04.html

William Morin, consultant and author of *Silent Sabotage*, has the same opinion. He sees the work world in a state of "values crisis," and organizations should get rid of their copies of Sun Tzu. "Operating a business should not be viewed as a battle."[389] Jeremy Bullmore, a marketing expert, thinks "macho marketing" has gotten completely out of hand. "I don't know whether marketing agencies just talk [tough] to make themselves feel manly with their—'Identify your target; invest in an arsenal; concentrate your fire-power; nuke them into submission'." Military strategy such as Sun Tzu's, in his view, could perhaps be used with some very competitive companies. "But it's a rotten way to schmooze a punter."[390] There are some positive signs appearing in the media:

- A firm called Strategies & Tactics bases their "ethical conduct" on Sun Tzu's Moral Law. They say it inspires their "Portfolio Management and Risk Management Corollary": "regardless of philosophical or religious inclination, always employ resources in a moral and ethical manner. Be generous in supporting worthy endeavors regardless of material return."[391]
- Once, military adventures were often designed to obtain more resources to fight more wars. Once, business development depended on the favors of already rich men. This was the world in which Sun Tzu lived. It is why his teachings are more relevant to modern business than we might expect. Most of all, Sun Tzu understood

---

389   *Toronto Star* (November 17, 1995)
390   *Marketing* magazine (December 17, 1998). An example of Bullmore's macho marketing can be found in the releases of Silakhan Route. It "executes Expeditionary Marketing Campaigns" and develops applications of Sun Tzu in "contemporary competitive conflict" (*Business Wire*, November 3, 1998).
391   http://www.strategies-tactics.com/suntzuchp1.htm

that the most successful battles are those you do not have to fight. Modern businesspeople obsessed with military analogies would do well to remember that.[392]

- "Formulating construction export marketing strategies: Lessons from *Sun Tzu's Art of War*," by Sui Pheng Low, appeared in *Focus on Property and Construction in Singapore*. With C. S. Martin Tan, he wrote a Sun Tzu application for the construction industry that brought together "Western and Oriental strategic thinking."[393]

- In 1993, B. H. Boar wrote *The Art of Strategic Planning for Information Technology,* said by Amazon.com to be a "relevant, accessible and logical guide to strategy for information technology … integrating a variety of approaches to strategy formulation into an overall framework using Sun Tzu's and Machiavelli's philosophies as a foundation."[394]

- "It is important for the executive team to discuss strategic issues together frequently. By doing so you will become like any good team … you learn to 'read each other's minds.' This becomes essential when it's necessary for the company to react quickly to marketplace changes or execute a strategy with vigor."[395]

- Some think a "war mentality" belongs in wars and war-in-the-office models are nonsense. "Even allowing for the notion of a 'just war',

---

392   *Financial Times* (August 4 1999)

393   *Marketing Intelligence and Planning*, 1995, Vol. 13 Issue 2, p. 36

394   http://www.amazon.com/exec/obidos/ASIN/0471599182/002-1639198-8367219

395   *The Sun Tzu Strategy Newsletter*, second quarter issue (online) See: http://www.indiapolicy.org/lists/india_policy/1998/Jun/msg00157.html.

one may still feel a war mentality is not necessary or desirable for successful business life; whereas a war mentality is always likely to contribute to a successful war" (Wee *et al.* 1996, v–vi).

- Book reviewer John Regehr says, "*The Art of War* is packed with valuable advice if you're going to fight a land war. It's mostly a curiosity otherwise, and its continuing popularity must be due to the assumption that some of the same skills apply to business, office politics, and other adversarial situations. Seems like a stretch to me."[396]

While some of what we are seeing may seem innocuous enough, and some may well be helpful, little of the real *Ping-fa* can be found in the literature. There can be real danger when managers with a superficial understanding start dogmatic application of alleged "Sun Tzuisms," based on Sun Tzu myths about war and destruction. Real harm can result from an overly controlling, overly aggressive, win-above-all-else management style. Instead of improving performance, the application of bad practices—from whatever source—just does not make sense. And it could be leaving real human casualties in its wake.[397]

The *Financial Times* contained an excellent analysis by John Kay, a director of London Economics.[398] It dealt with the "profoundly misleading" analogies used by "business as war" proponents who use Sun Tzu as the fashionable, "New Economy" basic text. Mr. Kay is of the view that,

---

396   http://www.cs.virginia.edu/~jdr8d/books/reviews/artofwar.html

397   Which is part of the reason I have written this work. The same concern led Cleary to challenge Wilhelm's work on *Golden Flower* (1991, 5).

398   *Management Lessons: Managers from Mars*, 4 August 1999

while the "military analogy" has clearly influenced both thinking and behavior in the office environment, it is very limited in what it can offer executives today. He does see effects in style and behavior, some of which is helpful and some of which is not. Among the unhelpful effects he observes is the adoption of workplace machoism by women executives. They are no doubt guided in part by Harriet Rubin's *The Princessa: Machiavelli for Women*, wherein they may learn how to be a "canny fighter and steely sovereign."

Bruce F. Webster wrote *The Art of Ware: Sun Tzu's Classic Work Reinterpreted* in 1995. The Decus Canada reviewer expected "the classic joke of business as a type of warfare" but instead found good "advice on software development based on a classic of combat wisdom." Webster admits to having a difficulty with his sources as a "scorched market approach to business is unlikely to help anyone in the long run." Robert Heller says, "In many auto companies life is like a jungle. An uncivilized company is no more worth living in than a cannibal country. Even decent companies such as General Foods were in danger of forgetting that people are not pawns" (1985, 377–378).

In October 1998, *The Independent* looked at Microsoft, which had enjoyed an "impeccable image ... as the brilliant icon of the emerging information revolution." How did the first almost-overnight become "The Evil Empire," and Bill Gates "the world's richest public enemy," as both faced US government trustbusters? The fault must lay with PR agency Waggener Edstrom, they say. The agency's apparent use of Sun Tzu, among other things, contributed to a growing public perception of the company as "predatory and ruthless in crushing all rivals."

Of late, management theorists have succumbed to a need to reduce great complexities to simple formulae. They are easily identified by titles that suggest "seven strategies" or "twelve principles" that will help you achieve (your) wealth or (another's) loss. These texts are targeted at Western society's insatiable appetite for the sixty-second solution and "Eastern wisdom." We have, for example, Steven R. Cunningham's "Five Principles of Strategy by Sun Tzu." The Albrechts (1993, 48) say, "Americans tend to like their deals like their hamburgers, put together and ready to grab and consume ... unlike the Japanese who prefer to study each facet of any deal." And if a Westerner wants a "crash course in seminal business thinking" covering the "50 Books That Shaped Management Thinking," he or she can get it all (including *Ping-fa*) in a three hundred–page volume. Reviewer Anne Fisher wondered how the publishers were able to achieve that miracle. Happily, she was able to conclude, "It does work."[399]

Mastering the art of engagement takes knowledge and experience. It takes more than shedding cultural and experiential baggage. The skills that *Ping-fa* requires do not come from one book or even a weekend retreat. They require intense study, experimentation, and development. Appreciating *Ping-fa's* lines about leaving enemies intact and building strength—not on the backs of competitors, but with their willing participation—takes time. The message is really quite simple: "Engage for beneficial reasons only. Manage costs and losses. Finish quickly. Make sure everyone is better off in the end."

In the business and management genre, better analysts are asking basic questions about assumptions, values, and methodologies that have been taken for granted for a very long time. Such challenges bode well for growth in understanding. For illustration, the authors of *Added Value Negotiating* ask whether

> negotiation is a form of combat between two parties, with each striving to get the better of the other, or is it a form of cooperation that seeks a balance of both interests?(Albrecht 1993, 8)

---

399 *Business Life,* January 5, 1999

Kenneth Kaye (1994, 123) ponders "high performance teamwork," a methodology where one seek solutions in polarized environments, by locating the right "balance point." This is a *Ping-fa* resonance. Another related model suggests that success comes with honesty and openness:

> Effective negotiation is the result of comprehensive research, of building a well-reasoned position, of studying and fully understanding the other party's position—perhaps more fully than he or she understands it—then bridging the gap between your position and the other party's with a persuasive mutually satisfying proposition based upon facts, reason, and fairness rather than upon willpower, desire or deceit. (Steinberg 1998, 14)

It is a valuable line of inquiry to examine the practice of negotiation—one of the cherished icons of conflict management. But we need to go deeper, and critically examine not only methods, but models. The Albrechts for instance appear unwilling to challenge the validity of two parties seeking common ground separated by a conference table.

Many of our organizational and engagement models are built on assumptions that are as solid as bedrock. We are not tripping over the sort of out-of-the-box breakthroughs we are going to need if we are to advance organizational and managerial quality. And we do need radical change. We are experiencing serious losses and costs in business, industry, and government because we continue to adhere to obsolete models, tinkering on the fringes, and not really ever getting down to the fundamentals. A military observer says of this phenomenon that "we are concerned [only] with the reconciliation of effects and not in putting aside the cause of war."[400]

---

400 J. Krishnamurti. See: http://www.kfa.org/bl-12.html.

International Trade

By the year 2020, the World Bank predicts that nine of the world's top fifteen economies will be from what we patronizingly call today the "industrializing" world including China, India and Indonesia. (Kiernan 1995)

The *Financial Post and Financial Times* reports, "More than 200 of the world's top 500 multinationals have made investments in China averaging more than $20 million each. Many more appear to be very keen to enter this potentially huge market." *The Economist* speculates that China could easily have the world's largest economy by the second decade of the millennia. But Kiernan feels that adapting and succeeding in this marketplace will be "particularly difficult for North American executives, who tend to lack the necessary linguistic, cultural and attitudinal skills for this job."

Westerners will find this a different business context. Business rules, values, and even etiquette may be challenging, especially for those who are accustomed to completing a deal over lunch, having met then for the first time. Businesspeople along the Pacific Rim are more likely to "see negotiation as an implicit, unstated aspect of a long-term relationship, not as a slam-bang problem-solving process" (Albrecht 1993, 59).

Kiernan suggests US academic institutions are unprepared for the effort needed to get managers and executives up to speed for this new environment—what he calls a "global snake pit," where even such business giants as McDonald's can have a major Beijing business deal canceled overnight (Kiernan 1995, 142). It *can* get nasty out there. The first sentence in *Conflict Management in the Asia Pacific* tells us, "Doing business in the Asia

Pacific is particularly fraught with conflict" (Leung and Tzosvold 1998).[401]

Lee Kun-Hee, chairman of Samsung Group, says: "Without understanding things considered 'alien' to Korean culture, Samsung can never compete." Okay so far. But then he says, "Knowing yourself and your enemies is the first prerequisite to becoming a warrior."[402] He means the "warriors" of *Sun Tzu: War and Management*. Says the chairman, "The business world is not unlike the battlefield [where] competition can be quite vicious and merciless, and clobbering the competitors is a common event. It is no great surprise war strategies have found a very receptive audience in the boardrooms of businessmen" (Wee *et al.*, 9–10). Michael Robert says that along the Pacific Rim some don't play fair.

> American industrialists should recognize the fact that maybe—just maybe—the Japanese do not want to play according to our rules. A better approach might be to spend time inventing a new game with new rules that are more to our advantage. When everyone ... plays the game according to the same rules, no one wins! After all, the object of competition is *not* to have an even playing field, but to design *a playing field that is tilted to your advantage,* and to design a playing field that paralyzes the competition. (Robert 1993, 117)

Dr. Wee Chow Hou of the National University of Singapore says Sun Tzu is popular in Asia but is the "top favorite" in China. To him, Sun Tzu is a useful tool in both macro and microanalysis, helping him understand and explain such issues as the strength of the Japanese

---

401   Though they say later that "East Asians place much less value on competition and conflict [than North Americans]" (Leung and Tzosvold 1998, 309)
402   *Businessweek* (February 28, 1994)

economy. Japanese companies such as Toyota, Nissan, and Honda, achieve global success, he says, because they, "began from a position of weakness, not strength."[403] *The Far Eastern Economic Review* (January 6, 1994) listed *Ping-fa* first among the favorite books of its Asian readers.

American executives who are trying to get up to speed by reading works by or about Asian tactics and practices may be in for some surprises. There are no guarantees that Asian "instructors" have themselves got it right; regardless, you have no way of knowing whether your business associates subscribe to the sort of view you have been reading about. Many Asian "experts" are convinced business is viewed and practiced by Asians as a sort of military campaign. Kent Calder's book on Asia-Pacific says that East Asians "place strong emphasis on indirection and psychological pressure, avoiding violent techniques except as a last resort." He follows this remarkable observation with the traditional *Ping-fa* misunderstanding about winning first and then going to war (1997, 128).[404]

Consider Wee *et al.*'s explanation for Japanese international economic success. They say it derives from their militaristic models and talent for copying. One needs only to look at the board game Go, quality control, quality circles, bonsai, and on-the-job training. They were all "borrowed" from others. They say, "*Sun Tzu's Art of War* may be the inspiration for much of Japan's economic success in the world."

Rosalie Tung's (1994) essay on Asian "strategic management thought" translates an incomplete understanding of *Ping-fa* into an Asia-Pacific business

---

403   See: http://www.gsansom.demon.co.uk/gs7.htm; http://www2.jaring.my/capa/article/89.htm; also *People Management* (October 23, 1997)
404   And as I point out elsewhere, the military interpretation of this line is absurd. If you have already won, you don't go to war.

strategy. In her view, the most preferred engagement strategy to be learned from *Ping-fa* is to "deal a swift and fatal blow." She suggests that among the "principles guiding the East Asian approach to business" are "transforming an adversary's strength into weakness, taking advantage of an adversary's or competitor's misfortune, and striving for total victory." She says traits considered negative in the West—such as passivity and taking advantage of someone's misfortune—are okay in Asia. Western ideals of morality and ethics are viewed differently along the Rim because, she says, "East Asians are a pragmatic people."

Michael Robert's *Strategy Pure and Simple* sets out, purely and simply, a comparison of values and styles between East and West:

> Whereas in America the system is geared to serving the needs of consumers, the system in Japan is geared to serving the needs of the producers. In America, the consumer is best served by innovating and holding down costs; in Japan the producer seeks growth to create employment as an integral part of nation building. Whereas cartels are thought of as being detrimental to healthy competition in America, cartels are encouraged in Japan. In America close buyer-vendor relationships are discouraged; in Japan, it is a fundamental concept of their success at quality improvement. (1993, 114)

Chin-Ning Chu, an "independent marketing consultant specializing in Asia," has a book called *Thick Face, Black Heart: The Path To Thriving, Winning & Succeeding*. Her publicist says this "powerful secret" answers the question of how countries ruined in World War II were able to spring back into global prominence. Some suspected it had to do with Confucianism, others on the rigidity of society and authority. Possibly it was

Ping-fa. The ostensible reason for consulting such unlikely sources is that Asians see no divergence between business, war, philosophy, and spirituality. Tactics used on a battlefield are just as applicable when it comes to winning in business, we are told.[405]

But one needs to be very careful in comparing words on pages with words that are understood, and actions thereafter that may or may not be based on either source. Asians may see very different messages in the words of their old masters. A recent book by Sterling Seagrave has the quite unsubtle title *Lords of the Rim*, yet it opens with a Sun Tzu quote on subtlety (VI.9)![406] One wonders whether Westerners, brash by design, will easily achieve understanding of the subtlety of the *Tao Te Ching* and *Ping-fa.*

Certainly there is evidence of changes in Asian style. *Asiaweek,* compiler of the "Asiaweek Power 50," sees the end of "recalcitrant regimes, entrenched interests and the dogged resistance of traditional whys and ways." They believe a failure to adapt, be responsive, and ensure integrity led to the toppling of President Suharto and Malaysia's Anwar Ibrahim. Today's "most powerful personages in Asia owe their authority not to armed might, astounding wealth or awe-inspiring titles."

Asiaweek says national leaders ought to be listening to what Confucius and Sun Tzu had to say, as evidently do the two most powerful leaders. They say South Korean President Kim Dae Jung and Chinese Premier Zhu Rongji exemplify leadership that combines a reform agenda with established, widespread backing. According to the

---

405 *Management* magazine (July 1996) says she earns "US$1000 a head for workshops for American executives on the secrets of Eastern thought." During an interview in March 1998 with Australasia *National Business Bulletin,* she made her militarist perspective clear ("bait the enemy, destroy the enemy, etc.").
406 Noted in *The Witch Doctors* by Micklethwait and Wooldridge.

Canberra Times of January 1999, China's successful application of the skills *Asiaweek* refers to can be seen in the growing close relationship between the Australian Defence Department and the People's Liberation Army.

If one can generalize about "Asian" social mores and business practices—and that is doubtful—we can say that individually and collectively we are witnessing evolutionary and in some cases revolutionary change. The economy is hot along the Rim, and new powers are emerging and consolidating. Ignorance of the East is no longer an option, if indeed it ever was. Soldiers, statesmen, and businesspeople are making a concerted effort to achieve a working knowledge of the area and its people, as Western peace and prosperity depends upon it.

We are seeing an impressive interest in Asian history, philosophy, and management practices. Business analysts study to discover the real reasons these countries are so successful in product identification, developing and deploying state-of-the-art engineering and technology, employee training and retraining, marketing, logistics management, and a host of other skills. There is a powerful interest in uncovering the secrets of Asia-Pacific successes, achieved in areas where Western economies have experienced dramatic market share losses, such as in automobile and electronic component manufacturing.

Still, we are a long way from understanding what makes Asia work and how an "outsider" can operate effectively within it. We need more guidance, such as that offered by Charles Handy (1994, 88), who learned how long it can take to develop cross-cultural business competence in South Malaysia. An associate, noting that Handy felt he needed a written agreement to seal a deal, almost walked away. "I had met a culture where negotiation was about finding the best way forward for both parties. Later I realized the 'Chinese contract' embodied a principle that went far beyond the making of lasting commercial deals. It was about the importance of compromise as a prerequisite of progress. It was about the need for trust and a belief in the future."

Another Pacific analyst (Micklethwait and Wooldridge 1996, 263) made the same observation: "Chinese managers like to boast that, in contrast to their legalistic Western peers, their businesses are based on negotiating relationships, not contracts. The chief assets of an overseas-Chinese business are usually its *guanxi* (or connections)." There is also advice available on the ways and means of building trust relationships. Lasserre and Probert (1998) say that even for the well initiated, there may be a need to call on the services of a "trusted intermediary [as] there is general agreement that European or American rules of business cannot simply be transposed to the Asian region."

But not all the experts agree that there is a need to bother with learning about the Pacific Rim or its resident cultures. The author of *The Tao meets the Dow* asks, "What is the missing ingredient in modern business leadership?" It is, he says, an "ancient Chinese secret."

Chinese philosophy—from the writings of the ancient military strategist *Sun Tzu* to the *Tao Te Ching* is all the rage in management and investment circles. Yet much of its message runs counter to the drumbeat of capitalism. Take, for example, *Real Power: Business Lessons from the Tao Te Ching*. It instructs the "wise business leader" that "yielding can be the equivalent of winning" —a negotiation tactic not likely to be kind to the bottom-line. *(Psychology Today,* May/ June, 1998 Vol. 31, No. 3, p.16)

The *Psychology Today* article quotes Dr. Eric Abramson, a Columbia University psychologist who studies management fads: "The fortune-cookie nature of such ancient counsel is often ill-suited to the complex, situation-specific management problems modern business leaders face." Notes the author, "The recent collapse of Asian markets may cause managers to stop looking for leadership lessons in fortune cookies—and go back to reading *Fortune*."

Fortune will not be able to, by itself, bring about a significant shift in Western perspective regarding Asian partners. To achieve "favored trader" status, Westerners will need to develop new insights, styles, and sensitivities. We will need to know more about "the rules of social behavior [that] clearly forbid one party to cause another to lose face" (Lasserre and Probert, 1998). We will need to better appreciate that the principles and values we take for granted about the East may be marginally correct, at best. As the Center for Strategic and International Studies discovered, "the most highly rated values among Asians were orderly society, group harmony and respect for authority." These data emerged from "100 noted Asian observers in Thailand, Malaysia, Singapore, Indonesia, China, Japan and South Korea."[407] Just how prevalent is the attitude, and belief, among Westerners venturing into the "Mysterious East" that they need to be superior in the techniques of contact martial arts and a militaristic, take-no-prisoners Sun Tzu?

Military Affairs and Infowar

The military likes Ping-fa, and they sometimes get it right, which is really quite amazing given the commentary they've had to work with.[408] They like his tactics, his strategies, his relentless pursuit of victory, and his instructions about fighting only when winning is a certainty. But they also sometimes get *Ping-fa*, and

---

407   *New Straits Times*, Malaysia (June 26, 1998)
408   *Ping-fa* is first on Air Force Chief of Staff General Ronald Fogleman's "Enlightened Warriors" reading list. See: http://www.afmc.wpafb.af.mil/HQ-AFMC/PA/leading_edge/mar97/page15.htm and the "Professional Readings" list of the Quartermaster Officer Course at Fort Lee, VA.

China, awfully wrong. They imagine *Ping-fa* saying all sorts of things—such as one should always attack an incapacitated adversary, that wars are inevitable because of human nature, and that when you do go to war you should eradicate the enemy.

From the time Father Amiot brought *Ping-fa* to the West, the army has claimed ownership of it. Giles discovered that very quickly when he dared suggest there might be other ideas in *Ping-fa* than military ones. As the commentators have come for the most part from the military, the translations, interpretations, and classification have been predominantly military. There is a fair degree of evidence that *Ping-fa* has found its way into the duffle bags of a number of key Western military and political figures.

Napoleon is supposed to have read it, and some say Mao Tse-tung carried it on the Long March. Tang Zi-Chang said Mao considered *Ping-fa* "the great military theoretician of old China."[409] Certainly Mao's first two challenges to Chiang Kai-Shek's "Campaigns" were pure *Ping-fa*, though the third was not. We may never know for sure. We are told that, according to a "senior Pentagon official," that "Bejing's .... defense establishment ... applies the theories of Sun Tzu...on how to extract advantage when an enemy deceives himself and how best to capitalize on an enemy's mistakes" (Halper 2010, 230).

In some cases the evidence is not at all clear. Jay Luvaas's *Napoleon on the Art of War* makes no mention of *Ping-fa*. Harrison Salisbury's (1985, 172) *The Long March* says Mao read *Ping-fa*, but his "military text for the Long March was *The Romance of the Three Kingdoms*." The autobiography of General William C. Westmorland had six listings for *Sun-Tzu*, who he called "The Clausewitz

---

409　From *Problems in the Strategy of the Revolutionary War in China.*

of the Orient."[410] Interestingly, Clausewitz is not among his references.[411]

Despite a commentary that has hardly varied since the time of Father Amiot, and despite generations of students at military academies having pored over the text and written uncountable term essays on it, elements of contradiction and confusion remain. And that contradiction and confusion extends beyond *Ping-fa* to China, and indeed, to Asia as a whole.

Michael Handel says that, according to Fairbank, the Chinese art of war is much the same as that practiced elsewhere. Research will "show up the sinological fallacy as to China's alleged uniqueness." But he allows there are differences that come from China's geography and history, leading to a Chinese

> approach to war that includes, (1) a tendency to disesteem heroism and violence, not to glorify it; (2) a tradition of land warfare that prefers defense to offense and stress that exhausting an attacker or the pacification of a rebel as less costly that their extermination; and (3) a tie-up between militarism and bureaucracy, rather than commercial expansion, least of all overseas. (1992, 168)

Here are some other examples of Western impressions about China, *Ping-fa*, and the business of war:

- Secretary of Defense Cohen. "For the foreseeable future, there are few who will have the power to match us militarily or economically, but they will be students of Sun Tzu and the Art of Warfare, dedicated to exploiting the weaknesses

---

410   Colonel Harry Summers USA (Ret) says the "Chinese Clausewitz" is really General Liu Chi, who became Emperor Gaozu, founder of the Han dynasty.

411   See Westmorland's *A Soldier Reports.*

of our very strengths. The more reliant we become upon computers and information systems, the more vulnerable we become to cyber-terrorists who will conceive unlimited ways to cripple our infrastructure, our power grids, our banking systems, our financial markets, our space-based communications systems. So we have to remain muscular enough to deal with and deter conventional threats and agile enough to anticipate and defeat attempts to send poison arrows at our Achilles' heels or, more appropriately, poison pills at our databases."[412]

- Ambassador Hughes. "Our 'nodal analysis' of key strategic points in ocean shipping ... seems to have been neglected, even as the Chinese have increased their study of these matters. This should come as no surprise. For it is a concept which they have successfully employed for literally thousands of years. The principle of their great military strategist, Sun Tzu, is that the surest way to defeat an enemy is to make sure that you do not have to actually go to war to defeat him. This is to be done, under the lessons of this master of strategy, by rendering us unable to support our technically superior fighting capacity through a control of the ocean commerce necessary to support it in actual conflict. In times of actual conflict 80 percent and more of our supplies and weaponry and personnel must move by ocean commerce. We are only as strong as

---

412   Secretary Cohen at DoD News Briefing at April 1998 Eisenhower Institute Leadership Dinner. See: http://www. defenselink.mil/news/May1998/t05051998_t428ike_.html.

our weakest link in this vital commerce. That weakest link is the Panama Canal."[413]

- "Shortly before the air war against Iraq began, Brigadier General Russell Sutton was reported as saying, 'The last thing we want to do is try to meet Hussein head-on. This is pure Sun Tzu'."[414]

- Asked what business book best applies to his unit's work, Brigadier General Thomas Matthews says his soldiers are writing the real book. "Let's put it this way," says the commander, a district sales manager for Lucent Technologies, "the art of war is very mature. It goes back thousands of years to Sun Tzu. The art of peace is much newer. We're learning about it here."[415]

- On August 22, 1999, the UK's *Observer* ran a story about alleged releases of US secrets and China's neutron bomb capability. Said the US Defense Intelligence Agency's Houston Hawkins, "Tzu's complex, Zenike doctrine of 'mosaic' intelligence and dis-information posits the possibility that the Chinese wanted the US to know what it had."[416]

It's not entirely clear (given the numerous ways people are able to use the same words and mean entirely

---

413   Ambassador Hughes, in a June 1998 hearing before the Committee on Foreign Relations, US Senate, on "The Panama Canal and United States Interests"
414   Reported in *Forbes*, 12/9/91 Vol. 148, Issue 13, p. 154
415   Congressional Record, June 1996.
416   W.P. Strobelin said the same thing in *U.S. News* (online) on June 7, 1999.

different things) what these speakers are really saying, and what their impressions really are.

Consider as further examples, the liberties of meaning that are taken in regard to several other key terms. "Strategy" means the way one conquers in military terms. "Fighting is the central military act: all other activities merely support it. Engagements mean fighting. The object of fighting is the destruction or defeat of the enemy. The concept of the engagement lies at the root of all strategic action, since strategy is the use of force, the heart of which, in turn, is the engagement" (Howard and Paret 1976, 227). Martin van Creveld has similar definitions: "The essence of war is fighting." He says everything else is prelude or results exploitation (van Creveld 1991, 97, 161).

Newt Gingrich (1984, 224, 235) advocated that senior political and military officials study it to help them understand "the art of grand strategy." He wanted the United States to get beyond "tactical zigzags" that addressed "problems with an inadequate strategic visionary policy and framework." Gingrich is not speaking of *Ping-fa* as a system for strategic, sensitive intervention, but of Clausewitzian strategy, which is "a question of mobilizing *all* mental and physical forces and forging them into a mailed fist [whose purpose] was to crash down on the enemy, shattering his body and breaking his will" (van Creveld, 97).

According to Rick Lazio, "Sun Tzu states that, 'To fight and conquer in all your battles is not supreme excellence. Supreme excellence consists in breaking the enemies' resistance without fighting.' Through our resolve over the last 45 years, we avoided not only war, but nuclear holocaust. We ended a form of slavery for almost half a billion people. Shouldn't that rate a small party, if not a full-blown celebration?"[417]

---

417   Mr. Rick Lazio in the Congressional Record, September 1996 (House), speaking on behalf of House Concurrent Resolution 180

How much of these views can be laid at the feet of those articulating them, and how much on the feet of the commentary?

Ping-fa must strike discordant notes with military practitioners. There is simply too much that, if taken literally, makes no sense at all. That is perhaps why it is mostly out of favor with conventional land forces today, now deemed an anachronism overtaken by modern weaponry, military practices, and globalization. Colonel Harry G. Summers Jr. thinks *Ping-fa* is overrated. He says at the "bedsides [of American battlefield commanders should be] Carl von Clausewitz's *On War*. A commander can then shout with confidence at any enemy he might face, 'You S.O.B., I've read the book'!"[418]

Ping-fa's alleged thoughts on military tactics did resurface in the Persian Gulf War,[419] and they are mentioned in the South Pacific press from time to time. You might imagine we could be seeing the end of the military's love affair with *Ping-fa*. But then along came computers, information technology, and something called "infowar." Infowar is a war fought virtually, and quite literally on computer keyboards. It is about intelligence, and it naturally resonates with the work of a master intelligence gatherer and user.

Infowar[420]

- The "Information War-Cyberwar-Netwar" paper by George J. Stein. "Strategic level netwar brings us within sight of Sun Tzu's elusive 'acme of skill' wherein the enemy is subdued without killing by attacking his ability to form or execute a coherent strategy."[421]

---

418   See: http://www.airpower.maxwell.al.mil/
airchronicles/aureview/1986/mar-apr/summers.html.
419   For example, Joseph J. Romm in "The Gospel According to Sun Tzu." *Forbes* magazine, 12/9/91
420   Also known as "Network-centric warfare"
421   http://www.infowar.com/MIL_C4I/STEIN1.html-ssi

- "Information Warfare: Will Battle Ever Be Joined?" A lecture by Lawrence Freedman.[422] "Sun Tzu is much beloved of modern 'cyber-warriors.' His interest in the possibilities of a bloodless victory led him to many observations on how to acquire and use information, including concealment, confusion, deception, dissimulation, and generally staying inscrutable."

- *Some Cautionary Thoughts on Information Warfare* by R. L. DiNardo and Daniel J. Hughes. "Sun Tzu's argument that, 'to subdue the enemy without fighting is the acme of skill' assumes that your enemy is willing to allow himself to be subdued without fighting. History tells us that governments are seldom so cooperative."[423]

General Peter J. Schoomaker of US Special Operations Command says, "Today it's less Clausewitz and more Sun Tzu." He sees the *Ping-fa* "acme of military victory" as "the ability to use information, deception, psychological warfare and electronic warfare."[424] Alvin Toffler views information as a weapon, and he is enthusiastic about its impacts.

No genius in the past—not Sun-Tzu, not Machiavelli, not Bacon himself, could have imagined today's

---

422   Professor of War Studies at King's College, London. Speech given at the launch of the International Centre for Security Analysis in October 1996. http://www.infowar. com/MIL_C4I/ICSA/ICSA1.html.
423   http://www.infowar.com/MIL_C4I/dinardo.html-ssi
424   *Armed Forces Journal International* (February 1999). Schoomakes goes on to say his "troops are highly motivated individuals who are really 'leaning forward in the harness.'"

deepest *powershift:* the astounding degree to which both force and wealth themselves have come to depend on knowledge. Knowledge is a key weapon in the power struggles that accompany the emergence of the super-symbolic economy (the 'Third Wave'). (1990, 17)

At a United States Air Force event, Toffler argued that the rules of international relations of the past three hundred years are obsolete. He declared that war planners must "replace deterrence and mutually assured destruction with force-backed, anti-war strategies for the turbulent world to come." The future military will face "a world of Sun Tzu technology in which the best victories are those that come without combat and in which information superiority can prevent or even win wars before they begin."[425]

"The best victories come without combat" and "winning wars before they begin" certainly sound like the sort of thing we might find in *Ping-fa.* But Toffler, like Newt Gingrich, is not talking about sensitive intervention. He's talking about a new wave—a wave where the means may be new but it's the same old objectives.

There is a very grave difference between Toffler intelligence and *Ping-fa* intelligence. The "spies" of *Ping-fa* gather intelligence to *prevent* engagement, or to ensure that if an engagement is necessary, it is limited in scope and duration. Toffler and company use technology in intelligence gathering to *prepare for* (eventual?) hostilities. To Toffler information means power,[426] and "power is inherent in all social systems and in all human relationships."

Infowar protagonist R. K. Newland says infowar enables "warfare unlike any other in the past, because it depends upon the quality and quantity of appropriate

425   http://www.foreignpolicy.com/ohanlside1.htm
426   This "power" is not Master Sun's "strength." It is "force."

data to positively change the behavior of the commander receiving it."[427] As Toffler, Newland, and Defense Secretary William Cohen evidently did not know, this was a central proposition in *Ping-fa's* 2,300-year-old methodology for engagement management. Though *Ping-fa* may have been there before him, today it is Toffler who has the army's ear. Rand Corporation analyst Glenn Buchan observed that Toffler's "Third Wave" jargon was in use everywhere in the national security establishment when the importance of information in future warfare was being discussed.[428] He and others have cast a decidedly military pall over new technologies that could equally hold promises for peaceful solutions.

S. J. Wray says infowar is all about "dominance over adversaries" and "resisting and fighting enemy advances." He says the Information Resources Management College defines infowar as information management in armed conflict. The National Defense University's Institute for National Strategic Studies is equally interested. Military experts there use computer-based simulations for strategic planning and learn how to disable enemies by the "creative" application of technology.[429]

Infowar has brought *Ping-fa* to the fore again as a sort of folk hero,[430] as computers and information technology present national governments with a whole new battery of threats. The American Institute for National Strategic Studies (AINSS) established the "Sun Tzu Art of War in Information Warfare Research Competition." They say they named the competition after Sun Tzu because of

---

427 *Tactical Deception in Information Warfare: A New Paradigm.* See: http://www.jedefense.com/jed/html/new/dec98/feature.html
428 http://www.foreignpolicy.com/ohanlside1.htm
429 http://www.ndu.edu/inss/siws/into.html; http://www.ndu.edu/inss/strforum/forum132.htm
430 Or "IW." Professor Fred Levien says the military is buckling under the forces of political correctness and is now calling it "information operations" (IO).

his conviction that "careful planning based on sound information would contribute to speedy victory." We see *Ping-fa* referenced in army publications, such as *The Craft of Intelligence* by Allen Dulles. And we are seeing that new tools (well, old actually) are being identified to combat these new threats. "Information" is gaining the reputation of a new "divine force":

On the battlefield, *cheng* is a holding force that puts the enemy on the spot, *ch'i* a flanking maneuver that fatally disrupts the enemy's strategy. That is how Genghis Khan fought, and also how Norman Schwarzkopf fought. It is now possible that information could take the place of *cheng*. (*The Economist,* June 10, 1995)

Conflict is an inherent human condition in Toffler's view. He calls it "an inescapable social fact." Such fatalistic views, strongly disputed in *Ping-fa*, were noted by Steven Metz of the US Army War College. He dismissed Toffler's *War and Anti-War* as a superficial "MTV clip, by failing to construct a psychological sophisticated notion of why people fight. [Toffler's] theory of anti-war is incomplete."[431] Toffler (1990, 28, 474) has little time for philosophy. He dreams of a new information-age "guerrilla army—blowing away the faceless bureaucrat-managers who run the old system."

Though not all infowar analysts speak of "blowing away" opposition—whether at home or abroad—most seem to agree information technology has brought a sea change to the rules and practices of military engagement. They imagine real possibilities for effective deterrence and—when offensive action is needed—achieving success without actual combat. Martin C. Libicki's AINSS essay on "Information Dominance" stated that *Ping-fa's* "winning without fighting" may at last be possible. But

---

431   http://www.foreignpolicy.com/ohanlside1.htm

before we declare victory we need to look carefully at what "winning" means to infowarriors:

The primary goal is to bend [an adversary's] mind to change, to mold it to see things our way and to achieve, where possible, our objectives with the avoidance of armed conflict. To meet this goal requires that the US must take actions that manipulate, deny, deceive, delay ... and yes, if necessary as a last resort, destroy an adversary's information systems. (Levien 1999)[432]

This is not *Ping-fa*. This is aggression using information technology, rather than weapons technology. Same activity, different tools. The military has discovered additional potential "benefits" in its studies of info tech. Information is a key ingredient in something called "non-lethality." Janet Morris believes the "area between when diplomacy fails and the first shot is fired has never been quantifiable before. [In this space, there could be] non-lethality, emerging not as a simple replacement for war or an extension of peace, but as something different—something radically new in global affairs: an intermediate phenomena, a pausing place, an arena for contest in which more outcomes could be decided bloodlessly."

"Non-lethal" weapons are those whose "primary purpose is not the taking of human life." They are deemed "defensive." We might, Ms. Morris suggests, "have protective devices built directly into the physical structure of an embassy, turning the entire building into a kind of transducer that can be tuned to create a defensive electronic shield." A "better" solution to the Temple Mount massacre in Jerusalem in 1990, she says, would have been to "have used an infra sound generator to break up the Palestinian crowd. If they vomited or defecated on themselves then that's better than anybody

432   http://www.jedefense.com/jed/html/new/apr99/
technology.html

being dead." In this field the high profile proponent is Winn Schwartau, who is the author of "Chaos on The Electronic Superhighway: Information Warfare." *Time*, in a July 1997 discussion of the "EMP gun," called it "the weird science of nonlethality."

Weapons of Mass Protection: Nonlethality, Information Warfare, and Airpower in the Age of Chaos says we can now have "weapons of mass protection" and "project high-precision power in a timely fashion." Armies will achieve results that are "life conserving, environmentally friendly, and fiscally responsible." They feel the *Ping-fa* authors would be proud of them, given their view that they "counseled that armed force was to be applied so that victory would be gained (a) in the shortest possible time, (b) at the least possible cost in lives and effort, and (c) with the infliction on the enemy of the fewest possible casualties."[433]

Are these changes being driven by "humanity," or are we seeing the effects of other factors, such as budgetary limitations, causing the military to become more creative in their use of new technologies? Certainly all the funds have not been available that experts, such as Alvin Toffler, consider essential. His "Third Wave War" laments the sad case of "dissipating defense budgets" that may have dreadful effects: "The chances for peace may be worsened as a consequence" (1993, 182). Military technology is "helping":

The future is bleak for the infantry, those that operate on a tight budget. A century ago, it was calculated that you had to fire a man's weight in bullets and shells to cause a casualty. This tonnage has increased several times in the last 50 years. But the tonnage has recently come down as much more efficient weapons became available. More cluster bombs and other ICM (Improved

433 Chris Morris, Janet Morris, and Thomas Baines at http://www.infowar.com/CLASS_3/MORRIS.html-ssi

Conventional Munitions) will be blasting away at smaller numbers of infantry. (Dunnigan 1993, 42)

But the real promise appears to be in the field of infowar. Not only might this sort of military preparedness be cheaper than what conventional war requires, but it also seems to have captured the imagination of politicians. New money may be flowing. James Adams, author of *The Next World War*, almost sounds excited when he describes what the "front lines" will look like in the next war. Andrew Leonard reviewed this book and said it read like a position paper for boosting government spending on the high-tech gadgets that infatuate the military-industrial complex (infowar.com July 28, 1998).

It's too bad Toffler can't widen his focus on the "new wave" of technology and get beyond conflict and destruction. Some theorists see all sorts of opportunities coming out of information technology. One pair of authors feel it offers new, beneficial prospects for "small-scale communities, indigenous knowledge, webbed education, and participatory democracy." They say it may be possible

for the community to visualize the pattern of change, to play out the effect of one or the other option, and decide which to choose on the basis of more foreknowledge than our ancestors ever had. (Burke and Ornstein 1995, 310)

To get us there, we will have to take a very hard look at social drivers—what moves us and what attracts us. And part of that analysis must include those philosophical "truths" about "human nature" and the "inevitability" of conflict that keeps us arming and jousting—long past the time when such activity made sense, if it ever did.

After he completed his extensive work on Baron von Clausewitz, W. B. Gallie said he wished that someone would work on the issue of war's inevitability. If someone would take on this task, he said they should

> concentrate on those crucial conceptual divides where competition (which is surely endemic in all life) passes into conflict and coercion, and where coercion passes into intolerable oppression and war. It seems to me more than strange, it seems to me ominous, that so little philosophical work has been done on these vital questions. (Gallie 1979, 141)

Gallie may be pleased to discover that Qin has already studied these questions, without the assumption that events must—irrevocably by some unknown force—pass into conflict.

Lieutenant Colonel Dave Grossman, a former army ranger and paratrooper, taught psychology at West Point. Now, he is a professor of military science who believes the world is a powder keg just waiting for a match. He says world tensions are maintained by vested interests and that something must be done. "Each act of violence breeds ever-greater levels of violence, and at some point the genie can never be put back in the bottle."

> I believe the time has come for our society to censure (not censor) those who exploit violence for profit. In A.M. Rosenthal's words we must "turn entirely away from those ugly people, defeating them by refusing them tolerance and respectability." What we must realize is that our society is trapped in a pathological spiral with all vectors pulling inward toward a tighter and tighter cycle of violence and destruction. (Grossman 1995, 327, 330)

Grossman speaks of the "why," with the conviction of *Ping-fa*. And Edward de Bono (1985) brings his special insights to the problem of "how." "The existing structures for conflict resolution at best are inadequate, at worst they are positively dangerous and may actually exacerbate conflicts. In structure and in idiom, they are part of our crude, primitive and antiquated approaches to conflict." Clearly, we need new, and perhaps rediscovered, models. "Our ways of resolving conflict tend to rely on the argument mode, which is a continuation of the conflict. We need to move towards a 'designed outcome' mode which consists of exploratory mapping followed by creative design."

Here, *Ping-fa's* theory and practice of engagement management may be useful. And if we look very carefully we will find other gems in the oddest places. Consider *Leadership Secrets of Attila the Hun.* Alvin Toffler calls it a "how-to book with a silly title," but it concerns a great (and apparently much misunderstood) military and social campaigner who had a good deal to say about how to do good things.

Author Wess Roberts (1993, xv) says Attila "symbolizes single-minded determination and concern for his followers." He describes Attila's leadership in words similar to what we find in Sun Tzu. Roberts says building great organizations is not that difficult. They simply need to focus on effective recruitment, training, rewards, and direction within an environment that both cares for and challenges its people. The last word here goes to J. G. Merrills (1998, 311), author of *International Dispute Settlement:*

It is clear that the destructiveness of modern warfare is such as to inflict suffering on an unprecedented scale. I have tried to show how the intelligence and resourcefulness that have produced contemporary weapons have also developed methods of dispute settlement that can make the use of force unnecessary. The present situation can and must be improved. The tools are already at hand.

Resonance: Contemporary Thought

In earlier times, we imagine that people of good intent routinely sought noncombative ways to solve differences. Workers (at all levels) could meet informally to discuss all sorts of issues without contracts and policy manuals in hand, or without the company of shop stewards or lawyers. This is, of course, all quite fictional. If earlier times were simpler, they were simple only in the distribution of power. It was all at the top.

Now power is distributed, and workplaces are consequently complex. They are characterized by structures and processes for rule formalization and functional specialization. Power elements have devolved from the top to both individuals and collective groups. It *may* have been simpler in the past when rules were centrally established and transmitted. Now rules are negotiated within strict parameters and formally agreed to. We have managerial performance accords and collective agreements. These systematic approaches to the organization of work extend also to the decomposition of what were once general activities into professional specializations. Managers "manage." They don't deal with personnel issues. The personnel department deals with personnel. And that department does not manage payroll; finance does that. Line employees do not deal with customers. "Client relations' deals with customers.

It may not be entirely nostalgic to imagine that workers were once much more "jacks of all trades." Routine work of all sorts was handled by employees who were told to just get on with the job. There was a great deal less worry about turf, and a great deal more concern about profit. When circumstances exceeded time or talent, help was provided through external agencies on an as-needed basis. This might involve legal services, marketing, organizational analysis, or general consulting services. Now these functions are fully institutionalized.

Overly structured organizations are the antithesis of free flow. They are characterized by polarity and third-party processes. Communication and cooperation are difficult. Creativity and energy are stifled, while fellowship and collegiality may be quite impossible. Walls are erected, and pathways are paved. For the most part, when worker groups meet with management today, the rules are anything but informal. Meetings happen on specified ground and with a set agenda. "Expert advisors" will be present, and even worse, they may be "management representatives." The objective of such gatherings is usually "getting it right" rather than "getting it good."

Negotiators know their job is to give up as little as possible and gain as much as possible. This is the basic method we use for contract negotiation, grievance administration, and a host of other formalized intergroup practices. In this environment, "special arrangements" or cutting a "deal" are issue resolutions that occur off-site. The conditions add up to what Pat Riley (1993, 24) experienced in 1982. At one GM plant, the labor-management situation got so bad the contract had "over four hundred pages of legal doublespeak—but it didn't serve as a basis for mutual understanding." In complete frustration, the company closed the plant. When they did, they left behind "more than eight hundred union-filed grievances and sixty contested firings."

Covey (1991, 158) says that there is just so much "negative energy" around that "people think of taking the legal approach to problem-solving, often at the first blush of a problem." Asks Albrecht (1993), "What else are we to make of the fact that there are 11 lawyers per 100,000 citizens in Japan, but in the United States the ratio is 281 per 100,000?" We may agree that we have a shared objective in solving differences, but we are guided by an equal belief in the rule of law and precedent. In the Asian environment, Lasserre and Probert (1998) suggest that "legal recourse is generally not a suitable method of trying to solve a problem: it brings the details of the dispute into the public domain [and] public opinion is most likely to side with the local party."

Steinberg (1998, 14) says, "In America the prevailing mood is one of intense adversarial conflict. We seem to be a society entrenched in deeply dug positions, tightly clutching our agendas, shouting across the battlements at one another, hurling edicts and ultimatums, ruled more by our emotions than by carefully reasoned thoughts and responses." Increasing polarization has been a boon to the disciplines of law, mediation, and management consultancy. It is almost a given today that groups need "facilitators." Negotiations frequently run into third-party conciliation or binding arbitration.

A study of conflict by Thomas and Schmidt, reported in *Academy of Management Journal,* found that "managers working only within their own country and in one organization spend a quarter of their time managing conflict and a good deal more time avoiding it" (Leung and Tzosvold 1998, 2). These are "workplaces-as-battlefield" domains that management theorists and journalists have fed on, and fed. In March 1999, *Canadian Transportation Logistics* carried an article on "supplier relations" titled "The Art of Supply Chain War." Drawing on his understanding of Sun Tzu, the author wrote about generals on battlefields, mobilization, the competition storming the gates, and finally, surrender.

Armbruster, in Jane Jacobs's *Systems of Survival,* gathered terms from the *Wall Street Journal* that were used to describe business events. They included: "hired guns," "impending carnage," "commandos," "a scalp in someone's belt," "ferocious opposition," "protect the castle," "hysteria," "war chest," and "scorched earth." Armbruster says, "Hostile takeovers and leveraged buy-outs have drained away management time and attention [as] threats and then battles could continue a year or more." Organizations suffer effects that are cataclysmic.

They bring "friction, misunderstandings, and rivalries ... while morale plummets, stress and anxieties soar."

The value of formalized workplace negotiations may be at an end. Collective bargaining remains the vehicle of choice for settling on tactical and monetary issues, but it is woefully inadequate for resolving the more difficult issues. Too, results are not always beneficial. This is, for example, the possibility that the will of one will be imposed on another. Among other things, "resentment is the residue" (Herman 1994, 126). Similar deficiencies are being experienced at the international level. *International Dispute Settlement* says, "The peaceful settlement of international disputes is the most critical issue of our time [given that] the use of force in certain disputes could result in the destruction of civilization." Though they see the situation as critical, they can't shake their axemaker mentality. They say, "It is difficult to imagine adjudication without law" (Merrills 1998, 292, 310). But some analysts don't think law and legal processes hold much promise in the conflict management area.

The zero-sum, win-lose view of life tends to treat every situation as though there is a fixed pie that is being struggled over, and a larger piece for me will obviously mean a smaller piece for you. Unfortunately, this is the way our legal system is set up, the way our management–employee relations are structured, and the way our political system operates. (Hoffman 1993, 7)

We are woefully incompetent at building organizations that eschew conflict. We are untrained in identifying embryonic conflict and full of uncertainty as to what should be done when we do finally see it. We tend to address conflict management and issue resolution with models derived from adversarial perspectives. Collectively more fatalist than we are prepared to admit, we often believe that full control is an unachievable dream and that damage minimization is a far more realistic target. Wedded to failure, we find it hard to get enthusiastic about achieving positive results. *The Tao of Negotiation* (Edelman and Crain 1993, 105) says, "Despite the obvious importance of preparations, an astonishing number of business people enter into negotiations fully prepared to 'wing it'."

There are a few nonmilitary *Ping-fa* interpretations and applications around. Terry Campbell and Heather Cairns use *Ping-fa* to explain flexibility in learning organizations. Clive Jeanes gives *Ping-fa*–based advice on how to improve customer service. Former Philippine President Fidel Ramos, who had been an infantry commander, says he doesn't necessarily see war when he reads *Ping-fa*.[434]

We read of the Thompsons of Coffee Mill Inc. in Maryland, Peggy Liu's Channel A, and Jim Green's community works. Someday such stories may become common. The Thompsons are avid followers of *Ping-fa*. Calling themselves "Warriors of Wall Street," they understand the importance of strength and quality but "don't see competition as the enemy."[435] Ms. Liu has built an Internet company that "bridges the US and Asia, offering chat forums, community calendars, business, health and spirituality content." All this work is, she says, consistent with *Ping-fa's* admonition to "join hands with allies."[436] Jim Green, who is active in Vancouver community affairs, says he has used *Ping-fa* for over ten years. "Always leave people with an escape route," he says.[437]

Ping-fa is being applied in areas ranging from architecture to environmental management to poetry.

---

434 *Manila Standard*, Philippines (July 1, 1999)
435 *Baltimore Business Journal* (October 3, 1997). In spite of the quite unmilitary content of the story, the journal was unable to resist titling it *Couple Declares 'War.'*
436 *Edmonton Journal* (August, 31 1996)
437 *Vancouver Sun* (January 22, 1994)

And a good deal of valuable work is being done on management structures and systems using more open, peaceful models. Imparato and Harari (1994, 130–131) suggest organizations should "look a customer ahead." They should perfect talents and processes that lead to sustainability and success, and use "group learning ... seeking out ideas ... encouraging open, constructive conflict (as problem analysis not blame analysis) and using technology."

They favor "inclusive organizations" that break down walls and barriers. And they—among other things—are clear on the broad responsibilities of the group and the individual while allowing everyone continually to recreate his or her job and make flexibility and change a way of life. They foster networking and collaboration across departments and disciplines. This is *Ping-fa* used in the workplace, as it was intended.

In somewhat of a departure from the traditional bargaining model, Carolyn Dickson (1997, 112) feels that winning is about finding a "new and better way" than what is being represented by the competing parties. Solutions then are something that come from some area beyond the stakeholders themselves. But this is still solution identification in a state of polarization. Ben Hoffman, who sees no enduring gain in winning by "coercing, overpowering, oppressing, or in compromising," says, "The consensus approach is the way of the future."

There are three essential elements that must be developed in any effort to build our Win-Win Competitiveness. People must be given: (a) The *skills* of conflict resolution; (b) The *tools* for conflict analysis and (c) The *systems* of conflict prevention (policy, procedures and mechanisms to support the application of the tools and the skills). (Hoffman 1993, 46)

The disciplines of conflict resolution and dispute settlement use models based on the levels through which they believe events evolve. At each stage of the evolution, different interventions are suggested. Edward de Bono (1985, 43) says, in conflict thinking, "Start with the design idiom because it offers the most. The next best would be the Problem-solving idiom. Then would come the negotiating idiom ... as a fall-back position. If all else fails then we are back to the 'fight' idiom." Another model sets out a situation–action continuum:[438]

Discussion–Conciliation (assist communications)
Polarization–Consultation (improve relationship)
Segregation–Arbitration/Power Mediation (control hostility)
Destruction–Peacekeeping (control violence)

The *Ping-fa* methodology did not give the world a solution. Solutions are organizationally defined to meet organizational needs. In engagement management, where intervention or nonintervention are deemed necessary, it happens before "Discussion." If resolution is not achieved, an engagement may be warranted. Then, a strategy is drafted, a leader appointed, and a team assembled. These activities are done according to strict rules, most of which are covered by Lipnack and Stamps in *The TeamNet Factor* (1993, 197).

Other parties must remain oblivious to this activity. Indeed, you will ideally achieve control and correction before the other is even aware of your concern. If events are at the stage of "Discussion," victory without cost may be impossible. Indeed victory itself will prove elusive. But effective engagement management, where there are shared interests and objectives, can bring about a "victory" without the dominance of one and subjugation of the other.

---

438   After Fisher and Keashly in Fisher (1997, 166)

Ping-fa advocates a holistic, organic model for interorganizational relations. Effective management involves an astute environmental awareness. One principle messages is "Gain knowledge and modify plans by circumstance." Consistent with pure Taoism, one watches, working continually to keep the urge to interfere in check. As we (in Taoism) know "how polarities work, wise leaders do not push to make things happen, but allow processes to unfold on their own" (Heider 1988, 3).

But the nature of the objects in engagement are a critical issue. They must be mutually beneficial. Mariah Burton Nelson did recognize the importance of intelligence in engagement, dedicating a chapter of *Embracing Victory* to the issue of assessment. But her notions of "victory" and process are obsolete, perhaps relevant to sports events and little else. "The most enjoyable competitions are between near equals ... with the slightly superior player challenged and the slightly inferior player having a chance to win ... in dignified, cooperative competition" (1998, 21).

Processes unfold most properly when one is full of knowledge—knowing oneself and others. Knowledge allows "unraveling and coordinating the patterns of continuity that emerge and persist in the natural, social, and cultural flux around us" (Lau and Ames 1998, 21). Establishing "continuity" is more than trying to find common ground as you sit across from others. By then, it may well be too late. *Ping-fa* says: Know your organization, know yourself, know the environment, know what is right and what you want to achieve. Proceed with caution and sensitivity. Achieve beneficial solutions for all.

Here *Ping-fa* anticipates Stephen Covey's (1990, 157) *abundance mentality*: the "bone-deep belief that there are enough natural and human resources to realize my dream, and that my success does not necessarily mean failure for others, just as their success does not preclude my own. Abundance mentality often makes the difference between excellence and mediocrity, particularly because it eliminates small thinking and adversarial relations."

His thoughts resonate with Edward de Bono's (1985, 5, 20) "exploration." Originating in part from Japan, he says it is based on the premise that parties jointly "explore" usefulness. "Both parties are interested in seeing the good points in the ideas of the other. There is an exploration instead of an argument." He speaks of "de-confliction," which is the "designing away or dissipation of the basis for the conflict. De-confliction does not refer to negotiation or bargaining or even to the resolution of conflicts. It is the evaporation of a conflict." He says the task is not easy. "Among other things, we need to change our perceptions, because we all live within 'patterning systems'." These could be likened to Jane Jacobs's "moral syndromes," where "Syndrome A" bears a remarkable resemblance to the themes of engagement management, while "Syndrome B" reads a lot like conflict management (Jacobs 1992).

Nelson and de Bono advocate conflict amelioration by the application of just the right tweak. Jane Jacobs calls this "tinkering." She views Lao Tzu as a "gift," presumably because the *Tao Te Ching* supports her thesis of achieving change through "syndrome-friendly interventions." But this is *Ping-fa*, not Lao Tzu. Though these management theorists have the notion right, their timing is not. Their interventions, or "course corrections," kick in when matters are actually quite advanced. There is already division, parties are in opposition, and there is the possibility or actuality of conflict. The purpose of engagement management is to achieve success before the conditions necessary for conflict emerge.

We are a long way from achieving real change in the workplace. We argue about what needs doing and how it ought to be done. We are very uncertain about whether real, sustained change comes from initiatives that are "bottom-up" or "top-down." We are really not even sure who is involved—our vocabulary speaks of "colleagues," "associates," "team members," and "partners"—but we have no clear definitions for any of this. There seems to be consensus that the master-servant model is obsolete, as is the staid organizational hierarchical model, but we have not come up their replacements.

But institutions and social structures can change if the political will is there. For whatever reasons, whether historical or contemporary, we all need a good shake. Neither "global warming" or "ice cap meltdown" gets our attention. Perhaps we too often tend to circulate in the stratosphere, where it is safer. There is also less chance up there of coming up with something really useful or of engendering dialogue. And the sort of change we are discussing here needs dialogue. A "grand plan for change" may be premature, but we can work to achieve change in our chiefs and leaders. We need them to understand that organizations can become healthier and happier places to work. A sound mission, defined organizational goals and values, clear guidance and control, effective empowerment, and crystal clear role definition are not desirable attributes. They are critical conditions. And when the organization is so prepared, it can then prepare itself to manage in engagement.

Do our organizations need improvement so that they can better manage themselves and conduct engagements when essential? That seems to be self-evident. But the challenge is great. In some organizations, ineffectiveness and counterproductive activities of all sorts are firmly entrenched. Robert Heller says, "Where the bland are leading the bland, all the behavioral scientists in the American universities will not improve performance" (Heller 1985, 237).

At this stage in the planet's history, we need new literature. We need to set out what we know and what we do not know. We need to expose cherished myths. We need to establish some fundamentals. But cognitive leaps will not come easily, and they will be forever frustrated if assumptions are not challenged. We need a collective admission of uncertainty and vulnerability. We need to examine our macro- and micro-economic models much more carefully and assess what really constitutes profit and loss. We are on the verge of space and in the midst of the greatest technological revolution the world has ever seen. The opportunities are more than global. They are galactic.

Annex 1: Ordeal by Fire

http://www.armory.com/~peterr/suntzu/szbook12.
html

Pan Ch'ao, sent on a diplomatic mission to the king
of Shan-shan, found himself placed in extreme peril by
the unexpected arrival of an envoy from the Hsiung-nu
(the mortal enemies of the Chinese). In consultation with
his officers, he exclaimed, "Never venture, never win! The
only course open to us now is to make an assault by fire
on the barbarians under cover of night, when they will
not be able to discern our numbers. Profiting by their
panic, we shall exterminate them completely; this will
cool the King's courage and cover us with glory, besides
ensuring the success of our mission."

The officers all replied that it would be necessary to
discuss the matter first with the intendant. Pan Ch'ao
then fell into a passion: "It is today," he cried, "that
our fortunes must be decided! The Intendant is only a
humdrum civilian, who on hearing of our project will
certainly be afraid, and everything will be brought to
light. An inglorious death is no worthy fate for valiant
warriors." All then agreed to do as he wished. Accordingly,
as soon as night came on, he and his little band quickly
made their way to the barbarian camp. A strong gale was
blowing at the time. Pan Ch'ao ordered ten of the party

to take drums and hide behind the enemy's barracks, it being arranged that when they saw flames shoot up, they should begin drumming and yelling with all their might. The rest of his men, armed with bows and crossbows, he posted in ambuscade at the gate of the camp.

He then set fire to the place from the windward side, whereupon a deafening noise of drums and shouting arose on the front and rear of the *Hsiung-nu*, who rushed out pell-mell in frantic disorder. Pan Ch'ao slew three of them with his own hand, while his companions cut off the heads of the envoy and thirty of his suite.

The remainder, more than a hundred in all, perished in the flames. On the following day, Pan Ch'ao, divining his thoughts, said with uplifted hand, "Although you did not go with us last night, I should not think, Sir, of taking sole credit for our exploit." This satisfied Kuo Hsun, and Pan Ch'ao, having sent for Kuang, king of Shan-shan, showed him the head of the barbarian envoy. The whole kingdom was seized with fear and trembling, which Pan Ch'ao took steps to allay by issuing a public proclamation. Then, taking the king's sons as hostage, he returned to make his report to Tou Ku.[439]

---

439   Hou Han Shu, ch. 47, ff. 1, 2: http://www.armory. com/~peterr/suntzu/szbook12.html

Annex 2: The Training of the Imperial Concubines

Sima Qian gives the following biography of Sun Tzu. Sun was a native of the Ch'i State. His *Art of War* brought him to the notice of Ho Lu, King of Wu.[440] Ho Lu said to him, "I have carefully perused your 13 chapters. May I submit your theory of managing soldiers to a slight test?" Sun Tzu replied, "You may." Ho Lu asked, "May the test be applied to women?" The answer was again in the affirmative, so arrangements were made to bring 180 ladies out of the palace.

Sun Tzu divided them into two companies and placed one of the king's favorite concubines at the head of each. He then made them all take spears in their hands and addressed them thus: "I presume you know the difference between front and back, right hand and left hand?" The girls replied, "Yes."

Sun Tzu went on: "When I say 'Eyes front,' you must look straight ahead. When I say 'Left turn,' you must face towards your left hand. When I say 'Right turn,' you must face towards your right hand. When I say 'About turn,' you must face right round towards your back." Again the girls assented. The words of command having been thus explained, he set up the halberds and battle-

---

440   Reigned 514–496 BCE

axes in order to begin the drill. Then, to the sound of drums, he gave the order, "Right turn." But the girls only burst out laughing. Sun Tzu said, "If words of command are not clear and distinct, if orders are not thoroughly understood, then the general is to blame."

So he started drilling them again and this time gave the order, "Left turn," whereupon the girls once more burst into fits of laughter. Sun Tzu said, "If words of command are not clear and distinct, if orders are not thoroughly understood, the general is to blame. But if his orders are clear, and the soldiers nevertheless disobey, then it is the fault of their officers."

So saying, he ordered the leaders of the two companies to be beheaded. Now the king of Wu was watching the scene from the top of a raised pavilion, and when he saw that his favorite concubines were about to be executed, he was greatly alarmed and hurriedly sent down the following message: "We are now quite satisfied as to our general's ability to handle troops. If we are bereft of these two concubines, our meat and drink will lose their savor. It is our wish that they shall not be beheaded."

Sun Tzu replied, "Having once received His Majesty's commission to be the general of his forces, there are certain commands of His Majesty which, acting in that capacity, I am unable to accept." Accordingly, he had the two leaders beheaded and straightaway installed the pair next in order as leaders in their place. When this had been done, the drum was sounded for the drill once more, and the girls went through all the evolution, turning to the right or to the left, marching ahead or wheeling back, kneeling or standing, with perfect accuracy and precision, not venturing to utter a sound.

Then Sun Tzu sent a messenger to the king, saying, "Your soldiers, Sire, are now properly drilled and disciplined, and ready for your majesty's inspection. They can be put to any use that their sovereign may desire; bid them go through fire and water, and they will not disobey."

But the king replied, "Let our general cease drilling and return to camp. As for us, we have no wish to come down and inspect the troops." Thereupon Sun Tzu said, "The King is only fond of words, and cannot translate them into deeds."[441]

After that, Ho Lu saw that Sun Tzu was one who knew how to handle an army and finally appointed him general. In the west, he defeated the Ch'u state and forced his way into Ying, the capital. To the north he put fear into the states of Ch'i and Chin and spread his fame abroad among the feudal princes. And Sun Tzu shared in the might of the king.[442]

---

441 Sawyer correctly sees Taoism here. He references Wu Tzu-hsü's comment that "I have heard that the army is an inauspicious affair" (1993, Translator's Introduction 152 and note 20).

442 Tang Zi-Chang adds, with no defined source, "The King of Wu, assisted by General Sun Wu, became the de facto leader of the League" (1969, 137).

Annex 3: The Story of Meng Chiang-nü

Meng's husband, Wan, a scholar, was taken from their home and carried away to help with the building of the Great Wall.

Meng, saddened by the loss of her husband, waited for news of him. Much time passed without hearing of his whereabouts. One night in her sleep he came to her and told her he was freezing to death. She awoke and made the decision to travel to the area where she thought he was working and take him clothes she had made for him. During her journey she almost froze to death in a snowstorm. A crow flew down next to her as she slept in the snow and, upon her awakening, showed her how to flap her wings so she could join the crows and fly to her destination.

Upon her arrival at the Great Wall she learned that her husband had died. She learned that he had been buried with many other workers in a section of the Great Wall. She searched the wall but couldn't locate his body. Anger arose from within her and poured out of her, causing lightning to split the sky and rain to pour from the heavens, washing away whole sections of the Great Wall. As the bones of the workers swirled about, Meng pricked her finger and asked that her blood penetrate the bones of her husband, Wan. She located his bones and wrapped them in the clothes she had brought for him.

The cruel emperor, Qin Shih Huangdi, was furious with her but taken with her beauty. The emperor gave her a choice of coming with him or being beheaded. Meng responded by asking for three wishes: to have her husband buried in the style of a prince, to have the kingdom mourn him for forty-nine days, and to give him a public funeral.

The emperor granted her the three wishes. After Wan's funeral she thanked the emperor and then threw herself into the sea, for she could not stand the thought of being with the emperor. The emperor commanded that her body be dragged from the sea, cut into pieces, and her bones ground into dust. As they threw her dust into the sea, thousands of little silvery fish filled the waters.

So today if you visit the Great Wall next to the Eastern Sea, you and others in China will remember the story of Meng and Wan.

Annex 4: The Inscription at Mount Langya

According to the Han's Great Historian, the first emperor of China had a tower built on Mount Langya. The inscription read:

A new age is inaugurated by the Emperor;
Rules and measures are rectified,
The myriad things set in order,
Human affairs are made clear
And there is harmony between fathers and sons.
The Emperor in his sagacity, benevolence and justice
Has made all laws and principles manifest.

He set forth to pacify the east,
To inspect officers and men;
This great task accomplished
He visited the coast.
Great are the Emperor's achievements,
Men attend diligently to basic tasks,
Farming is encouraged, secondary pursue discouraged,
All the common people prosper;
All men under the sky

Toil with a single purpose;
Tools and measures are made uniform,
The written script is standardized;
Wherever the sun and moon shine,

Wherever one can go by boat or by carriage,
Men carry out their orders
And satisfy their desires;
For our Emperor in accordance with the time
Has regulated local customs,
Made waterways and divided up the land.
Caring for the common people,
He works day and night without rest;
He defines the laws, leaving nothing in doubt,
Making known what is forbidden.
The local officials have their duties,
Administration is smoothly carried out,
All is done correctly, all according to plan.
The Emperor in his wisdom
Inspects all four quarters of his realm;

High and low, noble and humble,
None dare overshoor the mark;
No evil or impropriety is allowed,
All strive to be good men and true,
And exert themselves in tasks great and small;
None dares to idle or ignore his duties,
But in far-off, remote places
Serious and decorous administrators
Work steadily, just and loyal.
Great is the virtue of our Emperor
Who pacifies all four corners of the earth,
Who punishes traitors, roots out evil men,
And with profitable measures brings prosperity.
Tasks are done at the proper season,
All things flourish and grow;

The common people know peace
And have laid aside weapons and armor;

Kinsmen care for each other,
There are no robbers or thieves;
Men delight in his rule,
All understanding the law and discipline.
The universe entire
Is our Emperor's realm,

Extending west to the Desert,
South to where the houses face north,
East to the East Ocean,
North to beyond Daxia;
Wherever human life is found,
All acknowledge his suzerainty,
His achievements surpass those of the Five Emperors,
His kindness reaches even the beasts of the field;
All creatures benefit from his virtue,
All live in peace at home.

http://acc6.its.brooklyn.cuny.edu/~phalsall/texts/ssuma2.html

Annex 5: Works Consulted and References

Albrecht, Karl, and Steve Albrecht. *Added Value Negotiating.* Homewood, Illinois: Business One Irwin, 1993.

Alexander, Bevin. *How Great Generals Win.* New York: W. W. Norton, 1993.

Ames, Roger T., trans. *Sun-Tzu The Art of Warfare.* New York: Ballantine, 1993.

Aron, Raymond. *Clausewitz: Philosopher of War.* Englewood Cliffs: Prentice-Hall, 1976.

Autry, J. A., and Stephen Mitchell. *Real Power: Business Lessons from the Tao Te Ching.* New York: Riverhead Books, 1998.

Bishop, Donald, ed. *Chinese Thought: An Introduction.* South Asia Books, 1985.

Bloodworth, Dennis, and Ching Ping. *The Chinese Machiavelli.* New York: Farrar, Straus and Giroux, 1976.

Blunden, Caroline, and Mark Elvin. *Cultural Atlas of China.* Oxford: Equinox, 1983.

Bodde, Derk. *China's First Unifier.* Hong Kong: University Press, 1967.

Burke, James, and Robert Ornstein. *The Axemaker's Gift.* New York: Grosset/Putnam, 1995.

Calder, Kent E. *Asia's Deadly Triangle*. London: Nicholas Brealey, 1997.

Calthrop, E. F. *The Book of War*. London: John Murray, 1908.

Campbell, Terry, and Heather Cairns. "Developing and Measuring the Learning Organization: From Buzz Words to Behaviours," in *Industrial and Commercial Training*. Vol. 26, No. 7, 1994.

Cantrell, R. L. *Understanding Sun Tzu on the Art of War*. Arlington: Center for Advantage, 2003.

Chung, Tsai Chih. *Sunzi Speaks: The Art of War*. New York: Doubleday, 1994.

Clavell, James. *The Art of War by Sun Tzu*. New York: Dell Publishing, 1983.

Cleary, Thomas, trans. *The Art of War—Sun Tzu*. Boston: Shambhala, 1988a.

Cleary, Thomas, trans. *The Spirit of Tao*. Boston: Shambhala, 1988b.

Cleary, Thomas, trans. *Mastering The Art of War*. Boston: Shambhala, 1989a.

Cleary, Thomas, trans. *The Book of Balance and Harmony*. San Francisco: North Point Press, 1989b.

Cleary, Thomas, trans. *The Secret of the Golden Flower*. San Francisco: Harper, 1991a.

Cleary, Thomas, trans. *The Essential Tao*. San Francisco: Harper, 1991b.

Cleary, Thomas, trans. *The Book of Leadership and Strategy*. Boston: Shambhala, 1992a.

Cleary, Thomas, trans. *The Essential Confucius*. San Francisco: Harper, 1992b.

Cleary, Thomas, trans. *Thunder in the Sky: On the Acquisition and Exercise of Power*. Boston: Shambhala, 1993.

Cleary, Thomas. *Taoist Meditation*. Boston: Shambhala, 2000.

Cleveland, Harlan. *The Knowledge Executive*. New York: Truman Talley, 1985.

Cohen, E. A., and John Gooch. *Military Misfortunes*. New York: Free Press, 1990.

Cohen, Kenneth S. *The Way of Qigong (The Art and Science of Chinese Energy Healing)*. New York: Ballantine, 1997.

Cotterell, Arthur. *China: A Concise Cultural History*. London: John Murray, 1988.

Cottrell, Leonard. *The Tiger of Ch'in*. London: Evans Bros., 1962.

Covey, Stephen R. *Principle-Centered Leadership*. New York: Summit Books, 1990.

Creel, H. G. *Chinese Thought: From Confucius to Mao Tse-tung*. Chicago: University of Chicago Press, 1953.

Crump, J. I. Jr. *Intrigues: Studies of the Chan-kuo Ts'e*. Ann Arbor: University of Michigan Press, 1964.

Csikszentmihalyi, Mihalyi. *Finding Flow: The Psychology of Engagement with Everyday Life*. New York: Basic Books, 1997.

Davis, Erik. *Techgnosis*. New York: Harmony Books, 1998.

de Bono, Edward. *Conflicts: A Better Way to Resolve Them*. London: Harrap, 1985.

De Mente, Boye. *Japanese Etiquette and Ethics in Business*. Chicago: Passport Books, 1987.

Deng Ming-Dao. *Scholar Warrior*. San Francisco: Harper, 1990.

Dickson, Carolyn. *Creating Balance*. Greensboro: Oakhill Press, 1997.

Duyvendak, Dr. J. J. L. *The Book of Lord Shang*. Chicago: University Press, 1963.

Drucker, Peter F. *The Last of All Possible Worlds*. New York: Harper and Row, 1982.

Dunnigan, James F. *How to Make War*. New York: William Morrow, 1993.

Dunnigan, James F., and Albert A. Nofi. *Victory and Deceit*. New York: William Morrow, 1995.

Ebrey, P. B. *Cambridge History of China*. Cambridge: University Press, 1996.

Edelman, Joel, and Mary Beth Crain. *The Tao of Negotiation*. New York: Harper Business, 1993.

Evans, Air Marshal David. *War: A Matter of Principles*. London: Macmillan Press, 1997.

Fairbank and Kierman, eds. "Introduction: Varieties of the Chinese Military Experience," in *Chinese Ways in Warfare*, 27–67. Harvard University Press 1974.

Faligot, Roger, and Remi Kauffer. *The Chinese Secret Service*. New York: William Morrow, 1987.

Feng, Gia-Fu, and Jane English, trans. *Chuang Tsu: Inner Chapters*. New York: A.A. Knopf, 1974.

Feng, Gia-Fu, and Jane English, trans. *Lao Tsu—Tao Te Ching*. New York: Random House, 1997.

Fishel, John T., ed. *The Savage Wars of Peace*. Boulder: Westview Press, 1998.

Fisher, Ronald J. *Interactive Conflict Resolution*. Syracuse: University Press, 1997.

Fotion, Nicholas G. *Military Ethics*. Stanford: Hoover Press, 1990.

Gallie, W. B. *Clausewitz on the Nature of War*. Cambridge University Press, 1979.

Galtung, Johan. "Nonviolence and Deep Culture," in *Peace Research*. August 1995, Vol. 27(3) p. 21–37.

Gernet, Jacques. Translated by Raymond Rudorff. *Ancient China*. Berkeley: University of California Press, 1968.

Gernet, Jacques. Translated by J. R. Foster. *A History of Chinese Civilization*. Cambridge: Cambridge University Press, 1982.

Giles, Herbert A. *Gems of Chinese Literature*. Shanghai: Kelly and Walsh, 1922.

Giles, Herbert A. *Gems of Chinese Literature*. New York: Paragon Books, 1965.

Giles, Herbert A. *A History of Chinese Literature.* New York: Frederick Ungar Publishing, 1967.

Giles, Lionel, ed., trans. *Sun Tzu on The Art of War.* Project Gutenberg Etext #132 (originally published in 1910).

Gingrich, Newt. *Window of Opportunity.* New York: TOR Publishing, 1984.

Goodenough, Simon. *Tactical Genius in Battle.* London: Phaidon Press, 1979.

Greene, Robert. *The 48 Laws of Power.* New York: Viking, 1998.

Griffith, Samuel B. *Sun Tzu: The Art of War.* Oxford: Clarendon Press, 1963.

Grigg, Ray. *The Tao of Relationships.* Atlanta: Humanics Limited, 1988.

Grossman, Dave. *On Killing.* Boston: Little Brown, 1995.

Guenon, Rene. *The Great Triad.* Dorset: Element Books, 1991.

Hackman, J. R., ed. *Groups That Work—and Those That Don't.* San Francisco: Jossey-Bass Inc., 1990.

Halper, Stefan. *The Beijing Consensus.* New York: Basic Books, 2010

Handel, Michael I. *Masters of War: Sun Tzu, Clausewitz, and Jomini.* London: Frank Cass and Co., 1992.

Handy, Charles. *The Age of Paradox.* Boston: Harvard Business School, 1994.

Hanzhang, General Tao. *Sun Tzu's Art of War (The Modern Chinese Interpretation).* New York: Sterling Publishing, 1987.

Harris, Victor, trans. *A Book of Five Rings by Miyamoto Musashi.* Woodstock: Overlook Press, 1974.

Heider, John. *The Tao of Leadership.* New York: Bantam, 1988.

Heller, Robert. *The Naked Manager—Games Executives Play.* New York: Heller Arts, 1985.

Herbert, Brian, and K. J. Anderson. *Dune: House Atreides.* New York: Bantam, 2000.

Herman, Stanley M. *The Tao at Work.* San Francisco: Jossey-Bass, 1994.

Hesselbeing, Goldsmith, and Beckhard, eds. *The Organization of the Future.* San Francisco: Jossey-Bass, 1997.

Hoffman, Ben. *Win-Win Competitiveness.* North York: Captus Press, 1993.

Hollingworth, Clare. *Mao And the Men Against Him.* London: Jonathan Cape, 1985.

Hook, Brian. *Cambridge Encyclopedia of China.* Cambridge: University Press, 1982.

Horton, Thomas R. *The CEO Paradox.* New York: Amacom, 1992.

"How to Avoid the Wall in China," in *Mastering Global Business, Financial Post and Financial Times,* undated, circa November 1998.

Howard, Michael, and Peter Paret, eds., trans. *Carl von Clausewitz: On War.* Princeton: Princeton University Press, 1976.

Huang, J. H. *Sun Tzu—The New Translation.* New York: William Morrow, 1993.

Hucker, Charles O. *China's Imperial Past.* Stanford: University Press, 1975.

Imparato, Nicholas, and Oren Harari. *Jumping the Curve.* San Francisco: Jossey-Bass, 1994.

Jacobs, Jane. *Systems of Survival.* New York: Random House, 1992.

Jay, Anthony. *Management and Machiavelli.* London: Hutchinson Business, 1987.

Jeanes, Clive F. "Achieving and Exceeding Customer Satisfaction at Milliken," in *Managing Service Quality.* Vol. 5, No. 4, 1995.

Joint Chiefs of Staff. "JCS Pub. 1, Dictionary of Military and Associated Terms."

Kagan, Donald. *On the Origins of War and the Preservation of Peace.* New York: Doubleday, 1995.

Kaltenmark, Max. *Lao Tzu and Taoism.* Stanford: Stanford University Press, 1969.

Kaplan, Robert. *Warrior Politics*. New York: Random House, 2002.

Kaye, Kenneth. *Workplace Wars and How to End Them*. New York: AMACOM, 1994.

Keaney, T. A., and E. A. Cohen. "Gulf War Air Power Survey," a report commissioned by the US Air Force found at: http://www.pbs.org/wgbh/pages/frontline/gulf/appendix/death.html.

Keegan, John. *A History of Warfare*. New York: Alfred A. Knopf, 1993.

Key Sun. "How to Overcome without Fighting: An Introduction to The Taoist Approach to Conflict Resolution," in *Journal of Theoretical and Philosophical Psychology*. Vol. 15(2), 161–171, 1995.

Kiernan, Matthew J. *Get Innovative or Get Dead!* Vancouver: Douglas and McIntyre, 1995.

Kingwell, Mark. "Strategy Guide Lacks Power," a review of *The Lost Art of War* in the *Globe and Mail*, Toronto, April 23, 1996.

Kolko, Gabriel. *Century of War*. New York: The New Press, 1994.

Koller, John M. *Oriental Philosophies*. New York: Scribner's Sons, 1985.

Krause, Donald G. *The Art of War for Executives*. New York: Perigee, 1995.

Kuhn, Thomas S. *The Structure of Scientific Revolutions*. Chicago: University of Chicago Press, 1996.

Kwok, Man-Ho, Martin Palmer, and Jay Ramsay. *Tao Te Ching*. Shaftesbury: Element Books, 1993.

Lasserre, Philippe, and Jocelyn Probert. "Competing in Asia Pacific: Understanding the Rules of the Game," in *Long Range Planning*, Vol. 31, No. 1, 30–50, 1998.

LaTorra, Michael. *A Warrior Blends with Life: A Modern Tao*. Berkeley: North Atlantic Books, 1993.

Lau, D. C., trans. *Tao Te Ching*. New York: Penguin Books, 1963.

Lau, D. C., and R. T. Ames. *Sun Pin: The Art of Warfare.* New York: Ballantine, 1996.

Lau, D. C., and R. T. Ames. *Yuan Dao: Tracing Dao to its Source.* New York: Ballantine, 1998.

Lei Haizong. *The Warring States (473-221 B.C.): The Modern Period in Ancient China.* http://www. cic.sfu.ca/nacrp/articles/leihaizong/leihaizong. html.

Leung, Hwok, and Dean Tjosvold, ed. *Conflict Management in the Asia Pacific.* Singapore: John Wiley & Sons, 1998.

Li, Dun J. *The Ageless Chinese.* New York: Charles Scribner's Sons, 1965.

Lin, Paul J. *A Translation of Lao Tzu's Tao Te Ching and Wang Pi's Commentary.* Ann Arbor: University of Michigan, 1977.

Lipnack, Jessica, and Jeffrey Stamps. *The TeamNet Factor.* Vermont: Oliver Wright Publications, 1993.

Li Yu-ning, Ed. *Shang Yang's Reforms and State Control in China.* White Plains: M.E. Sharpe, 1977.

Low, S. P. "Formulating Construction Export Marketing Strategies: Lessons from Sun Tzu's Art of War," in *Focus on Property and Construction in Singapore.* 4:34–43.

Machell-Cox, E. *Principles of War by Sun Tzu.* Ceylon: Royal Air Force, 1943.

Machiavelli, Niccolo. *The Art of War.* New York: Bobbs-Merrill, 1965.

Mackenzie, Gordon. *Orbiting the Giant Hairball.* New York: Viking, 1998.

MacLean, Brian. "The Art of Competition," in *Canadian Bookseller.* Vol. 11, No. 8, October 1989.

Marrin, Albert. *Mao Tse-Tung and His China.* New York: Viking Kestrel, 1989.

McAlpine, Alistair. *The New Machiavelli.* New York: John Wiley & Sons, 1998.

McDermott, L. C., N. Brawley, and W. W. Waite. *World Class Teams*. New York: John Wiley & Sons, 1998.

McNeil, Art. *The "I" of the Hurricane*. Toronto: Stoddart Publishing, 1987.

McNeilly, Mark. *Sun Tzu and the Art of Business*. New York: Oxford University Press, 1996.

McNeilly, Mark. *The Six Principles from Sun Tzu and the Art of Business: Six Principles for Managers*. New York: Oxford University Press, 1996.

Merrills, J. G. *International Dispute Settlement*. Cambridge University Press, 1998.

Merton, Thomas. *The Way of Chuang Tzu*. New York: New Directions, 1965.

Micklethwait, John, and Adrian Wooldridge. *The Witch Doctors*. New York: Times Books, 1996.

Millis, Walter. *Arms and the State*. New York: The Twentieth Century Fund, 1958.

Min Chen. *Business Horizons*. Vol. 37 Issue 2, 42, Mar/Apr 1994.

Mintzberg, Henry. *The Rise and Fall of Strategic Planning*. Don Mills: Maxwell Macmillan, 1994.

Morwood, Peter. *Star Trek: Rules of Engagement*. New York: Pocket Books, 1990.

Nathan, Otto, and Heinz Norden. *Einstein on Peace*. New York: Schocken Books, 1968.

Nelson, Andrew H. *The Art of Information War.* Unpublished manuscript. 1994–1995.

Nelson, M. B. *Embracing Victory*. New York: William Morrow, 1998.

Nienhauser, W. H. Jr., ed. *The Grand Scribe's Records: Volume I*. Bloomington: Indiana University Press, 1994a.

Nienhauser, W. H. Jr., ed. *The Grand Scribe's Records: Volume VII*. Bloomington: Indiana University Press, 1994b.

Norris, Chuck. *The Secret Power Within*. Boston: Little Brown, 1996.

O'Connell, Robert L. *Ride of the Second Horseman.* New York: Oxford University Press, 1995.

O'Neill, Hugh B. *Companion to Chinese History.* New York: Facts on File, 1987.

Paquette, Laure. *A Comparative Study of Strategy and Time in Clausewitz's On War and Sun Tzu's The Art of War.* Master's thesis, Queen's University, July 1989.

Pascale, R. T. *Managing on the Edge.* New York: Touchstone, 1990.

Pascale, R. T., and A. G. Athos. *The Art of Japanese Management.* New York: Simon and Shuster, 1981.

Perla, Peter P. *The Art of Wargaming.* Annapolis: Naval Institute, 1990.

Peters, T. J., and R. H. Waterman. *In Search of Excellence.* New York: Harper & Row, 1982.

Pirazzoli-t'Serstevens, Michele. *The Han Dynasty.* New York: Rizzoli, 1982.

Porter, Michael E. *Competitive Strategy.* New York: The Free Press, 1980.

Quick, T. L. *Unconventional Wisdom.* San Francisco: Jossey-Bass Publishers, 1989.

Riley, Pat. *The Winner Within.* New York: Putnam, 1993.

Ringer, Robert J. *Winning Through Intimidation.* New York: Fawcett, 1974.

Robert, Michael. *Strategy Pure and Simple.* New York: McGraw-Hill, 1993.

Roberts, Wess. *Victory Secrets of Attila the Hun.* New York: Doubleday, 1993.

Rodzinski, Witold. *The Walled Kingdom.* New York: Free Press, 1984.

Rudnicki, Stefan. *The Art of War by Sun Tzu.* West Hollywood: Dove Books, 1996.

Russel, R. A. *Winning the Future.* New York: Carroll and Graf, 1986.

Salisbury, H. E. *The Long March.* New York: Harper & Row, 1985.

Salisbury, H. E. *The New Emperors: China in the Era of Mao and Deng.* Toronto: Little Brown, 1992.

Sawyer, R.D. *Chinese Warfare: The Paradox of the Unlearned Lesson.* http://www.unc.edu/depts/diplomat/amdipl_13/china_sawyer.html.

Sawyer, R. D. *The Complete Art of War—Sun Tzu, Sun Pin.* Boulder: Westview Press, 1996.

Sawyer, R. D. *The Seven Military Classics of Ancient China.* Boulder: Westview Press, 1993.

Schodt, F. L. *America and the Four Japans.* Berkeley: Stone Bridge Press, 1994.

Seabury, Paul, and Angelo Codevilla. *War: Ends and Means.* New York: Basic Books, 1989.

Silver, George. *Paradoxes of Defense: The Brief Instructions.* Circa 1600.

Simon, Hermann. *Hidden Champions.* Boston: Harvard Business School, 1996.

Smith, Kidder Jr. "The Sun Tzu Military Model Text," in *Sagehood and Systematizing Thought in Warring States and Han China.* Breckinridge Public Affairs Center, Asian Studies Program. Brunswick: Bowdoin College, 1990.

Steinberg, Leigh. *Winning With Integrity.* New York: Villard Books, 1998.

Teck, Foo Check, and Peter Hugh Grinyer. *Sun Tzu on Management: The Art of War in Contemporary Business Strategy.* Singapore: Butterworth-Heinemann, 1994.

Toffler, Alvin, and Heidi Toffler. *War and Anti-War.* Boston: Little Brown, 1993.

Toffler, Alvin. *Power Shift: Knowledge, Wealth and Violence at the Edge of the 21st Century.* New York: Bantam Books, 1990.

Torres, Cresencio. *The Tao of Teams.* San Diego: Pfeiffer & Co., 1994.

Tse, Angel, and Gregory E. Kesten. *The Art of War and the Art of Negotiation as Taught by Sun Tzu*. The InterNeg Group. Copyright 1996–2000. http://www.interneg.org/interneg/training/materials/sun_tzu.html

Tung, Rosalie. "Strategic Management Thought in East Asia," in *Organizational Dynamics*. Vol. 23, Issue 4, 55, Spring 1994.

Tushman, M. L., and C. A. O'Reilly III. *Winning Through Innovation*. Boston: Harvard Business School, 1997.

Twitchett, Denis, and Michael Loewe, ed. *The Cambridge History of China, Volume I*. London: Cambridge University Press, 1986.

Van Creveld, Martin. *Technology and War*. London: The Free Press, 1989.

Vassin, Vladimir. *The Eleventh Commandment*. New York: Vantage Press, 1995.

Waldron, Arthur. *The Great Wall of China: From History to Myth*. Cambridge: Cambridge University Press, 1990.

Walzer, Michael. *Just and Unjust Wars*. New York: Basic Books, 1977.

Watson, Burton. *Sima Qian—Grand Historian of China*. New York: Columbia University Press, 1958.

Watson, William. *China: Before the Han Dynasty*. London: Thames and Hudson, 1961.

Watts, Alan. *Tao: The Watercourse Way*. New York: Pantheon Books, 1975.

Watts, Alan. *Taoism: Way Beyond Seeking*. Boston: Tuttle Co., 1997.

Watts, Alan. *The Way of Zen*. New York: Vintage Books, 1957.

Wee, Chow-Hou, Khai-Sheang Lee, and Bambang Walujo Hidajat. *Sun Tzu: War and Management: Application to Strategic Management and Thinking*. Addison-Wesley, 1996.

Wenli, Zhang. *The Qin Terracotta Army*. London: Scala Books, 1996.

White, Bob. *Hard Bargains: My Life on the Line*. Toronto: McClelland and Stewart, 1987.

Wilhelm, Richard, ed. *The Secret of the Golden Flower*. London: Routledge & Kegan Paul, 1954.

Wing, R. L. *The Art of Strategy*. New York: Dolphin Doubleday, 1988.

Wing-Tsit Chan. *A Source Book in Chinese Philosophy*. Princeton: University Press, 1963.

Wray, Stefan John. *The Drug War and Information Warfare in Mexico*. Master's thesis at the University of Texas at Austin, August 1997.

Yang Hsien-yi and Gladys Yang, trans. *Szuma Chien. Selections from Records of the Historian*. Peking: Foreign Languages Press, 1979.

Zhengyuan Fu. *China's Legalists*. New York: M. E. Sharpe, 1996.

Zi-Chang, Tang. *Principles of Conflict*. San Rafael: T. C. Press, 1969.

Xuanming, Wang. *100 Strategies of War*. Singapore: Asiapac, 1993.

Other Media

The Art of War. Great Books Video. The Learning Channel. Walter Cronkite, ed. 1998

The Silk Road. China—Glories of Ancient Chang-an (Xi-an). Video. Central Park Media Corporation. 1990

China: Dynasties of Power. Video. Time Life's Lost Civilizations. Joel Westbrook, executive producer. 1995

The Emperor and The Assassin. Sony Pictures Entertainment Inc. Chen Kaige, director. December 17, 1999.

The First Emperor of China. Video. National Film Board of Canada. 1995

Sun Tzu: The Art of War. Video. Discovery Productions. Bethesda, MD. Distributed by Discovery Channel Video. 1994.

Wall Street. Movie. A Twentieth Century Fox film by Oliver Stone. 1987.

Index

417